TERRA   NEVM
S

Moren · Corneso · Oppis · Paphus
Medon
Greta
Pelin
Cydne
Candia

SINTE
Cyrene · Berniche · Pelusio · Shes
Pahara · Alexandria · ELCOL · ARV
Carcora · Cathena · Berton · Ptolomais · ELOCAT
Augela · Goram · Ammon · Caro
Berdoa · Ebaida · Serra
Sabia · Algueçet · Æorpzo · Cuiza · Jambut · Salata

Sinus Persi
Baharem

Gaoga reg · Geogan · Coale · Omot · Napara · Mecha · Ariadan · Saddock · Visardredan · Cora
Illarado · Labea · Saldace · Sancar · Sacolche · Siagar · Amacharan · uaha · ARABIA Fœlix
Nubia · desertium · Sobuha · Lacari · Warach · Elœnt · Zabid · Damear
N'uba · palus · Salent · Demba · Barnagasso · Camaran · Zacocora
V'anque · Sione · Darga · Dara · Corna · Zama · Decene · Diram · Abhadal · Meinberg · Uette · Carfur · MARIS
Danuic · Zigide · Sadie · Catad · Tenet · Fatigar · Valletta · Vugiat · Asum · Opin · Opane · Ptol · RVBRI
Ambian cantua · Sofa · Aroo · Orgara · Aren · Braua · Magadavo
Biafar · ABIS · SI · NI · A · Cercora · Cercora

PARS
Linag · Dembia · Barent · palus · Pate · Lamon
Gada · Vigier · George · Fabahen · Tacemiguo · Mombaza · Penda
Meraga · Iqua reg · Nore · Quiloa · Zanzibar
Leguda · Deba · Quilea · Adarno · S · Francisco
Manicongo · Falazur · Mozambique · Docomoro · Liena · Prassum prom · C del ambar
Damura · Camar · Gamba · Zuama flu · Madagascar
Galilia · Gebage · Amara · Dege · Quari · Deger · Phat

A dia · Junos · Messata · Juanca · Jmbaes · C de Corrientes · Cuata · de Juan de Lisboa
Gar · ma · Desa · C des Risque
Benami · Alagoa · Boligara · Vallenta
Mahambanar · Corada · Punta de S Maria
Caxneca · Postrera tierra de Nauidad · Punta primera de Nauidad
Baia hermosa y pesqueria · Los Romeros insula

Insula hæc Madagascar a nostris
S Laurenti vocatur, Plinio lib 6
cap 31 videtur esse Cerne, Ptol est
Menuthias

HEC PARS AFHRICE ANTIQVIORIBVS
MANSIT INCOGNITA

Terra Incognita

Published by Short Story Day Africa in 2015
Distributed by Hands-On Books

Print ISBN: 978-1-920590-91-8
E-book ISBN: 978-1-920590-99-4

Edited by Nerine Dorman

Cover and inside page design by Nick Mulgrew
Cover detail from Thomas Burke, *Cupid Inspiring the Plants With Love*, an engraving from a painting by Philip Reinagle: *New Illustration of the Sexual System of Carolus von Linneaus; ... The Temple of Flora, or Garden of Nature*
Detail on page iii from Sebastian Münster's map, *Africa, Libya, Morland, mit allen Kunigreichen so zu unsern zeiten darin gefunden werden.* (1544-1545)
Image on endpapers from Johan Bussemacher's map, *Afrique* (1600)

This book is typeset in Gestalt, Brandon Grotesque, Minion Pro and Bodoni

TERRA INCOGNITA

INTRODUCTION

INTRODUCTION

Over the past decade, the publishing industry has become risk-averse. The words "genre-defying" and "original" make agents and editors break out in a cold sweat – or so we're told. The industry is constantly described as conservative. Manuscripts are rejected for being too cerebral, unsellable in a market that wants only apple pie. An alternative publishing model has grown up around writers looking for new routes to readers. However indie publishers are often (unfairly) perceived as exploitative and the work produced by them as subpar.

It is in this climate that Short Story Day Africa was formed and, in the four years since inception, the SSDA team has developed a survival ethos: to subvert and reclaim. Reclaim the place of the short story. Reclaim a space for nonconformist writing. Subvert ideas about what it means to be a writer in Africa. Subvert ideas about what makes a story African.

No surprise then that, when we sent out the call for speculative fiction stories, we asked writers to subvert the idioms of both the genre and our vast continent. We received 116 answers to that call, around thirty up on last year's entries. The list was whittled down through a blind reading process, but also through careful curatorship. This meant that some of the stories that made it through the reading process, even some that scored highly, did not make it onto the long-list of eighteen. These were well-crafted stories, good stories, but we wanted stories that had interpreted the theme in unexpected ways.

As a result, around a fifth of the voices contained within these pages are being published for the first time. These voices appear alongside established writers, like Diane Awerbuck, who penned "Leatherman," this year's winning story. In fact, "In the Water", the story that took third place, is Kerstin Hall's first published story. Second place went to Sylvia Schlettwein for "Ape Shit", with "The Corpse" by Sese Yane getting a special mention. Needless to say, these eighteen are writers who are not afraid to bend rules, genre and language.

The nineteenth story in this collection did not come from the competition entries. "Hands" was written by Tiah Beautement, a member of the SSDA team, in response to a chronic and often debilitating condition she has lived with these past four years. In spite of the physical limitations imposed on Tiah she has never shied away from the challenges of co-running Short Story Day Africa.

In *Terra Incognita*, Short Story Day Africa is proud to present nineteen stories of speculative fiction. Contained within these pages are stories that explore, among other things, the sexual magnetism of a tokoloshe, a deadly feud with a troop of baboons, a journey through colonial purgatory, along with ghosts, re-imagined folklore, and the fear of that which lies beneath both land and water.

Terra Incognita. Uncharted depths. Africa unknowable.

RACHEL ZADOK
Short Story Day Africa

LEATHERMAN

Diane Awerbuck

For Clare

It was not that she was a prude. Joanna had just not found anyone she liked enough to relieve her body of its tight-wadded burden—the bud, the bouquet, the burning bush of her maidenhead. She wanted an expert, a light-fingered someone with a cunning tongue, but the hopefuls who knocked on the door were boys too young to know better, or her father's hairy, beery friends.

It was not the hair, really, either—it was the geography of it. Silverbacks, tonsures, furry-purry fright wigs: Joanna had refused to run her fingers through them all. But, more than that, it was the men's discomfort with their own topography that dampened her passion, the way one sucked in his gut when he passed her in Hatfield Street, or another whistled through nasal topiary when she skirted him on the steps.

And time passes more quickly when you're busy, as anyone who's ever attended a sickbed will say. Soon she hardly thought about her sanitary state. At *Allure* she researched features for the other women, invariably older, pencil-skirted, divorced. They smoked but never ate, and spoke in deep voices about the *Dirty Thirties* and *robbing the cradle*. Joanna couldn't see the point of younger men. Was it so much to ask, for someone she liked, who liked her too? She looked for him on the horizon, wished for him in the evening on Venus's unvarying machinery—the big-night star, the morning-after star—which should by rights have watched over her.

Joanna wasn't an idiot: she had known that a big city meant a certain amount of loneliness, but the Mother City was harder than she had imagined when she was back in Kimberley, mooning from the window of matric. She was unprepared for the carelessness of Capetonians, for sex-as-premise, for the difficulty of comprehending the unspoken rules, like iron filings rustling untouched on a sheet of foolscap. By the time you worked out the magnet's movements, it was too late.

The ticket to YDESIRE had been comped to *Allure* for publicity. "Oh, please. Take it," Siobhan had told her. Joanna found her dyed hair difficult to look at, brickish, hard against the hand. Siobhan breathed neglect and necrosis: her stomach was digesting itself. The editor fluttered her starved fingers. "Another fucking *art event.*"

During her lunch hour, Joanna had gone to The Emporium, searching for an outfit that would make her look like the girls she spied on in Mister Pickwick's: thinnish, hungover, imperfect girls who would skinny-dip in waterfalls with your boyfriend or produce large-eyed love-children with French seamen. They smelled of dirty panties and oily scalps, of snail-slick contamination, of sliding focused and impervious to some decided finish. Joanna in her slabbed flesh was unpierced, unmarked, a concentrated negation. She had looked under the rock and seen its workings. This was her last chance: really, the final countdown.

SOFTSERVE 4, said the invitation. Disbelieving, Joanna kept taking it out of her bag, like a guidebook. YDESIRE. The map of the Castle's innards was spread in pink on the reverse; the main building itself was an icon, an areola, a stamp for a club that had never let her in. Joanna imagined the pockmarked walls hung with fairy lights for this one bright night, translated at the witching hour. To-night she would dance on the heathen grass, twist under the tinselly stars, stretch out her sore back that had been slumped by plainness and office chairs. In a few years, Joanna knew, she would have a widow's hump. A Windows hump. *If this doesn't work, I'm going to be a librarian,* she told herself, as she made her way to the changing room with its corrugated door like a rocket ship and its promise of astral travel.

The clothes draped over her arm were doll-sized, made for aliens. She should have been used to it from the magazine (*GET HER LOOK!*) but it still took her by surprise, the Asian cookie-cutter that she saw descending on the dough of women's bodies. She began to struggle into a pair of animal-print pants. What had her mother called them? Pedal-pushers, like something out of an *Archie* comic. God, it was hot in here. Nothing worked, as if the shop was a stage set and backstage had been abandoned. Even the ceiling was still being built. Joanna scrutinised the digestive tract of the ventilation shaft—segmented, silver—and tugged at the pants. How reflective was it? Were the stick-insect salesgirls watching her wrig-gling against the seams?

She thrust her knees down into the pants like a drum majorette, and there was a ripping sound.

Joanna peered between her legs, a giraffe at a watering hole.

She had torn the material hymen.

She wouldn't be able to get them off again, either, a baboon with its paw caught in a biscuit jar. Joanna groaned and hauled the material over her rump in one last yank, and the teeth of the zip came to rest against her stomach. They burned cold as dry ice. She would have to buy the things now, and cut them off her. Not a drummie or a giraffe or a baboon: she had turned into some composite creature, tagged with metal and flagged with cloth.

But, surely, in a million other unseen changing rooms, her sisters were undergoing the same transformation. From the pods they would emerge the same light and laughing butterflies. She would go, she *would*, to fly in their rabble, to be flung against the smouldering streetlights. So she had no one to go with, and no car to get there. Big deal. Joanna hitched up the pedal-pushers and turned to look at her scrumpy, lumpen arse. She didn't need to sleep. The Pickwick's girls didn't. She would stay out all night and in the morning she would take the train back out to Observatory before anyone woke. She even had the timetable in her silly backpack, next to the roseate sprawling invitation. In the station the trains lodged, cold as revolvers, until four forty-five when the hollow-tipped passengers filled their chambers. Tonight they could wait for her: she had been waiting for them her whole life.

Joanna stayed late after work and did her make-up in the unisex bathroom. She could have asked the stylist to help her—Siobhan often had her hair done before a night out, wheedling, "Oh, darling, won't you give me a quick blowjob?" But at the last minute, Joanna had lost her nerve. She checked her tiny backpack and patted the carton of Siobhan's dribbly drinking yoghurt, like semen, that she'd fossicked from the office fridge.

The evening in the city was kind, the air soft and undecided, blowing possibility up from the harbour, sweeping the streets of bland diurnal debris. Behind the thick, whitewashed walls were secret gardens, art exhibitions, law courts, hotels.

For the first time they were hers. It made Joanna's heart hurt with pleasure. Every pavement coffee-drinker was a Barbara Cartland book cover; every dreadlocked backpacker was a boy she might kiss. She bounced through the Company's Garden with its raddled rose bushes, its glue-sodden street kids and bowed businessmen, circles of anxious sweat under their arms. Men watched her from the corners of their eyes as she swung her leopard-print hips, but she had wanted them to— hadn't she? It was a rule of the street that the more revealing your clothing was, the less attention you got.

The times Joanna really felt frightened were when she was wearing jeans and a long-sleeved shirt: the lack of willingness was what turned men on. They called to her from swerving, dented taxis, grabbed at their crotches, followed her in groups. "You look like a nice time," they told Joanna. Someday she would meet her man with his knife, but tonight her feet were springy against the curb, as if she was on the starting block of some magnificent race. Joanna felt the energy zing up through the bones of her feet, her knees, her thighs, and the hot pot of her pelvis: predestination.

She was nearly there. She would take a shortcut at the road that went past the Shack and the Mexican restaurant and that ridiculous showroom that sold only red sports cars. The path was mostly through grass—a meadow, really, a weedy overgrown plot surrounded by slanting high-rise reses. You never saw the students: inside, their dank and glugging drains; outward, the glassy facelessness.

Here the field was, knee-high and singing at sundown. Somehow the long, blond grass had escaped the severe manicure that was the sign of the city council. At the beginning of summer, the men were everywhere. They came with their reek of petrol and their masks: often at sundown, when rush hour was over, they set up their cones and tape on the highway. On Devil's Peak you saw them waxing a bare strip around the forest so that the scabbed pines oozed peaceful and resinous under their bark as night came on. The next day, from her Metrorail carriage, Joanna saw the shorn places within the city bounds as well, green lungs collapsed and spent, empty as wheat fields after the harvest. *One man went to mow,* she sang softly to herself. *He went to mow a meadow.* When they came too late there were fires, the flames creeping down the mountain every Friday evening until they made a cemetery of the city and the countryside around it. Joanna witnessed the empty tortoiseshells from the morning train too. NOW SEE WHAT YOU'VE DONE! begged Bambi on the signs blurred with passing.

Now she stopped, the blood pumping so hot in her feet she wanted to kick off her shoes. A whole field of grass, intact. The seeds chorused and swayed, interspersed with bunny-eared stalks. Joanna felt the medieval pull, boys under haystacks, bladders of cider in the end-summer heat, the unified rustling of the parched grass. And—oh, God—the smell. Joanna looked around to see if a soul would appear at a res window, but she was alone. She put her face closer to the grass and felt the saliva bursting under her tongue. She wanted to lay her cheek on the sweet earth or nuzzle the soil, like an astronaut home from the moon.

But up close the ground was hard and scabbed. Joanna squinted at it in the dusk. There were bricks here—the abandoned foundations of a building. The bricks were dark red, pentacled, Mayan. Animals had pissed on the remains: cats, and people, marking their invisible territory. She smelled it, quest and threat, the pheromonal tattoo.

Joanna stood up too soon, and the blood sang in her head. She inhaled one last time—surely this air came from somewhere else, some other good and happy time—and then she carried on up the road that would take her into town.

It was a mistake, she saw right away, from the banner over the Castle doors: FEELS SO GOOD INSIDE. Her pants, her make-up: awful. Everyone, everyone, was there in groups: the Pickwick's girls with their faces streaked with silver paint and their chests bare. They had been hired to stand at the entrance and feed punters shots of tequila. Around their necks were strings with plastic tot cups that twitched and dribbled between their boobs. Joanna couldn't look away from those puckered nipples, those sides of flesh. *All you can eat*, she kept thinking. A*ll you can eat*. She wanted to run her fingers—*prrrp*—over their xylophone bones, and tap their hollow insides.

Inside was worse: sacrilegious. The open space of the parade ground had been blanketed with art installations and the hideous merriment of bunting, like a drunken uncle singing *Happy Birthday*. People were jostling along the pathways in moonlit groups, peering at the pieces. Her ears hurt: in her back teeth the generators grumbled. The human shrieking against the boom of the music was panicky, hysterical, people jumping on each other's backs, sticking their tongues down each other's throats. Joanna had read that your mouth was sterile when you woke, but even that seemed unlikely. How did people ever kiss or hold hands? Touching spread a thin layer of filth over everything. The fingernails of ordinary men made her shiver. Joanna kept her prissy hands in her pockets, sure that her purse would be lifted by a lantern-eyed lingerer. Contact was contagion.

She tried to choose a path out of the babbling maze, but was stopped in her tracks by a giant moon. There were people inside it like invading ants, feelers twitching, papering over its cracks as the thing inflated. The artist stood by, drunk, in dungarees. "Stand back, baby!" he called to Joanna. "I don't know how big this thing is going to get!"

If only. There was nothing for her here.

Joanna wanted to sit down and relish her sorrow, but when she moved into the cool, damp rooms, there were shaky video installations occupying the spaces. The audiences squashed the unredeemed flesh of their backsides onto the benches: children bumbled in and out, avatar-blue in the flickering light. *This is not art,* thought Joanna. It reminded her of the station concourse, the grey and blocky lives of the commuters, everyone waiting for something else. Not Cape Town station but a Brueghel painting: not vice, just avarice. She found that somehow there was candyfloss matted into her hair and she batted at the sticky mulch, maddened, like a cat.

She pushed her way back out and chose a cobbled path that seemed less crowded. Through the clumps and strands of her ruined hair, she saw a clearing ahead, filled with a neat and gargantuan construction, a meeting of scaffolding and high wire. It was a perpetual motion engine, Joanna saw when she straightened up—or not that, but a performance, where the actors were acrobats. They were using their bodies to power the machine, their knees bicycling up and down, the parts whirring and clicking. They balanced, dived, returned.

Joanna leaned in to read the sign pegged on the machine: ODD ENJINEARS. She wished for the same merging of iron and flesh, like the little men her father had said lived inside wristwatches, turning the cogs. Here they were, come to life, with their bendy legs and bowler hats, each acrobat serenely partnered and rehearsed. They were slick with sweat: they had been going for hours, suspended, dependent, walking on air, and the end was nowhere in sight. The stragglers gathered around the performers clapped, chatty and jaded, blind to the effort that appears effortless.

Something nipped at her ankle, and Joanna pinwheeled, propped up only by the few people in front of her. They turned and smiled at her outfit and she wanted to smack them. *I'm not asking you for forgiveness, you smug fucks!*

She strained over their heads to see what had bumped her, and a furry little man with a wheelbarrow sped off. He was wearing earth-coloured lederhosen over gartered stockings. With one pistoning arm he pushed at the wheelbarrow and the tall thing in it. Why did men always do that for carnival—dress up in women's underwear? Was it meant to be funny? *Secretly they hate us.* She didn't enjoy wearing a bra, either, but somebody had to be in control; somebody had to say no. Otherwise, chaos.

She rubbed her grazed ankle, her backpack banging her ribs, and made a face at the small fuzzy man. He had already turned away, hunched over his barrow. Fucking pedal-pushers. And that selfish prick. He had delayed her evacuation plan. Now she would have to wait until she could put her weight properly on her foot again before she could go home. At least the trains were still running.

Joanna looked for somewhere quiet to sit, but she was distracted by the man with the wheelbarrow, who zigzagged back across her vision. He was so close she could smell the petrol in his ragged bush of hair. Then he was off, running in demented circles, drawing and redrawing private lines of desire like a spell in the sand. The sculpture he was pushing was a towering Babel of glue and paper, Joanna saw now, crisp as a clean serviette, begging for the lick of flame. It looked like a trellis of grotesque flowers, a zombie corsage, a ladder to God. There were other sculptures here and there over the Castle grounds, portable pyres of glue and wire and paper, in a pattern that could only be seen from the sky.

The capering man reminded her of someone. She marked his enormous bristling head, the narrow shoulders, his goatish legs stiff in their garters. His name would be Boris, she was sure, Boris or Viktor or Rumpel-fucking-stiltskin, a homunculus in tights. He looked like he fucked anything that moved. He held the barrow lopsided as a dance partner, pushing against it, the wheels fleeing him with agreeable squeals. It made her feel its weight dragging at her own wrists, the gravity of warm pipes and work well done. A hundred years ago this is what it must have been to handle a gun—some smooth tool that felt familiar in the hand, the way the right penis might. A tingling recognition began in her navel, like the singing of the grass, an earthy urge that made her want to grab the little man by the arms and shake agreement into him.

At last he seemed to make up his mind—here, no, here—according to some celestial mind-map. He set down the wheelbarrow, heaving, his hairy chest running with sweat. He looked around with the impudence of the well endowed, gauging his audience. Joanna gazed at him. *This is your last chance*, she told the universe. *Make something happen. Make this worth my while.*

The man scratched inside his lederhosen and produced a red lighter. Joanna knew by the sick tipping in her stomach what he was going to do. It was the same feeling she got when she saw the lawnmowers on the verges of the forest.

He bowed to her and held up the plastic lighter like Liberty. He flicked the ridged wheel and she felt its clitoral corrugations rub against her own thumb, the lemming lurch of destruction. Joanna moved closer, her ankle throbbing. She wanted to see it all, every detail of the roaring destruction after so much preparation. She wanted to grab his hairy-knuckled hand and shove it into her crotch.

The paper flowers went up fast: he'd designed it that way. He stepped back, unhurried, and the flames soared up into the sky and the full circus night. The smell of scorching forest came to her, as close as she was, and Joanna stopped herself from shielding her face. She felt the same vicious joy under her breastbone: to take and make and master—and to break, to crack and smother.

The man kept stepping backwards, prancing horsey steps, and turned to her, smiling and deliberate. The hair on his head didn't stop where it met his features,

Joanna saw. It was just thinner in places, whorled like crop circles, then glossier and fuller at the sideburns. It grew down lazily over his neck, sprang from his nose and his ears, meandered gently over his chest and must have trailed down into the gusset of the garter belt. *Promises, promises.*

He peeled down the straps of his lederhosen, a blacksmith on a break. The leather flapped around his groin. He stroked the hair down on his stomach and then shook his hands, flicking sweat and smut from his fingertips onto her. *Black magic,* thought Joanna, and wiped her face. He nodded his odd-shaped head.

"Sjoe! I need a rest."

"You need a smack."

"What?"

"You hit me with your wheelbarrow."

He grinned, demonic. He reminded Joanna of Punch from the old puppet show, his face set in wicked rubbery lines that recessed his eyes so deeply she couldn't tell their colour. Around each socket were three precise wrinkles that fanned out whitely where the soot hadn't settled. He smelled like a wet dog.

"Sorry. You were camouflaged." He ducked his big head at her pedal-pushers. "Did it tickle when you painted them on?"

"At least I'm not in fishnets."

He really was incredibly hairy, a happy satyr. The thick fur on his thighs was compressed by the diamond weave of the tights: she wanted to stroke it like a Labrador.

She stuck out her hand instead. "Joanna."

He held out his filthy left hand in response, sinister, awkward. She saw that his right was withered and clawed.

"Hili."

His hand was hot. *Well, of course it fucking is. He plays with fire!*

"Is that Israeli?"

"No. Further, ah, south."

Joanna could smell his armpits, some sharp, bittersweet scent, and felt the synapses blistering in her brain, old pathways being cauterised, new ones being laid down. She wanted to grip his biceps and bury her nose in the clump of damp hair there. Her mouth was watering.

Hili glanced over at the wheelbarrow. It wasn't going to burn. Joanna could see his mental calculations, the coins dropping into worn slots. She shivered.

"Do you want to walk around?" he said.

"I'm just about to leave, actually." *If my legs are still working.*

"Why don't you stay? We can talk. I'm hungry, and my work here is done." He didn't say, "You look like a nice time."

"Okay. You can walk me to the gate." She fiddled in her tiny backpack. "I have a yoghurt…" *Thanks, Siobhan. I'm glad we got something out of your eating disorder.*

Joanna pulled the lips of the carton apart and squeezed an accommodating V for his slick mouth. She saw on the low ridge of his forehead that his eyebrows were singed.

"Oh, God. I'm sorry. It's sour."

Hili held onto her hand with his paw. "That's the way I like it." He drank in gulps, his Adam's apple shadowed by sworls of hair. Joanna thought of her father's friend, who had shaved his face and down his neck a little way and then given up, the clear and hateful boundary designating intention, like the poster of the neatly sectioned cow at Hough's Meats.

Hili, Joanna realised, *liked* his fur.

He crumpled the carton and tossed it. "Let's go."

She leaned on his arm, the hair squeaking under her fingers. She felt a pleasant relinquishing of control, a sleepy, tidal desire like the sea that used to lap in the Gat of the Castle, drenching the outlaws who knew to hold their breath, drowning the ones who screamed. Was it better to survive and suffer, or to surrender?

They walked out together through the Castle gates. She had suggested he leave her there but they kept going, under the moths' streetlights, under the rabbit's moon. By the time they reached the meadow, she thought, *I was meant to come back here.*

They walked into the honest grass and faced each other: Joanna was taller by a head. She shrugged out of the ridiculous backpack, and Hili put his arm behind her and tipped her over, a gentle version of the way the boys used to trip the girls at

Kimberley Junior. On her back, it was all as she had imagined—a Café del Mar video, a song by Sting, the sweet grass closing over her head, like hiding in a laundry basket.

Hili stood up again, angled, architectural. His smell was very strong now: Joanna felt her nostrils flaring to take in more. And, because they had arrived, she knew what it was.

He was made of the grass itself, the seasonal uprising, the earth's dirty vegetable urge.

She tore off her shirt and lay back. He was busy disentangling himself from the lederhosen, a parachutist coming in to land. Joanna fingered the stiff hide where he let it fall next to her, the pucks and gathers warm from long settlement against the hinges of his body. What animal had once worn it?

"You can't wash leather," she said.

"No."

The stockings were next: how had he put them on with only one hand? Joanna saw that his dick had been shoved inside one of the stocking legs, to keep it down and out of the way. Did all men have penises this long? She struggled to sit up, feeling the stalks stuck in her hair like runners, as if she was growing into the ground, penetrating the earth in search of Persephone. *I am about to be ploughed,* she told herself. *Ploughed and furrowed. The good earth. The fertile earth. The flaming trellis.* Her teaspoon of bright blood would trickle out onto the soil here in the meadow and seed it for the next season. When she walked through it on her scissoring legs in September, she would know firsthand its heat and pain and growth.

Joanna unclipped his garters. The *snick* of their letting go was loud: there was pressure on her eardrums, the night air, the reversed juices of the grass like blood running the other way along their vessels, the ancient mammalian impulse.

His penis was the only part of him that wasn't covered in hair. It sprang up, freed from the stocking top and smelling of resurrection, eager and eternal and purplish-grey. Joanna reached out and touched the hard, shiny head at the end of the hose. The penis waved agreeably at her and produced one lubricating droplet, clear as venom. *More,* it said. *Harder, and more. You know what to do.*

She lowered her face to the fork of Hili's thighs, her lips already parted, and then she caught a flash of movement from the corner of her eye. Distracted, Joanna turned her cheek aside. His tortured hand again, the claw, flailing as if in a fit. He started making a sound, half hum, half growl, a wind-up monkey with sand in its works. It sent her back to a description she had read for an article on Van Hunks and Table Mountain. The entry was about the Devil—the Father, the witches called him. They said that Beelzebub's semen was ice. Would it feel like that with Hili—a snakebite searing and then numbness as the poison spread?

He pushed her back down, frowning, impatient. The rough ground under her shoulders made Joanna wriggle. The corners of the flat stones were digging into her, but she didn't want to move away. She put her hand on the pelt of his chest: it was hitching. She didn't mind the low moans, the soft panting-growling, or the flecks of spit. Hili kept licking his lips, his eyes so bright that they burned. *What colour are they?* Joanna's brain kept interrupting. *Are they brown or blue or black?*

From his stocking top Hili now pulled a small folding knife, the kind men got for Christmas but never used. "Leatherman," he said, and held it up in his left hand, steady even as the rest of him shook with excitement. He smiled and his teeth were yellow, with an old dog's striations.

She held the zip of her pedal-pushers away from her skin for him, and he flicked the blade under the cloth. He was going to divide her, known and unknown, cast off the bit of skin that stood between Joanna and experience. Hili yanked the blade through the fabric and her pants ripped and stuttered. Joanna pictured herself doing star jumps, bouncing high on the tiny trampoline of her virginity, a girl in a tampon advert, touching the sky.

And the pedal-pushers were gone: Joanna had shed her old skin. She stretched her grateful arms up over her head and closed her eyes: she was ready. Her back clicked back into place, her spine aligning with the stars, the music of the spheres rustling in concert with the grass as Hili lowered his hairy torso onto hers—and then she felt the rushing cold night air.

Joanna opened her eyes.

Where was he? Was this a joke? *Oh, wilt thou leave me so unsatisfied?*

"Hili?"

Silence. The grass, shifting. And there—the sound of someone running, breaking the stalks, and sobbing.

"Hili! Where are you going?"

And his voice came back to her, rough and despairing. "The bricks!"

Joanna angled her head and looked between her parted legs. She was lying across the old foundations of the vanished house, its long stone bones set into the surface of the earth.

She reached down with her fingers and felt along the scabbed and civilised threshold where no tokoloshe could enter. Then she lay back empty-handed, untouchable.

Diane Averbuck wrote Gardening at Night, *which won the Commonwealth Best First Book Award (Africa and the Caribbean) in 2004. Her work has been translated into, among other languages, Mandarin, German, Russian and Swedish. Averbuck's short stories are collected in* Cabin Fever; *a story from this collection was nominated for the 2014 Caine Prize. Her latest highbrow-horror novel is* Home Remedies. *Her doctorate on trauma and humour is coming soon, right after she finishes her new spec-fic series, co-written with Alex Latimer.*

CAVERNS MEASURELESS TO MAN

Toby Bennett

Raw stone bore down on the light of the single miner's lamp with all-engulfing shadows. Jacob Lunga could feel the granite throat constricting every time he blinked the blood from his eyes. He was bent double and rushing into that darkness as fast as he could, drawn by the retreating light.

He wasn't sure if he knew the man in front of him. After the explosion, every-thing around him had degenerated into chaos.

His ears still rang and it was difficult to think. After images played over his vision: Fefo's hand protruding from the collapsed stone; and Segokgo's head snap-ping back as the bullet hit. For all he knew, he was running into more trouble, but there was no going back—the explosion had seen to that. Bad enough to face AK-47s and R1s, but someone had decided to set off the dynamite.

Jacob ducked beneath a ledge of low-hanging stone, fighting to keep up with the guy ahead of him. He almost slipped on the debris that choked the tunnel. Murky water had pooled in the middle of the narrow passage of the long-aban-doned mine. The dust thrown up by more recent drilling was a viscous mess just below the surface. The harder stone beneath the mud was slick, which made each hurried step a risk.

"Not so fast!" he called.

Whoever was up ahead didn't listen, he just kept moving forward, taking the light with him.

He had to keep up; wherever the other man was going couldn't be as bad as being left in the dark. No way to know that he wasn't running right up to the rest of the gang that had hit them, but he'd deal with that if he had to. He'd beg for mercy—if they didn't just shoot him first; he'd get no mercy from shadow and stone.

The light was all but gone.

He's moving too quickly!

It was hard enough to keep up in the confined space, but all these tunnels were new to him. Jacob didn't even know when his quarry might take a sudden turn.

I told Mahau we should stick to our own shafts.

No good crying over that mistake. Zama zama—taking risks was what you did.

For all I know it was Mahau who set off the dynamite... maybe this guy's running from me.

Jacob smiled at the thought and instantly regretted it. Even the brief contraction of the muscles in his jaw sent currents of pain jolting through him. Blood pumped harder in his ears, it felt like his head was going to explode.

My face must be worse than I thought. Lindi wouldn't like it if he was too scarred up.

The light was almost gone.

Jacob forced himself to move faster.

The fabric of his overalls hissed as it scraped against the stone at his back, a snake's warning from the twisting passages ahead of him. The ore in his bag banged against his knee. The bag was an impediment, awkward and heavy, but Jacob didn't think about dropping it. He had to get his ore out or else what had it all been for?

Is there even a way out?

The cave-in had sealed his way back, so he had to hope the man with the light knew where he was going.

The passage turned again and cut downwards; the light ahead was a lambent promise, barely enough for him to see the way ahead. Behind him, the yawning dark rushed closer.

He had to *move.* Jacob scraped some of the drying blood from his eye in a quick motion then threw himself forward on hands and knees. His breath came hard as he scurried through the narrowing passage.

It was strange to think that somewhere over his head the people of Johannesburg were having another day in the sun: paper boys and BMWs, traffic and noise all lost when one came down here. If he stopped now, the world would go on as if he had never existed. Lindi would find someone else and his daughter would call another man father. If he stopped here, he'd have sweated and choked for nothing. He might as well have just lain down next to the others and waited for the dust to settle.

The way ahead narrowed, which forced Jacob to refocus.

Can't get sloppy now.

He hissed as his elbow connected hard with the rock around him. New stars flashed across his vision.

His breath echoed around him, quick and desperate.

The tunnel had become dangerously tight and he had to push himself forward on his belly to squeeze through. The water helped him move quickly, but the stones in his bag dug mercilessly into his hip as he plunged onwards.

The light intensified as he got to the end of the short constriction in the passage.

The other guy had finally stopped. Jacob could just see the man standing at the other side of the larger chamber into which he was sliding.

Is he waiting?

Jacob got to his feet. The tunnel had opened up a lot. In fact, it was wider than any mining shaft in which Jacob had ever been. Here and there stalactites jutted from the stone above.

Jacob gave a groan as he stood upright. His head nearly touched the ceiling but it felt good to stretch his battered body.

"Hey, you. Stay there," he called.

The other man didn't turn around.

"Please just wait." Jacob hobbled forward, favouring his good leg.

The other man stood head bent, as if poring over the light he was holding, an elongated silhouette against the lamp's beam.

"Hey! You deaf or what? Speak to me." Two more steps, he had to bend to avoid a projection from the ceiling. "I said, are you deaf or something?"

He heard his own footsteps reverberating off of the stone, echoing back to him through the gloom. "I've got ore. Get me out and I'll pay."

Idiot! Jacob chastised himself as soon as his offer came out of his mouth.

If he's got a gun he could just take everything and leave you down here. It's not like you'd be the first skeleton left in a shaft. The image of Segokgo and Fefo rose unbidden from his memory.

Jacob squinted, trying to make more of the light obscured by the waiting man.

As he got a little closer, Jacob could guess why the other man had stopped. If their tunnel was wide, the cave beyond was massive. It looked as if there were several exits from the chamber ahead. The lamp light played over the distant walls, making long fingers of the rock formations jutting from the cavern roof.

Perhaps he's lost too.

The thought hit Jacob hard. His only hope had been that the other man knew where he was going. His thirst and pain sharpened as that hope dimmed. He licked his cracked lips and grimaced. The same dust he'd tasted for the past week, only now there was no water to wash it down.

I wonder if there's gold in the dust... The irony was palpable; unless he could find a way out, all the ore in the world wouldn't matter.

And if there is no way out? Jacob recoiled from the thought.

We can't just stand here guessing which way to go—there's no time.

He set his shoulders and stiffened his aching jaw. If the other guy didn't know the way out then he'd take the light. They couldn't just stand around waiting for the batteries to…

Jacob gasped in horror as the light ahead dimmed then went out.

No!

He tried to rush forward, but only succeeded in striking his head on one of the stalactites.

He dropped to the cold floor, his head hammering.

An age passed before he could register anything other than the inky infinity around him.

Jacob wasn't sure if the sobbing he heard was his own or if it was coming from the other man. The sound seemed to resound from all around him, making it impossible to guess which way he should go. The only sensations that seemed certain were the chill of the wet stones under his hand and the warm creep of blood down his temple.

Jacob mastered himself as best he could and crawled in the direction he *thought* he had last seen the light.

When I last saw the light. A cold morning, the sun just a hint on the horizon when we slipped down the ropes into the shafts? The last time I saw the sun?

The memory was thin and unsatisfying, yet it was enough to keep him scrabbling over the damp floor. The ghost of the sun was enough; he didn't dare think of not seeing Lindi again or holding Ejaj in his arms once more. If he dwelt on that, he wouldn't be able to take it, so he kept his mind fixed on the remembered light, the promise of a morning that everyone he loved had seen.

The sobbing stopped, to be replaced by the sound of slow dripping and ragged breathing in the dark.

"You there man?" he called and the stone gave him the same question for an answer. "If you're there, speak to me!"

"Ya." The response was guttural but clear. Jacob wondered if he wasn't the only one with a damaged jaw. "Where are you? Can you get the light working again?"

"Ya."

"Then turn it on. I can't see where I'm going."

"Ya."

Jacob waited. The darkness remained unchanged and the rhythmic sound of the water wore at his jagged nerves.

"Are you still there?"

"Ya."

Jacob ground his teeth in frustration. "You understand me?"

"Ya."

"So stop stuffing about!"

"Ya."

Still nothing.

Jacob started to crawl forward again. "Just give me the lamp. Maybe I can fix it."

"Ya." The word came from right next to him and Jacob started despite himself.

"I told you to stop stuffing about!" Jacob lunged forward to catch the other man but his grasping arms closed on empty air.

Worse, he was falling forward into blackness.

At the last moment, a hand gripped his own, dragging him back from what he now realised must be a ledge.

He was too panic-stricken to do anything but let himself be pulled back and led to his left.

For a brief moment, he imagined that he saw a flash far below him. Had the lamp fallen down there? Was that why the other guy wasn't turning on the light?

"Wait! Not so fast!" Jacob yelled to the man who led him away from the ledge. He cast about with his other hand and shuddered with relief to touch smooth stone next to him.

At least that explained how he was being led. His companion must be feeling the wall just like he was.

But what does that matter? We'll never get out. Even if he wasn't lost when he stopped how can we find our way without any light?

Jacob slowed, but the man gripping his hand just kept tugging him forward and it made as much sense to be led as to stop in the dark and wait for the end.

"You think you can find the way out?"

"Ya."

Jacob chose to believe that the sound was assurance. His fingers bumped along the wall, reminding him of when he was younger and he used to walk next to his old school fence, letting a stick tap against the thick wire.

He hadn't gone to school for very long; there had always been the need to make money. What they taught in classrooms didn't help anyone for a long time.

The ore in his bag swung against his leg, something solid, something he could touch.

Such a stupid reason to be down in the dark, but for all that he'd die before he let the bag go.

The path began to rise and Jacob dared to hope they weren't as far from the surface as he'd imagined.

"Much longer?" He didn't expect an answer anymore but the sound of his voice was a comfort.

"Ya," came the predictable response.

The rock was closing in on both sides now. Jacob could feel it like the pressure of an angry gaze, a malicious weight pressing on the borders of perception. His eyes ached for light. It seemed to him that there were small flashes of colour in the dark around him, but whenever he tried to get a fix on them, they vanished.

When he'd first joined the gang, Mahau used to tell him about people going mad in the dark. If you didn't see anything for too long then the mind plays tricks, Mahau had said. Then he'd turned his lamp out just for a second. His first time down, with a head full of ganja, the threat of losing the light had been scary, but he hadn't come close to imagining what really happened when he stared into the dark for too long. It wasn't just the wisps of colour; every so often it felt like he saw faces staring from the blackness. As the nightmare march continued, he thought he heard voices: his mother scolding, Ejaj's laughter.

The tunnel began to wind down again ever so slowly. It took him some time to even notice.

"We should be going up," he protested.

"Ya," his guide agreed, leading him down.

Jacob stopped and briefly considered trying to pull free and run back, but his near fall and the hopelessness of being left in the dark alone made that impossible. The man tugged at his hand and he started forward again.

"My name is Jacob," he said after a while.

"Ya."

"Who are you? You should tell me in case only one of us makes it." The man in front didn't respond, so he pressed on, "I don't know who you work for, but please, if you do get out and I don't, I need you to find my wife Lindi, Lindi Lunga, we live at—"

"Ya."

"Can't you say anything else? I need to know that you will do this for me. I need to know if you need me to find someone for you."

"Ya."

"Ah, fuck you man!"

"Ya."

Jacob fell silent again and focused on putting one foot in front of the other. He wondered if his guide had been a half-wit before the explosion.

If he's a half-wit, why are you following him god knows where?

His father's face grinned at him from the dark.

Trust the old goat to ask the hard questions.

They might have walked for minutes or hours; Jacob had no way to know. The blood had stopped flowing from his head and was becoming hard and itchy on his skin.

He couldn't let go of his guide's hand or stop touching the wall, so he forced down his discomfort.

At first he thought he was imagining the light coming from ahead—it was barely there, just a red tinge to the darkness. As they moved forward, the illumination intensified. It was probably still no more light than one might see when the moon was hidden behind clouds, but to Jacob's straining senses it seemed almost overwhelming.

"We've done it," he whispered. "You know the way from here. There must be a shaft up if there's light!"

"Ya."

Jacob squeezed the other man's hand. "Thank you." The tears were warm on his face.

I'm going to make it!

They turned a corner and Jacob expected to see a shaft of sunlight, but instead he was surrounded by gleaming crystals scintillating with various colours. The point of each jutting crystal sparked with precious light, perhaps no more than the gleam of a firefly for each.

He blinked in the sudden brightness, struggling to adjust. His companion swam in his vision, a gloomy blur amid the galaxy of flashing stone.

"What's this?" he exclaimed, trying to reach out to the pulsing wall. The man holding his hand dragged him on quickly, heading back into the gloom of another waiting passage.

Jacob's thoughts whirred. Had he gone mad in the dark? What could cause the light? Perhaps if they were close to the surface and sunlight was shining on the tops of the crystals. That had to be it, like when one of the old glass Coke bottles he remembered from his childhood caught the light.

The stones couldn't be glowing on their own, could they?

Jacob tried to keep track of the way they were going. If gold was worth something then how much would people pay for crystals that made their own light? If he got up top, he'd have to find a way back here.

He was so intent on looking for ways of returning that it took him a while to notice how pale the hand holding his own was.

That was strange. He'd never seen a white guy underground. They stuck to working in legal operations or with the kingpins up top. They were the ones behind it all or they worked for them anyway, big guys, ex-soldiers most of them, but this guy was as thin as Jacob was, from the looks of him.

Jacob opened his mouth to comment on this new realisation when they stepped out onto a wide ledge. Above them a cluster of the bright crystals clung to a distant ceiling, glowing like a small sun. Water gushed from the rocks to Jacob's left, forming a white-flecked waterfall that cascaded down into a deep-cut valley arrayed with heavy-capped mushrooms the size of trees.

Jacob caught sight of a white worm sliding between the pallid stalks of the alabaster fungus. The long body's undulations made him think of a maggot. At such a distance it was impossible to tell how large the creature actually was, but he imagined it must be longer than the tallest man he had ever seen.

A maggot bigger than a man.

Jacob stared in horror as the *thing* slithered through the dense growth, only to stop at the base of a huge wall constructed of black stone that rose around a distant city.

If the city had once contained life, it was now dark and still—a mausoleum, monument to another time when the light of the crystals had been brighter and warmer, when the city's folk had farmed the disordered rows of knotted fungus. Not one lamp shone in the windows below, not slumbering but dead, picked over by its forgotten scions.

"Do you see this?" he asked the man next to him.

The *man* next to him.

Jacob turned to regard his guide in the half-light.

Not white but pale, colourless as milk—a skin that had never seen the sun.

Blue veins pulsed beneath his finger. And, as he followed their path up the long skeletal arm, he caught sight of a gaunt face tight with hunger.

There were no eyes, just a flat expanse of pale skin, recessed into the skull. Below that was a thin nose, little more than a slit and an over-sized, misshapen jaw brimming with yellowed teeth.

The creature spread its lips wide and put its head on one side as if considering his question.

"Ya," it said.

Toby Bennett was born in 1976 in Cape Town, South Africa. He holds a degree in philosophy from the University of Cape Town. He has had a varied career that has included graphic and web design, database administration and technical writing. His true passion lies in creative writing and to date he has written nine novels and appeared in various collections of short stories.

I AM SITTING HERE LOOKING AT A GRAVEYARD

Pwaangulongii Benrawangya

I love coffins. I often go to the coffin shops in Barkin Lafia to watch them being stacked on top of each other in graceful columns. I take great pains to make sure nobody discovers this preoccupation—there are things that are mine alone. But there is something big, something romantic that always eludes me at coffin shops. I love coffins, but seeing a coffin with a corpse in it arouses in me a feeling that only poetry can evoke. It is the hunger for this feeling that makes me turn to reading every obituary I can find and taking down the date and time of all the nearby funerals.

The first corpse I ever saw was my brother's. I slept beside him on a mat on the floor of our room on the night he died. I touched the body; it was cold. The eyes were open, dreamy and askance. The face was pale and suffered. My father said he died of malaria. I was ten years old then. Everyone cried, but I didn't. All I wanted was to see the corpse again and again, but they held me back; they said a child must never see a corpse.

Evil. Evil is here. Please take the child away. This is not good for him. They were too close. He may be tormented.

At dusk one day, not so long after my brother died, I sat alone on the veranda of our house when I saw bats. I gazed at them flying away to the trees on the other side of our house. I remembered my brother. I felt myself growing wings within to fly away with them to look for him. I cried then. I became sick and I didn't talk to anyone. They said I was sick for four months.

I began to go see corpses and coffins after I recovered, and have seen many since. The last funeral I attended was a big one. One would know it was going to be a big funeral by merely reading the obituary:

> *With heavy hearts, the family of Adama announces the sudden death*
> *of our father, grandfather, great-grand father, uncle, brother, in-law and*
> *friend, Chief Dr Albert Adama OFR, who passed on in a London hospi-*
> *tal after a brief illness. He was aged 84 (1929 – 2013).*
> *He is survived by Jude Adama (SAN)*
> *Paul Adama, CEO Loolap oil Ltd*

Prof Lalatu Adama and many grandchildren amongst whom is Ambassador Lukas Jude-Adama.
Funeral arrangements are as follows:
Service of songs at St Andrews Catholic Church, Ungwar Yelwa, at 6pm.
Burial at Ungwar Yelwa cemetery on November 13, 2013. Time: 10am prompt.
NB: no African time.
Reception follows immediately at the family house 19 to 24, Goronba Street, Kakuri, Kaduna.

Chief Dr Albert Adama was a big man. He died in a big hospital, in a big country and was given a big burial in a big cemetery.

I arrived at the cemetery before everyone else, and stood at its entrance when the corpse was brought in a long motorcade, in a blue ambulance. The blare of sirens filled the air. When the pallbearers alighted, I thought they were the man's sons, because of their colourful dress. They marched to the ambulance and lifted the coffin onto their shoulders—a big, glittery coffin. I had never seen such a coffin in my life.

I stood in the crowd looking at the coffin. Big, shiny and golden. A warm glow began to surge through me. In my mind, I saw myself walking through the crowd, past the security men, with my eyes fixed on the coffin, which was resting on a stool beside the grave. I imagined reaching it and standing before it like a hunter coming face to face with big game; then opening it. Chief Dr Albert Adama lay there, still. I imagined dragging him out onto the ground, then climbing into the coffin, lying in its sweet smell. Then I would close the coffin and let the warm darkness spread itself all over me.

From him we come, to him we all return. May the soul of the departed rest in perfect peace. Amen.

Amen. Amen.

After the burial, I left the cemetery alone. I walked home thinking about that big, glittery coffin.

My father once told me that dying is pleasant when living becomes sore. Each time we talked about my brother's death, my father always said in a solemn voice that being born poor in this place was like courting death. You sit, unnoticed, looking at the world creating and inventing without you, feeling what an impotent man feels when he sees a pregnant woman.

Today is the burial of the girl who died on my street. I stand behind her wooden house where the grave has been dug. An agama lizard and a chicken with her chicks stand on the red earth at the mouth of the grave. The chicks peck at ants. The chicken scatters some earth backwards, putting its beak into the hole it leaves. I am alone here, save for two women passing by, returning from the farm with bundles of sugarcane on their heads. A breeze is blowing, carrying the smell of the fresh opened earth. I think of my mission here: to see a coffin.

One of the women turns to the road that leads out of the street and bids the other goodbye. They will not be attending the girl's burial. Everyone on the street thinks she was a witch.

Two men emerge from the lower end of the street. I move away from the grave when I see them; the girl's remains will soon be here.

The men at the graveside look into the hole. One of the men—a tall, slender man—turns to his friend, a short albino with tribal markings on his cheeks.

"This grave is too deep," he says. "Ah, do you people want to bury three persons in the same grave? This is more than six feet."

The albino raises his head. He looks at me quickly with the eyes of you-are-not-supposed-to-hear-this, and faces his friend again. "Yes," he says, "it really is. But she should be buried like this."

"Why? Everyone should be buried the same way."

The albino was irritated. "Didn't you know she was a witch? She bewitched her father to his death."

The tall man looks into the grave. He says nothing.

"The deeper they go into the ground," the albino says, "the lighter their power becomes."

The albino is interrupted by deep voices, voices like booming drums, coming from the street. A group of men are approaching. Six of them are carrying something collected in a mat. They look like a procession accompanying a coffin to a burial, but they are not carrying a coffin.

When they arrive, the men drop the mat on the ground and gather into a group around the grave. They talk in quiet tones.

The girl lies on the mat, lifeless. The pre-noon sun shines on her almost-naked body. A piece of black cloth covers her from her neck down to her genitals. No coffin, no coffin. Anger swells in my heart. No coffin?

The men finish talking and turn to surround the mat. They lower the mat with its contents into the grave and begin to fill it with stones, each man vehemently throwing their own. Afterward the albino and six other men shovel earth into the grave.

I notice the chicken scratching near the opening to the street. Beside her, her chicks fight over a dead millipede. Suddenly she squawks and runs, opening her wings for them to hide beneath. I look up and see a hawk diving. It grabs one of the chicks and ascends into the sky, leaving the chicken running around. Her remaining chicks run from her and attack a living millipede. They peck it in quick succession. They seem to be avenging their sibling.

Something ate one of us up, so we started to eat up another thing.

Something ate my brother. Another thing ate the girl.

The men collect their working tools and leave, with the albino trailing behind them. I leave the graveside and walk into the street. A faded green shirt and a long black skirt are clipped on a rope, held up by two bamboo sticks at the front of the girl's house. These were the girl's clothes—I had seen her wearing them.

I start to walk back home, disappointed by the coffinless burial. I look into the sun shining above the street, as I used to do with my brother when we were kids. Its rays beam into my mind and illuminate my imagination. I see the girl, standing on her toes under the sun, looking up to it and stretching up her hands to grab it. She wears her green shirt and black skirt.

I came to this street during the rainy season of 2006, a few days after I left the ref-ugee camp at Barkin Dutse. My parents' death was still sitting big in my heart. They had been killed by rioters, who were killing people because of their beliefs. I hadn't seen how my parents were killed. I didn't know where they were buried.

One afternoon, sitting in the tent at the camp, I tried to imagine the rioters killing them. They were kneeling before the rioters, who were carrying machetes, sickles, guns and gallons of petrol. They stood, their eyes bloodshot. Mother was crying but my father would not. African men don't cry. Even before death. They are not white men, who cry over everything—a broken pencil, withering grass. A small insult can make them cry like children and women.

My father was an African man. He bent his head and looked at the ground. One of the rioters approached and flashed his torch on him. He did not raise his head…

I didn't miss anything at the camp except the coffins. I wanted to smell death around me again.

A strange, murky excitement glowed in me the first time I saw the girl on our street. Dressed in her green shirt and long black skirt, she carried herself in silence. She walked burdened.

She passed along the street without talking to anyone. *Is she parentless, sick and helpless?* One day, standing under the neem tree, I saw her return to her wooden house. There were tears in her eyes, rolling down her face. I couldn't stop thinking about her after that.

The only time I ever spoke with the girl was in a dream the night after a state of emergency was declared on Barkin Lafia. The riots had begun again. Soldiers were everywhere, with guns and armoured tanks, but people were being killed anyway.

I dreamt I was in my room at dusk, just finishing a painting, when she entered. She wore her green-striped shirt and long black skirt. I stood and hung the painting on the wall. "Sit there," I said to her. I pointed at the plastic chair opposite my small mattress on the floor.

"No, I'll not sit down," she replied. "I know you've being longing to speak to me."

"That's not true," I said. "Who told you that?"

"No one told me. I just know."

"Wallahi—it's not true"

"Look at you in here all day." She pointed at my painting.

I saw I had painted a coffin lying open on the ground. At the coffin's side was a pair of slippers and, at its head, a standing winged figure: an angel, looking away from the coffin towards the heavens.

"Tell me," the girl said, "are you afraid of the soldiers outside?"

"I won't break the curfew," I said, "but I'm not afraid of them. I'm always working in here anyway. I'm an artist."

"Artist? So you studied at the university?"

"I didn't study at the university," I said. "I was in college studying fine art. I dropped out in my second year. But I'm not just a painter. I'm trying to be an *artist*. I mean painting, novels, poetry."

"I love poetry," she said, excited. "I used to read a lot of poems. Oswald Mtshali's 'Nightfall in Soweto' is my favourite."

I picked up a towel on the mattress and cleaned off a drop of paint from my arm. "I have a lot of favourites. Langston Hughes' 'Night Funeral in Harlem', Celan's 'Fugue of Death', Thomas Gray's 'Elegy Written in a Country Churchyard'…" The names rolled off my tongue.

She chuckled. "The first poem that made me cry was AE Housman's 'To an Athlete Dying Young'. I read it one term in secondary school."

"That's a nice poem," I said.

She sat on my floor. "Something funny thing happened that term in school. The teacher who introduced the poem to us died. The principal chose me to read a poem for the teacher at the candle night we held in his honour. And I read that poem. I cried that night. He was a real athlete dying young. On this continent, many athletes are dying young."

She stood and walked to the painting on the wall, and held it with both hands. She peered into it again and again, deeper and deeper, like a priestess in a divination.

"Do you like my work?" I asked her.

Silence. She turned from the painting and looked at me, her faced pinched. "No," she said. "It's poor, but I like its intention. It reminds me of my father."

"Your father?"

"My father loved angels. He was obsessed with angels." She embraced herself and began to shiver. I walked over and led her to a chair. I placed my hands on her shoulders. Her body was cold.

"Father used to say that angels live on that neem tree in front of my house. But we didn't believe him. He said they were peacekeeping angels, angels who are tired of their mission in Africa. I asked him if they were African angels. He would chuckle. He said that Africa doesn't have angels. Blacks can't be angels."

"That doesn't make sense," I said.

"He would say things like, 'Do you want Heaven to be underdeveloped?' Or, 'Do you want God to be president of a third-world country?' Father said angels are white, and that the ones on that tree might be European Union angels. He would laugh and laugh and laugh.

"Each time Father talked like this, my mother would drag me to our room and whisper, 'Be careful before you begin to get tormented like your father.' She would hang her rosary on my neck and pray over me."

"Why was your father tormented?"

"A prophet once told my mother that demons will torment Father and me. Me, I don't believe that prophet. Father was a good man. I know how it all began. We read in the newspapers that the government was planning a retrenchment in the textile company where Father worked. Those days, he arrived home earlier than before, he talked less and less. We knew his worry.

"At night he would wake up smiling. If anyone asked him why, he would say angels are here. They look like the sun. They shine like the sun. They burn like the sun."

The girl hunched over in the chair. "One morning he stood at the door, his eyes on the neem tree and hands on his belly as if it was aching. My mother went over to him, held him on the shoulder. 'Dada, why are you like this? Are you tormented?'

"He smiled and said, 'Nana, I've just swallowed an angel. It hurts there, it hurts down there. It burns like the sun.'"

"Where is your father now?"

She gave a frail smile. "He went with the angels during the Sharia riots," she said. "Five years ago. The afternoon he went, the street was empty. Everyone was inside our house. Father stood with us at the window where we were watching the street. Suddenly, a figure on fire struggled down from the top of the street—a man set on fire by some rioters.

"Father turned and looked at us, starry-eyed, and smiled and said, 'Look, it's an angel. An angel wearing the sun's clothes.' He raced to the door, kicked it open and like a child jumping in the air, he approached the figure. 'I've seen an angel,' he said, over and over. He reached the person on fire and embraced them.

"I wanted to run to my father but my mother held me, I could hear the pounding of her heart. The rioters were nearing them. The rest were two bodies blazing under the sun."

She rose from the chair and walked towards a lantern I had lit in the corner. The light outlined her thin frame.

"I'm sorry about your father's death," I said.

"Sorry? Come on, be happy. How many people die with an angel?"

"What about your mother?"

"She moved out of the house the next day. She said to me that morning that one day I will begin to see and court angels too. She went away."

She walked close to me and gazed in my face. "Are you hungry?" she asked.

"No," I said. "I am not hungry."

"You can't lie."

"I'm not hungry," I snapped. "I know when I am. I am not a child."

"You are a *child*. You are hungry and tired. Tell me, you are hungry and tired."

"Tired? Yes I am. Hungry? No, I am not."

"You look hungry. Does this continent make you feel hungry?" She leaned to touch my face. "You know you are an artist; you have to leave this continent. Artists should not be hungry. Hunger imprisons true creativity."

She sprang away from me and ran towards to door. "I will go and cook," she said, excited. "I will bring you some food before the curfew hour comes and stay with you. Tomorrow we will go to the neem tree under the sun. Angels will be there. We need to see angels."

"Why?" I asked her. "Why do we need to see the angels?"

"Yesterday a hawk came into my yard and took one of my chicks. I want to ask the angels and find out why it did that. I want to ask them why it had to be *my* chick."

She stepped out of the room into the darkness. She never came back.

One November evening, a few months after the dream, I was seated around the hearth in the compound in which I lived. We were peeling melon seeds for Mama Ishaku and chatting—everyone was talking about a fight they had seen between the girl and an electrician. I had been attending a funeral at Leda Galadimawa when the fight happened. The stories astounded me. What caused it? How was it fought? I probed Ishaku, who was seated beside me on the bench. He threw a small piece of wood into the fire. "You know that the girl's house doesn't have any source of light," he said. It was a statement rather than a question.

"I know that," I said. "She has been rejecting the lamps that they have been giving her."

"That was how it started. The electrician had drawn power into her house from her neighbour's house this afternoon while she had been out." He looked into the fire before us and hunched forward, as if the remainder of the story was in the fire, which was eating the wood he had thrown into it earlier.

Then he asked, "Do you know that that girl is strange?"

"Tell me what happened."

"This evening when power was restored and she saw that her room was illuminated, she began to cry. She took a plank and broke the bulbs in and outside her house. When the electrician came and confronted her, she punched him in the eye. He retaliated, then they fought. But what was most surprising about it was that she kept shouting something about angels. Gaskiya, she was calling angels."

I remained seated on the bench, wordless. I stared into the fire—its yellow, blue and white flames. I did not know when everyone, including Ishaku, left the fireplace. Alone in the compound, I walked to my room and looked at the sky. It was big and moonless.

Nobody saw the girl after the incident. Her house remained locked.

When I saw the girl again, she was not the girl. She re-emerged into the street wearing a new dress. She walked to the top of the street as per her custom, but now she now sashayed. She wore a smile like a gold chain. She walked past us at the street's borehole, where we stood with our jerry cans awaiting our turns to fetch water. All the boys in the queue were looking at the girl except Ishaku, who stooped beside us playing with the sand. As we struggled back to get positioned in the queue, Ishaku walked to my place.

"The girl now has a lover," he told me. "Gaskiya ne, I've seen them many times at night."

I had to find out more. I went out on a moonless night during a power outage, travelling from my compound amid the chirps and blinks of the nocturnal insects to the neem tree, hoping to see them—she and the lover. I squatted under the tree. My heart was pounding and, as the minutes passed, I saw them. Like bodiless figures they came down the street in the darkness. They calmly walked in that night as if the darkness were a friend. As they come close to where I squatted, I could see the lover's right hand on her waist. An icy spirit ran through me. I decided to walk past them then heard Ishaku, in a voice that was not his, telling her: "Angels are no more here. Allah! They've gone to the other side. I will go and find money, then take you away. Far away. We will be with the angels there. Bazan barki ba har sai mun je wajen."

I stopped walking as the icy spirit made my body cold, almost cold like my brother's corpse. They continued conversing, not noticing anyone's presence.

"Do you really like me?" she asked him. "Do you like me so much? Look, angels used to be on this neem tree but they aren't anymore. Where are they? Where did they go so soon? I want to see an angel. Help me see an angel. I don't want to die."

I ran away without hearing how Ishaku responded. I did not sleep that night.

The next morning Ishaku was found dead on the mound of rubbish behind our compound. A music box was on his chest, its rope around his neck. His eyes were opened like my brother's. I did not touch him. I did not cry. I only gazed at his body. He looked like my brother's corpse. Dead people resemble each other. The corpse was carried into the compound, to his aged, widowed mother.

The funeral was on the evening of the Friday. I was in the compound before the crowds arrived and had a good seat to watch the activities—especially the coffin.

On this street, death brings more friends than life. When everyone was seated on the benches, four boys carrying a coffin on their shoulders marched into the compound. The girl walked behind them. Her eyes were swollen and tearful. She motioned to the boys to drop the coffin in the centre of the audience and knelt beside it. I felt that icy spirit in my chest again. I could feel my brother's cold corpse rubbing against my body. I sat there, shivering, gazing at the coffin.

There on her knees, with her hands raised, she began to speak to the corpse. "You!" she screamed. "You lied to me! You promised to take me away, to renew my being, to refresh my essence collected in the warmth of those angels. But here you lie, lifeless as those promises." She placed her hands on the coffin. "This coffin is for you. I kept it in the coffin shop at the bottom of this street for my own death, but you need it now more than I. You were there for me and here I am for you."

Everyone around was lost in her actions. I began to feel that strange, murky excitement I felt the first day I saw her on the street. Turning away from the coffin, she let out empty laughter, then dropped to the ground, beating her thighs. She began to cry—a strong groaning. It was the strangest cry I had ever heard, as if she was going to die.

She didn't stop crying for many days. She sat on the ground outside her wooden house crying and beating her breasts. Sometimes, sitting under the neem tree with her leg spread out, she screamed. Everyone said the cry was no longer for the death: for a rash grew across her face, her legs were swelling and her breasts were bigger. Was she pregnant? Had insanity crawled into her being like a guinea worm?

My father once said that being born poor in this place was like courting death. Every time I think about this, I see the girl in her faded green striped shirt and long black skirt standing in my mind. I see my brother's corpse lying on that mat. Each time I think about what this statement means, I feel a severe hunger to see a coffin. I feel cold hands reaching for my body and my body growing cold.

Pwaangulongii Benrawangya studies literature at the Ahmadu Bello University, Zaria, Kaduna State, Nigeria. He was invited by Chimamanda Adichie to the 2013 Farafina Writing Workshop in Lagos.

HANDS

Tiah Beautement

His hands are elegance personified. Peeping from between the stacks of the Cape Town Central Library, I watch as this man's fingers slip along the bindings, dip among the pages. Controlled, smooth, knowing—these are hands that are skilled. Should I be in position to accept a lover's attention, these would be hands I would court. To touch, to hold, to caress, to dream…

Pain flares down my arms, asserting its dominance over my flesh. There is no escape from its grasp. The talons are fused to my being, as the beast consumes my physical capabilities, leaving me with many desires and no means to fulfil them. My ex-husband's solution to the changed me—divorce. Now he may freely copulate without the guilt of adultery. And while I am unable to do the same, I can still observe.

I mentally push above the burn in my limbs and move closer to the source of my fascination. The man in the stacks pays no notice. Either oblivious, or simply accustomed to attention. The rest of him is the sort that would be admired by the general populous. Although being handsome might not be worth much. There are those who have tried to reassure me—"At least you still have your looks"—as if this makes up for six piano-less years.

I creep closer, intending to get a better look at the pads of this man's fingertips, hoping for tell-tale signs of calluses acquired by playing a musical instrument. But my focus wanders, noting what is not happening. A minute passes, and another, and still he doesn't… "You don't breathe."

"I do," he says. Calm, without a glance from the pages. "I'm merely discreet."

Fear gives a kick to my belly, but my instinct for survival has long been dulled by the ache. "No, I've been watching you for some time and you've yet to take a breath."

The book shuts.

I wait.

"If I didn't breathe, I couldn't talk."

"The air doesn't travel further than your throat."

He turns, looking me in the eye. A momentary flash of an elongated incisor sends a bolt of panic through me, but then I remind myself I'm in the library, for heaven's sake.

"And do you think it is wise to discuss throats with me?"

Fuck it. It is the way he states this warning, with pedantic dry tones reserved for a dull child, that hits the one remaining nerve that has not been deadened by six years of torment. The one still capable of becoming irritated and frustrated with men who walk freely on the streets while cautioning women to conduct themselves with care: *don't go out at night, use the buddy system, have pepper spray, don't! Don't! Don't!* Maybe he is, but maybe he isn't, but *I'm not taking this shit.*

The faux apology drips sweetly from my lips, "Oh, I've embarrassed you. Shame. If you didn't want to talk about it, you only had to say."

A twitch of an eyebrow is the only hint that my words have had any effect. Then his features mask themselves into the overconfident air often acquired by men who've never doubted they have the upper hand. "Not going to scream?"

Fuck. "Would there be any point?"

He sets the book back on the shelf, without taking his gaze off me. Numbly, I watch the bound pages slide into place, perfectly. "I'll take that as a no. Perhaps, then, you'd care to join me for a cup of coffee?"

Coffee? What the hell... But then I consider the offer. Six years ago I'd have refused, but now confined within a cage of aching tissues comes the freedom of no longer placing such a high value on remaining alive. *It will make a more memorable obituary, at least.*

We end up at an eccentric café, known for its mismatched chairs and crockery, which brews beans a step above the average commercial fare. After placing our orders, we sit at a rickety table, whose peeling paint reveals wood etched by time. In the quiet, we study each other. I cannot decide if what I've observed is true or not. Yet if he is, it isn't all that inconceivable, I suppose. Humans tell the same stories even in our future history. Each tale is a recycling of the one before, containing a kernel of truth built on the misunderstood.

Now this potential kernel of truth is before me, thanking the barista as she sets our drinks upon the table. When she is back behind the counter he says, "Why were you watching me?"

"Your hands," I say, curling my own around my mug. "I used to play the piano."

"Why did you stop?"

I hold out my ruined palms, giving him a brief look, before trotting out the onerous explanation. How it isn't deadly, but is degenerative. The battle to try to stay engaged, as my interests and pleasures must be sought in increasingly smaller, simpler things.

He nods as I pause to sip my drink. "I can smell the meds."

I sniff.

"No, it's not that bad. I'm simply wired to notice these things. It—" He offers a rather wicked smile. "Impacts the taste."

Shit. I glanced down and see his mug is still full. "You're not drinking."

"Coffee no longer agrees with me, but I enjoy the aroma and it's an excellent method of keeping my hands warm."

And your offer of coffee had given me such optimism.

He waits, his face presenting a smile of perfection. *Trust me,* his body language seems to say. Perhaps this is how he convinces people to offer their throats. My ex-husband plays a similar game, soothing people into handing over their investment portfolios to his self-interested care.

"I have questions," I say.

"So ask."

I do, even as I wonder if I've read the whole situation wrong. *Maybe he is a liar, having a laugh?* Yet there is something about the timbre of his voice that makes me want to believe, which only leads to suspicion. It is his willingness, however, to say, "I don't know," to some of my queries—How did your kind begin? How many of you exist? Were you ever human?—that begins to ease my distrust. Snake-oil salesmen and politicians always have a retort, regardless of its factual accuracy.

He is so old, yet his memory is incomplete, just like mine. More questions emerge, each one bringing hope a bit further out of the abyss where I'd banished it, until hope asks, "Is it true your blood cures?"

"If it did," he says, "wouldn't we be selfish asses, keeping it all to ourselves? Imagine, a donation here and there and cancer could be beaten, malaria extinct. Alas, our accelerated abilities to heal are not as simplistic as magic blood."

And this is why hope should never be allowed to breathe.

But I refused to show disappointment; be too much like giving pain another victory, so I ask, "And living forever?"

"Not quite. Harder to kill. Nobody lives for eternity."

For some reason, this answer is comforting.

A tentative friendship develops, first over cups of coffee, which leads to games of chess. Odd perhaps, but it is such a pleasure to be around somebody who could be content in the moment, even if my enjoyments are small. There is no pressure to be the person I was, simple appreciation of who I now am. I discover he plays the piano, but I don't mention the one stashed in my studio flat. I can't have everything exposed. Not yet. Instead he displays his talents by commanding the instrument in underused bars. We attend a few concerts at the Kirstenbosch gardens, he lounging in the grass, I propped up in a nest of pillows. At times our hands find themselves gently interlinked. There has been a brief kiss here or there, but nothing further. We rarely discuss the burn, shadowing my every moment.

"Might you invite me in?"

I pause with my hand on the latch. "I could, but don't expect anything."

"What do you mean?"

"I mean just that. I can offer a hot cup for your hands, but that will be it."

He tilts his head, as if considering. "All right. I accept your generous offer of a warm mug. If you have hot chocolate, even better. The smell is delicious."

Shit.

Inside, I busy myself with the kettle at the kitchenette, bracing for questions at the instrument taking up most of the space. There is nothing else to remark on except for my bed. *Don't remark on my bed.*

"Take a seat," I say, gesturing to the two barstools, the only islands of conversational neutrality.

He ignores them, crowding behind me.

I fumble for the mugs.

He stretches out one of his exquisite hands, running the back of it along my cheek.

"I want you," he whispers.

"What do you mean?"

A knuckle trails down my neck, curves over the shoulder, along the arm until reaching my fingertip. "As a man. A lover."

I thought he'd understood. "Not possible, I'm afraid. Nothing personal. Just how it is."

"Don't you miss it?" His thumb has begun tracing shapes on the inside of my curled palm, softly-softly as if the skin might tear. He has no idea.

But who could? I clumsily uncap the coco. "My missing it or otherwise isn't the point. It simply is what it is."

"But if I could help. A thirty-minute to an hour reprieve from the pain. Would you want me, as a man?"

The kettle clicks. I turn away and slosh the liquid into the mugs. He lightly places his hands over mine.

Warmth creeps up my arms, mingling with the burn. But this heat is different, pleasurable, despite the constant aches. "How?"

His lips brush the line of my neck. "A small nip."

I twist away and settle on the piano bench, for there is nowhere else to flee. I slide my warped fingers along the keys, careful not to press. I glide my hands over the white and black, slipping along their lengths. Considering.

He says, "What are you thinking?"

So many things. I keep my eyes on my ruined digits, playing out their soundless melody. "I'm not sure I understand."

He crosses the room, takes a seat beside me. I flinch. He acts as if he doesn't notice, placing his hands next to mine and mimics the inaudible song. Odd how this makes me more nervous than the day we met. Rejected one too many times, perhaps.

He says, "What don't you understand?"

"You'd drink from me?"

"Ah, well, not quite. You only need the bite to absorb the venom." He lets out a soft chuckle, which seems weighted, far from mirth. "I suppose I'm much like a mosquito, except I won't leave an itch."

Wordlessly, we play a few more bars. "Look," he says, "the point is you would feel very good for a time. For some, it lasts a few hours. But it would be enough."

The words hang. His fingers shift. It takes me a moment to see where he is going, then I understand and move to take the lead. Relief dissolves my nervousness, as we map out Strauss's *The Blue Danube*. Delight steps in. This is flirtation between fingertips. But I am reluctant to allow hope to rise.

I say, "Wouldn't you be tempted to keep drinking?"

"No. I've recently eaten."

Our hands brush.

Yet.

"Really? Isn't it still hard, with the vein right there, to resist?"

He shrugs as our hands continue moving in perfect duet.

"What are you not telling me?"

"It's nothing."

"It must be something." I still. "What? You don't mix food and sex?"

"I think we should drop it."

I turn to face him, the burn intensifying at my abrupt movement, causing me to snap. "Oh no, I'd like to hear this."

He shifts, gaze not meeting mine. A rarity. "Look, don't take this the wrong way, but you wouldn't taste nice."

Laughter bursts out, causing pain to radiate from my ribs, running along the spine until it rattles against my skull. But I can't stop laughing; it is all too preposterous. He's told me how he feeds. How the numbing effect of his bite leaving his human-of-choice mistaking his careful sips for a wicked after-make-out hickey.

He gives me a mischievous grin, and finally his eyes meet mine. "It has no reflection on you as a person."

"No… reflection… stop… you're—" The aching laughter takes over.

Concern crosses his face. He reaches out and carefully rubs my back until my breathing returns to normal, but my outburst has left my sides feeling bruised.

"I'm sorry," he says.

"Don't. Everything has a price, but sometimes the discomfort is worth it. What is the point if I cannot even laugh?"

"The point is, you could laugh, and more. Let me help."

"You don't know that for a fact. It might even be too messed up for even your bite."

"What is the harm in trying?"

Hope.

Instead, I offer a joke. "Well, for starters, you said so yourself, I'd taste bad."

"Would you want me to feed from you?"

Heat floods my face. Has my inability to be intimate left me yearning for whatever scrap I can take? "I can't believe we're having this conversation."

He cups my cheek, thumb stroking the thin skin beneath my eye. "Nor I, to be honest." The words are soft. Much like his touch. "But I'm attracted to you and, I believe, you are to me. I wish for us to become lovers. You have a practical objection. I've provided a practical solution. It's as simple as that."

"It isn't simple. You have to bite me for it to work."

"Are you honestly telling me that you're afraid of a small nip?"

Fear, I thought I'd left you far behind.

I offer him my neck.

Pain retracts. Not so much tamed, but like a snake, coiling up, biding its time to strike. Skin tingles, liberated to enjoy the caress of the air, the pressure of his touch. Delight. Delicious. Dangerous. This reprieve from my viper could oh too easily become my heroin. Until now I've never fully appreciate how much living hurts until being granted this parole from the beast. Hope screams for more.

Afterwards, under the covers, naked, he holds me against his solid self, while the viper extended its fangs, reasserting its dominance among my cells. A small prick of regret begins to bleed. Now it is harder to forget what is I have missed.

"We can't do that again," I say.

He brushes the hair from my face, bringing his lips close to my ear. "Did you not enjoy it?"

"Too much."

He falls silent, holding me still in his strong, yet careful embrace until the pain's jagged teeth has me clenching my own. Then he rises, fetching a glass of water and the various containers brimming with modern chemistry. Deftly he uncaps, unzips and pops, placing what I request into my curled palm. When the last pill has been swallowed, he sits on the edge of the bed, beside me, our clothes still on the floor. His naked form, beautifully constructed, radiating health, virility. While mine is a vessel curling inward, prematurely aging, courting inevitable decay.

Wordlessly, he waits. Through his gaze I detect something that is not quite pity. More, deeper—yet less.

The quiet begins to grate against my over-stimulated nerve endings, the drugs not catching up. I lifted my gaze to the ceiling, hoping my voice won't betray how close I am to tears.

"Please understand, it would not be right to allow myself to be dependent on you. It is too... there is too much wrong with needing somebody like that. You would become addictive in a way you do not deserve."

He plucks up my misshapen hand and places it on his muscular thigh. There my hand sits, intimately close to his penis, still glistening from our coupling. His elegant index finger—the very one that had so recently plucked at my nipples, stroked my clitoris, dipped deep inside to tease a spot that left me screaming, now traces the edges of my claws. "I wouldn't desire such a relationship, either. To be wanted for only that."

I release an unsteady breath. "Then you understand. Not again."

His finger continues to trace: up down, up down. Seconds pile up, pushing time along. The quiet stacks itself until I can nearly taste his words of farewell.

"I could change you over," he says. "No longer human, your ills would be history."

My throat closes as hope tries to rise.

"Only if you wanted, of course."

Chill sweeps my skin.

He runs his palm up my bare arm, as if trying to iron out the goose flesh. "It would give you permanent freedom from the pain. Independence."

My body goes still, warily watching his words collect on a mental table of choice, now challenging the grim reaper's opaque promises.

Yet.

"Nothing is that simple," I say. "There is always a cost."

Hope lets out a small cry.

"Yes." He lifts my palm to his lips—so close to those teeth that have scraped against my flesh, entered my veins.

A kiss.

"But you could handle the burden of time. You are not easily bored despite your circumstances. Your curiosity is one of depth. Unlike most, you are rather suited to this life. It is only the pain that has caused you to be so blasé over living life."

I consider the pain, whose presence over the years has both plagued and tutored. It had taught me the consequence of hasty decisions. Revealed the ramifications of hope—the very one crying to be freed. But I have seen the dangers lurking behind the silky language of cures. So I give pain a poke, and inquire about our future. In reply it creates a vision of unending moments spinning outwards, twining itself into a rope of years, until it curled, wrapped around, morphing into a noose.

"I need to think about it," I say.

Time he gives me. Three weeks, to be precise.

"Have you considered my offer?" he asks. We are back in the coffee shop with the mismatched chairs, he cradling a mug of hot chocolate with a pale pink marshmallow bobbing in the milky brown.

I draw my mug of coffee closer, breathing deeply, as if gathering courage from the heat. "I don't understand why you offer."

He frowns. "You can't see why I'd want you to be rid of the pain?"

I sigh. "It is more than that. What if I find I don't suit such a change?"

"You've contemplated ending your life because of the pain. What's to stop you doing from making the choice later?"

I wave him off. "Really, that's a side issue."

He leans in, jawline hardening. "Then what's the issue?"

"I don't understand if you have this ability then… it seems selfish to accept when… It isn't like the condition is fatal. Frustrating, yes. But when there are so many people dying—tuberculosis, pneumonia, starvation—why not save one of them? To offer this to me seems unnecessary. Or that there is something else."

He clucks his tongue. A muttered oath. "It isn't about saving. Or a price. Yes, I am selfish. I want you to be free. To have a choice of being with me or not."

"Like God, you want those that love you to have free will."

"I am far from God!"

I rear back in my seat.

Quieter, he says, "I want companionship, not devotion."

"And wouldn't I be beholden to you?"

He raises a brow. "As you are to your ex?"

Touché—to bring up the man on whom I still depend for medical aid. I consider defending myself. Instead, I say: "You could help people."

"No, I couldn't. They'd cease to be people."

"Still, you'd save them."

"From what, exactly?" He shoves back his chair, placing ankle on knee. "What if they don't want to be saved? What if they miss humanity? What, pray tell, am I to do if the endless years lead to boredom? When boredom leads to harm? Am I to be judge and executioner as well?"

"Isn't that what you are doing now?"

His foot slams down. Leaning forward, he says, "Again, you are missing the point. It is natural for humans to die. Even what I'm offering would require your humanity to cease."

"I still don't—"

"I do. I've watched people. For years. Most claim that if they had more time they'd learn new languages, master an instrument, write that book supposedly dwelling inside. But that isn't true. You are a rarity. You do not require being passively entertained."

"No, I'm not. Most people are busy. Working. Raising families."

"Nonsense. Time is there and instead of using it, they sit and watch the television, go to the next club, take the next bet, needing more and more of something they can't even name until their search for the next rush has them creating havoc for no reason other than the spectacle it brings. Longevity rarely does the world favours."

"So it is for the greater good you let most of world's population suffer? I'm not sure if I can take such a stance. What then?"

"The greater good, eh?" Amusement crosses his face. "Now that is a different matter altogether. I welcome this debate. Go on, tell me how you'd use a set of fangs for the greater good."

The conversation runs in circles. We chase it up and down. Frustration builds as he plays the devil's advocate.

"It isn't fair," I blurt.

He folds his arms across his chest. Smug. "No, it isn't, but you still eat while others starve. You still use private health care while others go without. You still sleep alone at night while others shiver on the street."

"But this is bigger than that."

"No, it isn't. And you are missing the point."

"Which is?"

"That the offer is there. You have a choice. Why not consider taking it?"

I leave.

He does not follow.

The next day he phones. "It's your life. I'll enjoy your company, human or otherwise," he says.

Days go by until a flare-up sends me to bed. Now here I am, studying the ceiling while he watches me from the windowsill. And what exactly have I accomplished by indecision? In avoiding the obligation of sainthood have I, instead, been acting like a martyr clinging to a hair shirt?

He says, "Have you made a decision yet?"

Slowly, I shake my head.

He says nothing in reply.

Lying back in the pillows, I close my eyes. The pain slithers under the skin, tunnels through the delicate soft tissues, and leaves burning tracks in its wake. Tentacles burrow, questing for muscle and bone; tiny hooks latch onto the nervous system. Fighting only makes it worse, tensing the body, bunching and scrunching until every cell howls. Instead, the body must inhale. Long, deep breaths, stretching the lungs, rib cage and belly, welcoming in the unwelcome while refusing to panic. Acceptance is the only way to remain sane.

He says, "Why do you wait?"

"Is there a rush?"

"I only ask because it seems pointless to torture yourself."

I open my eyes. He is frowning from his perch.

I ask, "Are you bored?"

"As I have said many times, I am not easily bored."

"Good." My eyes flutter close.

"But I do know when someone is avoiding confrontation."

I flinch.

"If I didn't know better, I would say you were waiting to die."

I say nothing. I have already confessed to being tempted by death in moments of weakness. Seductive promises of peace, an airy lightness, floating outside the self. Or no self at all. A utopia most youth would not understand.

At one low point I became engrossed in a macabre study of methods to end my life. But not one book could promise that death would achieve the release I craved. Some, in fact, foretold eternal damnation.

An utter lack of afterlife I can handle. *The end* as dull as switching off the television. Circuits disconnected, wiring fried. Nothingness. But being infinitely doomed to remain in my current state, or worse, is too horrific to contemplate. So I wait.

"If it's too much, I'm happy to provide a temporary reprieve," he says.

"Thank you, but no. That would only cloud the issue."

He drops audibly to the floor. Footsteps reveal his shift around the room. He is being courteous. A scrape across the wooden floors. A settling as denim meets leather. The piano bench.

"Would it be too much if I played?" he says.

"I would enjoy the music. Thank you."

"No headache, then?"

"No, not tonight."

The music begins—Chopin, one of my favourites. Inwardly, I smile as the nocturne spills into the melody. It is as if he is trying to woo tonight. Nobody has made so much effort to please in years. Not that I blame them. Even my ex-husband, selfish bastard though he may be, I understand. Being with a person with more woes than a hypochondriac is wearing, even for the most devoted optimist. This man is not an optimist, however. I intrigue, he has said. This is pleasing, apparently.

The composition shifts. Schubert.

I clear my throat. "I can tell the difference, you know."

"I know," he says, without disruption to the tempo. "I enjoy that about you."

"That's something, I guess."

"It is. Now, hush. I like this part."

I comply. Happily so.

"Why do you insist on keeping it?" my ex-husband asked, after I demanded he have my baby grand moved to my current studio flat.

"Because it is mine," I said.

He had shaken his head, grumbling how the instrument consumed too much of the inarguably limited floor plan. I knew better than to explain my foolish hope.

The piano falls silent. "More, please," I say.

"You could play, yourself, if you'd allow me to help."

"I don't want to have this discussion right now."

"Why not?"

"I'm still weighing the costs."

"You could weigh them as you play."

"We'd only end up having sex," I say.

He chuckles. "I wouldn't mind."

Nor would I.

Yet.

The piano goes quiet.

"Please," I say. "Another piece."

He replies with Handel's mournful *Sarabande*.

I bite my lip. This impatient melancholy being displayed tonight is new. Then again, he has never seen me this bad before. I force my eyelids open and shift on the pillows so I can witness his hands in action. They move along the keys with precise, fluid grace.

The notes begin to beckon, then they argue for me to acquiesce.

So tempting to rid myself from pain, my constant companion. For even in slumber it stalks me. Shadows chase after the dreams while the medication swirls, sending the subconscious tumbling head over heels into the burning pit.

Except once.

Those moments we coupled were the first time I'd been liberated, free of those tentacles, those hooks, in years. Joy of *being*. Then he and I had created a different pleasure, revelling in mutual desire and sensual touch. Since then memories of us, his body inside mine, slip along my consciousness, leaving me longing.

Selfish.

True.

The notes reach out and taunt me. How I miss having the music under my command. It was once my life. For six years I've tried to enjoy it through the hands of others. Not the same. Akin to watching a steady stream of erotic films, with no hope of your own release.

I take a deep breath, exhaling a decision.

The piano halts.

There is a scrape as the bench is pushed back. His deliberate footsteps cross the floorboards, telling of his approach. His weight dips the bed. One of his talented fingers touches me behind the ear, wanders down my throat. My nipples tighten, heartbeat increases. He inhales sharply.

Lips brush my ear.

"Say yes," he whispers.

Tiah Marie Beautement lives on the South African Garden Route with her husband, two kids, Orwell-the-dog and a small flock of chickens (four of which want to be house pets). Her second novel, This Day, was published by Modjaji Books in September 2014.

MARION'S MIRROR

Gail Dendy

I

It happened on a Friday morning. At 5.47am to be exact. Outside it was still dark. And it was winter—the sort of Highveld winter when the landscape appears to disintegrate into a powdery ash prior to the dawn.

Marion had been awake for almost an hour. That wasn't in itself unusual, as this had been the pattern for more than two months, but now the lack of sleep was becoming chronic. She'd been concerned that, only the night before, she'd begun to hear things, a carthorse, for instance, lumbering through the private driveway of the block of flats where she lived. Of course there was no carthorse in Killarney, no leather strapping, no nosebag, no wooden side shafts. Yet the sound was absolutely distinctive with its *clip-clop* of hooves, proceeding somewhat unsteadily as though the horse was, in fact, slightly lame. And had she not heard a whinnying as of a horse? And a metallic pawing at the tarmac that covered the driveway like an oozing, black fleece?

She sat up and turned back the bedcovers. Her dark-brown hair fell below her shoulders in a disorderly tangle, partly covering her breasts and partly accentuating the ridges of her shoulder-blades. *I must get it cut again*, she reminded herself. She'd thought that for some time, but had done nothing about it. Somehow her life had got in the way of—well—her life. She was a receptionist in a busy office of architects. She answered the phones, placed calls, took messages, made tea and coffee for clients, organised everything necessary for meetings, and tidied the magazines on the enormous, square coffee table which dominated the reception's entrance. In recent months, Marion had felt that if her life could be depicted as a movie, it would be short and uninteresting. As the weeks wore on, she'd harboured fears that the movie would soon be filled with a procession of flickering black and white—as intelligible to her as hieroglyphics—before snapping off into complete darkness.

This, more than anything else, was causing Marion's careful façade of efficiency to evaporate. She went off to work determined to enjoy her day but, halfway through the morning, her hands would begin to shake and her head feel as though it was whirling. No amount of coffee or energy bars seemed to help. At home, even her flat reflected her state of mind, with dirty washing lying in an ever-growing mound in the laundry-basket, and dust accumulating to the point where the horizontal struts of the dining-room chairs were turning white.

Marion heaved a huge sigh, and reluctantly got out of bed. She noticed, as if for the first time, that her nails—once a great source of pride—were bitten and broken. The skin on her face was taut and dry, and she knew that there were faint beginnings of indigo half-moons defining her eyes. Her life had become burdensome to her. That was the bare truth.

Only the night before, Marion had tried to shake off her increasing lethargy.

Yes, she'd told herself, *it's my lousy sleep patterns. All I need is a good night's sleep, and everything will be different.* After all, she'd gone to bed between 10.30pm and 11 for years, and fallen asleep almost instantly. Every morning she'd rise at 5.30, brush her teeth, wash her face, and do twenty minutes of gentle yoga. After that she'd have breakfast, and dress for work in front of the mirror.

But this day, a Friday morning apparently no different from any other, was when it happened. Despite her intense drowsiness, she forced herself to perform her usual routine. Finally, she chose her clothes—a dark-blue two-piece suit with red piping round the edges—intending to match them with a creamy-white blouse and either red or navy shoes. The mirror, a full-length free-standing one mounted on tiny wheels, could be moved and re-angled with ease. She went over to it and straightened it. The bevelled edge, usually smooth as ice, appeared to have a slight chip in it so that she cut her finger. She flicked her hand to lessen the pain. *Damn! That's all I need! I can't have a bloody stain on me. And of course the senior partner is going to be there before me, so I can't avoid him.* She sucked at the cut. The blood tasted salty, and she winced.

She adjusted her skirt and looked in the mirror. Startled, she looked again. There was nothing there. No image, no shape, no familiar face. Just a view of the wall behind her with an old wooden clock mounted next to a Diego Rivera poster. Marion treasured that clock, for it had belonged to her mother, who had died when Marion was seventeen. Similarly, she'd always loved the poster. It depicted a woman burdened by an enormous wicker basket chock-full of calla lilies which, with the aid of an almost-unseen man, she was endeavouring to heave on to her shoulders and secure in place with a broad, blue cloth.[1]

Marion blinked a few times and massaged her eyelids. The poster was there, as always, and the clock which, in contrast to the digital clock next to her bed, appeared to have stopped. But where was her reflection? She moved closer to the mirror. Surely she was mistaken? She placed her right hand on the glass and flinched at its coldness, its razor-smooth glaze. When she lifted her hand away she could briefly see the outline of her fingers and a palm print, but both of these soon evaporated, leaving little more than a smudge. *Perhaps it's a trick of the light,* she thought, although she could feel her heart rate quicken and her face blanch before becoming flushed. *A cup of coffee, perhaps.*

She entered the kitchen. Through the window she could see the sky with variegated streaks of pampas white, butter yellow and ballet-slipper pink which preceded its turning to a hard-edged, polished blue. The gardens of the flats across the road boasted a mixture of bleached grass patched with hoarfrost, while on the corner there was an oily clump of burnt charcoal left by a group of squatters who would regularly light a fire at night in a rusted half-barrel, leaning over the open flames for warmth. Marion turned on the kettle. It soon began its familiar thrum as the water heated up, followed by the eventual rush of steam from the spout and the friendly *click* of the switch as it turned itself off. She poured her coffee, and walked slowly back to her bedroom.

The mirror stood as it had when she'd left it. Nevertheless, she avoided looking at it. She put down her cup of coffee on her bedside table, and tentatively extended one arm to where she ought to have seen its reflection. Again, there was nothing. It was all so odd. She took a deep breath. What should she do? Call a doctor? What on earth would she tell him? Should she call the optometrist? No, her eyes were good. There was the clock, its hands frozen at twenty-eight minutes to one. It must have stopped after midnight. She peered more closely at the mirror. The Diego Rivera poster was sharply in focus, the woman's blue cloth wrapped horizontally and tied with a knot beneath her chin and so allowing its ends to drop vertically, evincing a clear sign of the cross. Everything else in the room looked as it always did. Marion rubbed her forehead and tried to calm herself. *There has to be an explanation*. But there was no time to dwell on this any further.

Fifteen minutes later she was manoeuvring her car out of the parking garage of her block of flats and into the traffic stream. There on the corner of Riviera Road was the newspaper seller. She had a soft heart for him, for he wasn't a young man anymore. Whenever she could, she gave him food, or clothing. She waved at him, but he ignored her. Did he not see her? Admittedly, he'd been counting out change and another motorist had started hooting, either to alert him to sell a newspaper, or out of irritation that he stood straddling the white lines and so was a danger to both himself and the traffic.

Having arrived at work in Illovo, Marion parked in her designated bay and took the lift up from the fourth basement to the second floor. By now it was nearly 7.42am. The office opened formally at eight, but she always needed to be there early. At that moment the senior partner walked past, accompanied by one of the new architects.

"Unusual for Marion not to be in by now," he said, shaking his head. Alarmed, Marion waved at him.

"I'm here, Mr Malone!"

"She's usually very punctual," continued Mr Malone. "I suppose she got caught up in traffic this morning."

"One of the robots was out in Rosebank," confirmed the new architect. "There was a helluva backup. Christ, I could've *walked* here more quickly than it took on the roads."

Marion raised her voice. "I'm *here*, Mr Malone."

"We all need to get out our bicycles," continued the new architect.

"*Here!*" insisted Marion. But they had walked right past her and on into one of the boardrooms.

Just then, a client arrived. He gestured to her to open the glass front doors, which she did. At that moment Mr Malone emerged from the boardroom.

"Ah, Marion! I thought you weren't in yet." His voice rose slightly as it had a tendency to do when he was anxious. "Organise coffee for us, won't you? Oh, and perhaps some breakfasty things, like rolls and muffins or something."

Marion hadn't realised that she'd been holding her breath. Now she let it out in one lengthy exhalation. *Everything's all right. I was probably half asleep this morning. How ridiculous.* And the rest of the day passed by without any further peculiarities.

That evening, she was rather annoyed at having returned home late. It being Friday night, she'd hoped to meet some friends in one of the trendy little restaurants in Parkhurst for drinks and dinner. But a meeting scheduled at the office for 4pm had dragged on until nearly 7pm. After that, Mr Malone had insisted that the clients stay for drinks, causing Marion to have to wait for another hour and a quarter. Yes, she was paid (and rather well) for weekend overtime, but the money never really made up for ruining her social life. In fact, it had led to an acrimonious break-up with her boyfriend.

Once inside her flat, Marion switched on the lights, slammed closed the security gate, double locked the front door, and kicked off her shoes. Normally she would have gone into her bedroom to change into something casual, but for reasons she didn't care to articulate, she avoided doing just that. In any event, she was hungry, and so went into the kitchen and microwaved a frozen meal which she ate while perched on a somewhat rickety bar stool at the kitchen counter.

A quandary now presented itself. She needed to have a bath, but then of course she also had to fetch a change of clothes from the bedroom. This meant passing in front of the mirror. She turned on the light, and peered tentatively around the door. Everything looked as it normally did: the bed with the rumpled pillows and the duvet and blanket thrown partly back, the bedside table, the comfy chair, the free-standing lamp and, in the far corner, the small desk with her laptop. But— how peculiar—the wall clock showed the time as 11.50pm. Had she misread it that morning? She was certain it had stopped at twenty-eight minutes to one.

The cupboard where her clothes were kept was against the far wall, with the mirror standing at right angles to it. Taking a quick breath, Marion marched smartly across the room, and grabbed her fresh clothes. She intended not to look at the offensive mirror but, out of curiosity, she paused, turned, and gazed directly into it. The light from the streetlamp outside gave the impression of the mirror being a fathomless pool of dark blue water, striated here and there as though by a faint wind dragging across its surface. She could almost hear the water trembling.

She studied the mirror carefully, but she simply wasn't there. And, startlingly, there was only the dirty outline of the wooden clock and the Diego Rivera poster, as though someone had pried them off the wall. She spun round. There they were, the clock with its silvery hands, and the poster with the lilies in the basket burning white and yellow against a background like hardened mud. But the wall clock now showed the time as five past eleven. How could a clock run backwards?

Marion's chest heaved. From her throat there emitted a strange, rasping sound unlike anything she'd ever heard. In a panic, she tore off her clothes, switched on the oil heater, and threw herself onto the bed where she soon lapsed into a tossing, dreamless sleep.

II

On waking, Marion felt sweaty. The heater had made the room unbearably stuffy. Her mouth seemed to be lined with fur, and her tongue was exceptionally dry. Her body was stiff, no doubt from having lain awkwardly sprawled across the bed. Thank goodness it was Saturday, a time when she normally slept in. The wall clock's hands showed the time as 10.30. Which way were its hands turning? Fortunately, apart from power failures, the bedside digital clock could be relied on. It showed just after 9am. It was a good thing Marion hadn't slept any later, for she had arranged to go shopping with her neighbour.

As she got up, Marion noted some unusual sounds emanating from outside her flat. At first she was convinced that she heard the tumescent piping of a rooster. And now, clearly discernible, was the whinnying of a pair of horses and the metallic clink of the clasps of their bridles, followed by an energetic, muscular stamping at the ground and then the increasing speed of hoof-falls as the animals broke immediately into a canter outside her front door. She looked about her. *I'm going to prove to myself that everything's all right*, she admonished herself and, almost jauntily, went and stood in front of the mirror. Its bevelled edges looked like ribbons of silver. Light flowed in from the north- and east-facing windows of her bedroom. Marion looked in the mirror, and screamed. It was completely blank. She was not there, and neither, for that matter, was anything else. Although *she* could see every object in her room, the mirror could not.

What would she see if she turned the mirror so that it faced the outside world? Although she knew it was illogical, she decided to test this out. The little wheels on the mirror's base made this easy to do.

What she saw startled her. Looking eastwards, she saw not the familiar edge of the Killarney Mall, but what appeared to be a recently constructed stone building with a large signboard reading, in bold capital letters: 'AFRICAN FILM PRODUCTIONS'. *I must be dreaming*, thought Marion. *Whoever heard of a film studio in Killarney?*[2]

She turned the mirror northwards and gaped in disbelief. Instead of the various high-rise flats and buildings opposite, there was simply open, empty veld with what appeared to be a twisting cart track running across it. And there, plodding dutifully between the shafts of a roughly made wooden wagon, was not a horse but an ox. The wagon—which looked like something from the Great Trek—was loaded with heavily tied bundles as well as with an enormous, highly polished bureau the like of which Marion had only ever seen in museums. The animal's progress was laboured, its weight shifting heavily from side to side. With one hand, the man at the reins disinterestedly flicked his long whip above the ox's head, while with the other he fingered the edges of his broad-brimmed and rather greasy-looking leather hat. Marion watched as the wagon jolted along before turning off on to a side track which led into the distance.

Curiously, the mirror showed a different season altogether. Instead of winter, it depicted a hot, steamy summer's day, perhaps getting on to late in the afternoon, with swollen, dark skies presaging a particularly heavy cloudburst. Turning away from the offending mirror, Marion realised that her mother's old clock now indicated a quarter past ten. It had to be—it *was*—running backwards. She examined the poster. Was it her imagination, or did the woman look younger and thinner than before?

Marion felt more confused than alarmed. She felt her forehead to see if she had a temperature. Her face was warm, but not unduly so. The idea of a relaxing bath—the one she ought to have had the night before—revived her spirits. Now that she thought about it, there was the mirror on the front of the small bathroom medicine cabinet which she could use to confirm that everything she was experiencing was simply some sort of hallucination.

She took her underwear and clothing, ran into the bathroom, and closed the door. *Now*, she said to herself, *let's see.* She let the taps run, closed her eyes momentarily, opened them, and looked into the mirror. Yes, there was a reflection. She existed. Her face, though, appeared somewhat elongated and was a rather unpleasant shade of green, with a ridge running vertically down the middle. Her skin, in contrast, seemed overly soft and puffy, as though it was too large for her face and lifted by a subcutaneous layer of fluid, or possibly pus. And her eyes. They were set far apart, one on each side of the dividing ridge, and were undeniably small and dark black in colour. In fact, they looked like two recently unearthed pebbles. And where were her eyelashes? She couldn't see them at all, for there was a sort of extra fold of skin around each eye, almost like a flap. Even worse, through the rising steam from the bathwater she could see her scalp, enlarged to the point of being swollen, on which the skin looked thickened and unnaturally hairless.

Marion screamed. The reflection in the mirror was impassive. And then her face dropped completely out of sight.

III

The bathwater was warm and soapy. How enormous the bath now seemed. Marion tried to sit up—her neighbour would soon come knocking—but her hands, which looked more like flippers, slid unobstructed along the enamel surfaces and failed to grasp the metal handles on each side. Where were her legs? All she could see was a tapering oval which divided at its base into two hook-like fins. Along most of her body, her skin—if one could call it that—was dark green, but by the time it reached the 'hooks' where her feet should be, it was coal black.

Marion knew that she needed to be dressed and ready for her neighbour's call. Her agitation, however, led to little more than a great deal of thrashing. After several attempts, she managed to wedge her fin-hook feet beneath her and wrest the top half of her body on to the ledge of the bath. By dropping her head over the side, she was able to use the force of gravity to manoeuvre herself out of the bath altogether and to land on the bathmat with a resounding *plop*.

The bathmat, which had always felt soft and fluffy, now scratched and pulled at her. Worse, she struggled to move off it. After a great deal of twisting and turning, she reached the tiled floor. Using her flippers, and pushing with her hooked fins, she retreated from the bathroom back to the bedroom, a journey which took her a full fifteen minutes.

Exhausted, she came to rest, rolling over on her side and slumping her heavy head. Her one eye, moving independently of the other, gazed at the wooden clock. Its hands were whirling backwards, fairly slowly at first, but then with ever-increasing speed. Simultaneously, Marion's other eye located the mirror and, in its reflection, she observed the outside world. What was happening? Trees were living and dying almost simultaneously, their fruit and flowers blossoming, falling and re-attaching themselves to their branches in an unending sequence. Fields altered swiftly from season to season in a flurry of colours. Broad, heavy rivers were geomorphologically pushed up on to flat terrain where they became mere trickles of water. Within seconds, ravines turned into tiny mountain paths. Eventually, all these phenomena occurred with such dizzying rapidity that Marion saw nothing but the blurred sequence of an unstoppable regression of aeon after aeon.

In desperation, she turned her attention back to the wall. There was the Diego Rivera poster but now it, too, was changing. The dark-skinned woman who had previously been forced to exist upon her knees, her face pointed downwards towards the earth, her body oppressed by the crippling weight of the basket with its sensuous abundance of bright calla lilies, was now—although with immense difficulty—managing to stand upright. The basket tumbled from her back, strewing lilies in a profusion of green, yellow and white all over Marion's bedroom floor. It was as though she had been released from servitude.

Marion had to be careful not to be crushed by the weight of the flowers. One had hit her on the side of the head so that she felt momentarily dazed. Many of the lily stems were wet, as though newly harvested, leaving blisters of water congregating in random clumps on the parquet.

The woman, appearing to show contempt for the flowers rather than awe at their perfection and magnificence, kicked at them with her bare feet so that they skidded ahead of her. She looked about, noting with evident satisfaction the bedroom and its furniture. She saw the cupboard standing partially open and with Marion's dresses in view. She smiled, threw off her fringed shawl, walked over to the dresses and picked out the most stylish of all. Holding it against her body as though assessing whether it would fit, she turned her head, saw the mirror, marched across to it and swivelled it round to face her. The sunlight streamed onto the glass so that the woman's skin glowed. Her expression, for so long inscrutable, likewise lit up, and she smiled broadly showing her strong, white teeth.

At that moment, the doorbell rang. Simultaneously, there was a loud knocking.

"Marion! Marion!" It was the neighbour.

The woman looked up. "She's coming!" she called, and strode to the front door. Without having a key, she nevertheless unlocked it. The door flew open as with massive force, flooding the flat with a wall of seawater which brought with it silt, pebbles, beach sand, barnacles, rocks, seaweed, shells, silver and brown fish, and shards of bleached driftwood, all of which smashed through the walls and into every crevice of the flat.

IV

When Marion regained consciousness, she was being tumbled by the force of the foaming seawater down the funnel of the stairway of her block of flats. Various images appeared and disappeared before her eyes—doors and doormats, corridors, ceiling lights, windowsills, pot plants, arches, banisters—everything passing by in rapid succession, much like a roll of film being spooled out of a projector at immense speed.

Without the strength to resist, she was carried along by the force of the deluge which sluiced out into the street, except it wasn't a street at all, but a stretch of sepia nothingness in which she was forced along, sometimes breathing water, at other times air (it didn't seem to matter which). The salt stung her body. She tried to ease the pain by rubbing her flippers against her, but all that happened was that raw, pinkish patches appeared. The pain was immeasurable, and she gave out a prolonged, piercing cry.

An expansive, white light was shone into Marion's eyes, its unfamiliar brightness causing everything else around her to appear black.

"I think she's coming, said the dark-skinned woman. Her hands were firm, but gentle, and from time to time she wiped the sweat off the mother's face. "Keep pushing," she urged, "you're doing well."

A spasm of pain wracked the woman's body.

"Not long, now," said the midwife encouragingly. "Breathe, breathe. Yes, that's *wonderful*—that's excellent! Keep breathing! It won't be long! We're nearly there."

The mother nodded and grimaced, turning her eyes first to the silvery hands of the wooden clock mounted on the wall, and then to a spray of freshly picked calla lilies arranged in a tall glass vase near the window.

The midwife stroked the mother's hair. Her voice was low and soothing. "It won't be long," she repeated. And then, almost as if to pass the time, she asked, "What'll you call her?"

The mother smiled. "Marion," she answered. "We'll call her Marion."

V

It happened on a Friday morning. At 5.47am to be exact. Outside it was still dark. And it was winter—the sort of Highveld winter when the landscape appears to disintegrate into a powdery ash prior to the dawn.

Marion awoke. She had slept well. That wasn't in itself unusual. Her job as a sought-after architect was one in which she revelled. The night before, she'd imagined hearing things: a horse, for instance, prancing about on the driveway outside the bedroom window of her enormous country home. The sound was absolutely distinctive with its light *clip-clop* of hooves. Marion swore she could smell the sweat of the horse's flanks.

The hall clock chimed. It took only a few minutes for Marion to throw on the nearest clothes to hand.

Flinging open the front door, she was just in time to see the horse, snorting and eager, rear up on its back legs—the veins in its neck pulsating—before propelling its muscular body forward at great speed, kicking off clumps of sand and gravel which disintegrated behind it in a blizzard of grains. The drumming of its hooves through the crisp, cold air could easily be mistaken for a beating heart, and its progression was much faster than anyone could anticipate, almost as fast as time itself.

---

[1] The poster is Diego River's *El Vendedor De Alcatraces* (1941).

[2] African Film Productions, set up in 1913, was located on the site of the present-day Killarney Mall.

Gail Dendy's first book of poetry was published by Harold Pinter in 1993, with six subsequent collections appearing in South Africa, the United Kingdom and United States. She won the SA PEN Millennium playwriting competition and was shortlisted for the Thomas Pringle Award 2010 (short story) and the EU/Sol Plaatje Poetry Prize 2011 and 2012. In 2014, she was longlisted for the EU/Sol Plaatje Poetry Prize and for the Twenty in 20 Project.

HOW MY FATHER
BECAME A GOD

Dilman Dila

My father was a god, though he looked like any other old man. He had a thick white beard, and a bald head with tufts of hair above his ears. He had no wrinkles. His ribs showed. His gait was slow, shuffling. He always wore large, green earrings, a rainbow-coloured necklace, and a black goatskin loincloth. He looked ordinary, but I knew he was a god. This was confirmed the day he showed me the egg-shaped thing. The object stood on two, bird-like legs that were taller than he was, and it had a pair of wings that were so large my father must have skinned twenty cows to make them. I wondered where he got the hide, for he had no wealth to buy cattle.

"It's buffalo skin," he said.

"You don't hunt," I said.

"I paid a hunter."

I frowned, but was too courteous to ask how he had paid the hunter. He was so poor he could not afford to buy a chicken.

"I sold him a trap," he said.

It had to have been a unique trap for this hunter to pay with twenty buffalo hides. I did not press him about it. The egg-shaped object enthralled me.

"Can it fly?" I said.

"Not yet. But one day, it will take you into the sky to become the bride of the sun."

I giggled. "Is it a new type of bird?"

He smiled. "No. I call it a bruka. Do you remember Bruka?"

I nodded. Bruka was an eagle. A boy had tricked it with a chicken, and it had come to the ground. Then he had jumped on its back and rode it through the skies. Yet this egg-shaped thing had no life. How would it fly?

"Will you put the spirit of a bird in it?" I said.

"No. I am still making its—" He paused. "I don't know what to call that thing." He pointed at a box-shaped object fixed between the wings. "For now, let's just call it a heart. It will make the bruka fly, but it needs special sap for it to work. I haven't yet found that sap."

We were behind a hut that looked like a fallen tree trunk. He called it the ot'cwe, the house of creation. My family had banished him from the homestead, so he lived alone in this hut. The walls did not have the beautiful red-and-white designs Maa had painted on our home. The walls here were cracked, and full of drawings of the things Baa tried to create. The grass-thatched roof had holes that leaked when the rains came. I wished I were old enough to help him with repairs so he would not sleep in a place worse than a kraal. When the rains became too heavy, my mother allowed him to sneak into her bed. I could hear them giggling all night. She had to be careful or else my uncles would beat her up. They once thrashed her when they discovered she had prepared a dish of goat meat for him. They insisted he should eat only their leftovers, which they dumped in a calabash at the edge of the compound. He never ate that garbage. Maa secretly sent me with food for him.

"Lapoya!" Okec, my eldest brother, shouted from a distance, interrupting us.

He had come to the ot'cwe. A bush still hid me from his view. Baa gave me a look of surprise. They forbade anyone to visit him. They wanted him to live in isolation like a leper, hidden away from the eyes of the public, because they thought he was a lapoya, a mad man, and a shame to the family. Whenever I visited him, I made sure no one saw me. Why was Okec here? Had I made a mistake? Had he seen me?

"Hide," Baa said.

He lifted me onto a window. I jumped into the hut and hid in a giant pot. They thought Baa was a lapoya because he tried to make magical things that did not work, like this pot that would make water during droughts. Nothing he made worked, but I had faith in him. In the great stories, Lacwic, the creator, kept trying to make humans. Each time he failed, he instead created an animal or a bird, so we have all these different species. Eventually, he succeeded.

Baa was a god. He had to experiment until he came up with the thing he was supposed to create. He had spent all his life on this pursuit. Everybody laughed at him, but he did not stop. He could not stop.

"What do you want?" I heard him say.

"I have a husband for Akidi," Okec said.

When I heard my name, my flesh turned as hard and cold as a hailstone. Baa had ten sons. I was the only daughter, the youngest child from his third wife. Since he was a poor man, his sons had no cattle to pay dowry for brides. Because he had no mature daughters, there was no hope of wealth coming into the family anytime soon. His sons could not get married.

"She's still a child," Baa said. "She's too young to have breasts or to know that women bleed."

"Okot has offered a thousand head of cattle," Okec said.

A thousand? Only the Rwot's daughter could command such a rich dowry, not me. If it were true, then all my brothers would have enough cattle to marry.

"She's still a child," Baa said.

"That's why she's valuable," Okec said. "Okot lost his manhood. The ajwaka says he needs a wife as young as Akidi to regain it. That's why he's offering all this cattle. You can't refuse."

"If you mention it again," Baa said, "I'll cut off your head."

"You are cursed," Okec said. "Your madness has wasted our wealth. We now can't get married. This is our best chance. Don't say no."

My father was not listening anymore. I knew, for I heard him entering the ot'cwe. He sat on a stool beside my hiding place.

"We don't need your permission," Okec shouted. He remained outside. They feared to enter the ot'cwe, which they believed was infested with demons. "You are a lunatic, so your brothers will give the permission."

He stomped away.

I climbed out of the pot. Baa's face had wrinkled. I hugged him. His tears fell on my cheeks.

"I'll go to the forest." His voice crackled like dry leaves. "I'll find the obibi tree. Its sap will make the bruka fly. We'll go to the clouds, just you, me, and your mother. We'll start a new home up there."

I held him tighter. My fingernails dug into his flesh in anger. I was still a child, but I knew obibi was a myth, a monster that lived only in fairy tales. Before I could berate him for giving up, love drums started to beat. The musicians were already in our homestead, which was a short distance from my father's hut. My brother had come to ask for Baa's permission only as a formality. He had conspired with my uncles, and they had already organised the amito nywom feast. In the ceremony, boys gathered at the bride's homestead and danced larakaraka, and she chose the best dancer for a husband. Rarely did the bride choose a man only because of his dancing talent or good looks. Often, she would know her choice long before the function. In some instances, like this one, her family would force her to pick a boy they preferred.

"Akidi!" I heard my mother shout. "Run, my daughter! Run and hide!"

Baa charged out of the hut with a vunduk, a lightning weapon he had created. Shaped like a gourd, it was a ball with a long pipe attached to it. I followed him out, praying to Lacwic to make the vunduk work.

Maa ran through the bushes with three of my brothers chasing her. It reminded me of a hunt I once saw, where a group of boys chased a hare with bows and arrows. They did not catch it. My brothers, however, were faster than Maa. They overtook her, pushed her aside, and came for me. Baa pointed the vunduk at them and pulled a string that dangled from its ball. The weapon made a low sound, like a harp's string when strummed, but it did not produce lightning to strike my brothers. They kept running towards us. Baa pulled the string, again and again. My brothers started laughing at him.

"Run!" Maa was shouting. "Run, Akidi! Run!"

I ran. Unlike the hare, I could not outrun my brothers but I could hide. I saw a hole in an anthill. Someone had dug it up recently in search of a queen. I ducked into the hole and into a tunnel big enough for me to crawl on my hands and knees. I went in deep, where my brothers would not be able to get me. I snuggled in the darkness, trying not to cry. I felt safe until the mouth of the burrow darkened with someone peeping in.

"She's inside," Okec said. "Make a fire. We'll smoke her out."

"You'll kill her!" Maa cried. "Don't use fire! You'll kill her!"

The burrow went deep under the ground. It became so dark that I could not see. I groped, but as long as I could feel open space ahead, I did not stop moving. The voices became faint, until I could not hear them anymore. I feared a giant snake would swallow me or a hundred rats would attack me. Still, I did not stop. Such a fate was better than marrying Okot.

When the smoke flowed into the tunnel, I was so far away it did not bother me. The burrow widened, becoming big enough for me to stand. I ran, stumbling over the uneven, soggy ground. I ran for such a long time I feared the tunnel had no end, and that I would get lost in an underground maze. Still, I refused to cry. I went round a bend and saw a light. A draught of fresh air tickled me into laughter. The tunnel narrowed again. I went down on my knees and crawled out.

At once I wished I had remained inside.

I was at the Leper's Swamp. No one ever went there, not even powerful shamans. It was about the size of four large homesteads and deep enough to swallow a man. In the middle stood a black rock, shaped like the mortar we used to pound ground-nuts into flour. The rock was larger than three huts put together, two times taller than trees, and it had a surface as smooth as a polished pot. Every full moon, blood dripped out of it to colour the water. They called it Leper's Rock. Spirits lived there.

I ran away from the haunted water, to find a place to hide, but then I heard hunting dogs. They had picked up my scent and were coming after me. Wherever I hid, they would find me, though not in the water—they would lose my scent if I went there.

But there were spirits in the water.

The dogs came nearer. Their barking pricked my eardrums. My brothers were urging them to get me, and my mother screamed, "Run! Akidi! Run!"

I saw my face in the water. I resembled my father. He was a god. Surely, spirits would not hurt the daughter of a god. The barking grew louder, angrier, and I had no choice. I closed my eyes, said a prayer to the creator, and slipped into the swamp. The cold water stung my skin. Goosebumps sprouted all over my arms. I waited for something else to happen, for fire to consume my body, for spirits to strike me dead. Nothing happened. I swam fast, through papyrus reeds. Frogs and fish swam with me. I took it as a sign that Lacwic had answered my prayers. The spirits would not harm me. I reached the middle, where I climbed onto the rock. Still, the spirits did not do anything to me.

Long ago, a thirsty leper had found a group of girls at a well. He had asked for a calabash to drink water, and the girls had laughed at him. One, however, had given him her calabash. After he had quenched his thirst, he told her to stay away from the dance that night. She had heeded the warning. The other girls did not. During the fiesta, this rock had fallen from the sky and buried all the dancers. The well from which the leper had drunk dried up, and a swamp grew around this rock. It was not just another fairy tale. The blood that seeped out every full moon proved it to be true. Red stripes stained the rock's surface.

I sat still in the reeds. The dogs whined on the banks. They had lost my scent. My brothers were shouting, my mother was wailing. Their voices came as if from another world. I longed to hear my father.

"Did she enter the water?" Okec said.

"She wouldn't dare," someone responded.

"Useless dogs!" I recognised Okot's voice. "Useless!"

A dog yelped in pain. Maybe Okot had kicked it.

I could not stand my mother wailing as though I were dead. I put my fingers in my ears, but that did not shut her out. I walked around the rock. The tall papyrus hid me from their view. On the other side, their voices were faint. I saw a cave and went in. The mouth was low, but inside it was bigger than a hut and I could no longer hear Maa or my brothers. I felt safe, and cried myself to sleep.

A dripping from further inside the cave awoke me. Something glowed on the floor and filled the room with a weak, reddish light. I was not afraid. Baa was a god, so this spirit would not harm me. I crept to the light, which came from a pool of thick blood. Above the pool, on the cave roof, hung a sculpture that resembled a cow's breast with three nipples. Somebody, or something, had carved it up there. Blood dripped out of the nipples.

Was it really blood? It looked to be thicker than porridge. When I touched it, the liquid stung me like a thorn and left a glowing stain on my fingertip. Blood could not do that, but sap could. Maybe it's what Baa needed to make the bruka fly and take us to a paradise in the heavens.

I ran out of the cave. The sun had sunk low into the horizon, giving the world a red tint. I had been asleep for far much longer than I had thought. I could not hear my mother, my brothers or the dogs. I crossed the swamp and crept through the bushes. By the time I reached the ot'cwe, darkness had fallen. A small fire flickered under the tree in front of the hut. My parents sat beside it like prisoners, their backs to me. Baa still had the vunduk, and held it as though it were a real weapon. Okec, Okot, and an ajwaka in a costume of bird feathers, stood around them. I climbed up a tree, silent as a cat, and curled up in the branches to hide.

"She's our sister," Okec was saying. "We can't harm her, but every girl has to get married. Why delay her happiness when a wealthy suitor is interested?"

"There are other girls in the village," Maa said.

"We are the poorest," Okec said. "We don't even own chickens."

"Work for your wealth if you want to marry," Baa said.

"You squandered our wealth," Okec said through his teeth. "You must make amends by giving us Akidi. Where is she?"

"Even if I knew," Baa said, "I wouldn't tell you."

"I won't stop looking for her," Okot said. "I'll marry her, whether you like it or not."

He walked away. The ajwaka said something to my parents in such a low voice that I did not catch it then followed Okot. My brother jeered, hissed insults, and went away too. After a while, my parents begun to roast maize. They worked in silence. I stayed in the tree for a long time, watching them, until I felt it safe to climb down. They did not notice me until I had crept right up to them.

"Baa," I whispered. "I found it."

They turned to me. Their faces were bruised from a beating.

"Akidi," Maa cried.

They hugged me tightly.

"The sap." I wrung myself out of their grasp. "It's in the Leper's Rock." I showed Baa the stain, which still glowed on my finger.

"The Leper's Rock?" Baa's eyes turned white in terror. "You were there?"

"Oh, my daughter." Maa's tears shone in the lights of the fire.

"Nothing happened to me," I said.

That night, I dreamt that my father's bruka took me to the stars, where I became a princess in a world whose sky was red like blood. My finger with the sap stain glowed while I was awake to give this world day. When I awoke, the stain had peeled skin off my finger, leaving a scar that I still have to this day.

My parents had sat up through the night, Maa armed with a machete, Baa with the vunduk, ready to defend me, but my brothers had not attacked.

"We shall hide in the Leper's Rock," Baa said.

They must have reached that decision while I slept. Maybe Baa also knew that, being a god, the spirits would not harm him or his wife. We set off before dawn. Baa took some of his creations, and I carried his tools and other materials in a sack. I wanted him to take the bruka, but it was too big and heavy. Maa packed a basket of food that she had secretly taken from the gardens during the night. At the swamp, Baa built a papyrus raft. We rowed to the other side just as dawn broke.

We hesitated at the cave, where a strong red glow spilled out. Was it spirits?

Maa took several steps away, her face tight with fear. "Let's wait a little," she said. "It's still dark."

Baa grinned at her then crawled into the cave. I wanted to follow him, but Maa grabbed my arms and made me stay with her. We sat on a boulder and waited. Baa took such a long time I feared the red light had eaten him. The sun rose. The red light weakened until it went out completely. Still, Baa had not returned.

"Baa!" I called, alarmed.

He crawled out, smiling, and brushed dirt off his knees and palms.

"There are no spirits," he said. "The light came from the sap. It seeps out of the rock and people think it is blood. It shines at night and goes out at sunrise. I'll call it the leper's blood."

I looked at the scar on my finger and thought of the red world in my dream. Had the Leper's Rock fallen from there? I did not tell my parents about the dream.

We settled in the cave, in a spot as far from the breast as possible, though it had stopped bleeding. By the time it started again, just before sunset, the pool had dried up.

Baa went to work at once. He made gloves that enabled him to touch the sap without it pricking him. I prayed that the leper's blood did not turn out to be useless. I wanted it to make the bruka work so we could escape from my brothers, but this made me think of the world in my dream. The blood red sky suspended over a land without vegetation or soil, without living things as I knew it, but full of black, mortar-shaped rocks. I suddenly did not want to go to that world.

Maybe Baa could create something else, like the cooking stone that used the power of the sun rather than firewood. I hated collecting firewood. I had to walk with other unmarried girls far from the village. The snakes did not scare us, nor did the monkeys or elephants. These were merely animals.

We did not fear obibi, for we knew they were mythical, but we dreaded the warabu. These were evil spirits in the shape of humans, with albino skin and black hair that was long and straight like a lion's mane. They kidnapped people and put them in black ropes of a strange material, which was harder than rock, and took them across the great desert to work as slaves in the land of the dead.

If Baa made a stove that cooked without firewood, he would become wealthy, for every homestead would want to own such a stove. With such wealth, my brothers would not force me to get married.

Baa did not want to make the stove. It would take a long time to bring him wealth. But if he had a super weapon, no one would dare touch me, so he concentrated on the vunduk. He worked fervently for the next three days. On the fourth, as he tried to make the vunduk shoot fireballs, he accidentally created something that worked. He moulded clay into an orange shape the size of my fist, mixed it with leper's blood, and put it out in the sun to absorb heat, but the ball was harmless. Instead of fire, it gave off the sunlight it had absorbed. The longer Baa left it in the sun, the brighter it shone.

Baa groaned in disappointment, though the ball could be a valuable source of light in every household. Back then we relied on kitchen fires and the moon for lighting. He called it the sunball.

"It's a step forward," I told him. "You made a ball that can trap the light of the sun. Don't give up. Now make one that can trap its heat."

That night we went to the mainland for firewood and food. We dug up wild roots and collected fruits. We stole hares from traps. As we returned to the swamp, we thought we heard someone following us. We hoped it was only our imagination, but the next day we heard shouting from across the swamp. People were singing and chanting. I could make out Okec's voice, and that of Okot, but the ajwaka's voice rang clear above that of everyone else as he led them through a ritual.

"He is preparing to enter the home of spirits," Baa said.

Spies had seen us during the night and now Okot and my brothers knew where we were hiding. They could not attack us at once, for they still believed there were spirits on the Leper's Rock.

We crept back into the cave. My parents did not know what to do. In a short while the ajwaka would finish the ritual and the men would row rafts to attack us. My brothers would then force me to marry that old devil.

"I know what to do," I said.

Before they could stop me, I put seven sunballs in a goatskin bag to mask their light then I crept out of the cave. The ajwaka had finished the ritual. The papyrus hid them from my view but I could hear oars as the men rowed in silence. I could smell their fear. I took a deep breath and went underwater, where I released the balls, one at a time. They sank to the bottom, right in the path of the rafts, and sent seven red beams jetting out of the papyrus. I silently crept out of the water.

"Demons!" the ajwaka screamed. "Go back! Go back!"

I clamped my hands on my mouth to stifle laughter. Their oars splashed frantically as they scrambled back to the other bank. Then I heard running. I finally laughed aloud. Even today, I laugh every time I picture men running from lights.

"They'll come back," Baa said. "Okot has enough wealth to hire Olal."

Olal was a famous sorcerer. Some claimed he was a god who lived among mortals. They said he could raise the dead, and that he once caused the sun to stand still because he did not want to travel after dark. If Olal came, red lights would not frighten him. Baa had two days to make the vunduk work, because it would take messengers a day to reach Olal and another to return with him.

Baa did not sleep for those two days. On the third day, when he pulled the string on his vunduk, it spat out a ball of flame as big as my head. The fireball fell in the swamp and, rather than frizzle out in the water, it rolled about as though it were a rat looking for an escape hole. The papyrus it touched dried up and burst into flame. By the time it lost its energy, half the swamp was on fire.

"People will stop calling you a madman," Maa said, watching the flames.

"You are a god," I said it aloud for the first time, and Baa laughed at me. His laughter sounded as though he were singing in a strange language. It reassured me of his divinity. Normal people did not have such beautiful, musical laughs.

"If I'm a god, then what are you?" he said, and laughed harder, but it turned into a coughing fit.

"Do you use magic?" I said.

"No," he said.

"Then how did you make this thing to trap the heat of the sun?"

He laughed and coughed. "How did the first woman learn how to cook?" he said. "How did the first farmer know how to plant? How did the first butcher know how to skin goats?"

I thought about that. Maybe in the future, making fire-spitting weapons would be an everyday activity. But knowing how to put the fire of the sun in clay was not the same thing as knowing how to skin a goat. If he did not use magic then he had special powers of his own, and that was proof that he was a god.

The fire died, leaving a black waste on the water, and revealing to us a turtle-man on the other side. He had a long, green beard that dangled over his chest, and hair that stood on his head like green flames. For a moment, I feared the fire had destroyed the home of a spirit, and now this spirit stood on the other side of the swamp, glaring at us. Surely that turtle's shell, that green beard and green hair could not belong to an ordinary man.

"Olal." Baa's voice was hoarse, as though with thirst. Other people stood in the far distance behind Olal, hiding in the bushes and behind trees. I could only guess they were my brothers, and Okot.

"Burn them!" Maa said.

Baa pulled the string of the vunduk. His hands trembled. He could not release it. Setting the swamp ablaze had been easy, but taking a life was something even gods hesitated to do.

"Are you Ojoka the madman?" Olal shouted at Baa.

"I'm not a madman," Baa shouted back.

"Did you burn the swamp?" Olal said.

"Yes," Baa said. "And I'll burn you too if you don't leave us alone."

"Do you know me?"

"Yes. You are Olal."

"So you should know better than to threaten me. I can kill you even if you are in the protection of spirits. But if you hand over the girl, we can settle—"

He did not finish speaking, because Baa released the string and a fireball flew over the water. Olal gaped at it for several heartbeats then he stepped away shortly before it landed right where he had been standing. The fireball danced on the ground, drying up the wet green grass and setting it all ablaze.

Olal waved a bull's tail at the fire. Maybe he was casting spells to put it out, but the ball of flame seemed to grow in intensity, and it sped faster from here to there, and the bush came alive with terror. Grasshoppers jumped away, frogs ducked into the water, rats scampered from their holes, and birds flapped away in panic. Okot and my brothers fled. Even Olal, seeing he could not fight the fire, dropped his wand and took flight.

Well, that is how Baa earned his place among the gods. Okot dropped all his plans of marrying me. He gave Baa three hundred head of cattle in apology and he lived the rest of his life with the torment of a lost manhood. Baa became famous and wealthy from his creations. His other two wives and his sons begged on their knees for mercy. He forgave them. I do not have to tell you all this, but if you are good children, I'll tell you of all my escapades in his house, especially my adventures in the bruka. I can tell you a story every night until you grow as old as I am. Just pray that the jok grants me a long life to tell it all.

Dilman Dila is a Ugandan writer and filmmaker. His work was shortlisted for the prestigious Commonwealth Short Story Prize in 2013, and longlisted for the BBC Radio Playwriting Competition in 2014 and the Short Story Day Africa prize in 2013. His films include What Happened in Room 13 *(2007), and the narrative feature,* The Felistas Fable *(2013), which was nominated for Best First Feature at AMAA 2014. He has published two short books,* The Terminal Move *and* Cranes Crest at Sunset, *as well a collection of speculative short stories,* A Killing in the Sun.

IN THE WATER

Kerstin Hall

I never had any great faith in traditional medicine. I believe in science and antibiotics and clean, cool, sanitary hospital rooms. I like American medicine and uniforms. There is security in a hypodermic needle and a saline drip.

My aunt disapproved of my derision, but she is dead now. I suppose that means that my drugs and I won in the end. No ancestors came to her aid when she was coughing her lungs bloody with the Taint. She wasted away within a week and they threw her oozing carcass over the edge. I was there. She was little more than bones by then and sank when she hit the water. Like a magic trick. Now you see her, now you don't.

So when I found myself knocking on the igqirha's door, I felt like a sell-out. But times were desperate.

Anathi does not advertise. Her practice is not secret, but she would never stick up a poster. She has no need to anyway. Everyone knows someone who knows her. As part of a dying breed of genuine practitioners, she comes highly recommended.

I waited outside in the still evening air, rubbing my hands together. The sounds of the city were subdued; Anathi's place was almost hanging off the edge. Being this close to the brink made me uncomfortable. There was a small alley between the buildings. Through it I could see the sea, murky brown in the light of the setting sun. The water splashed against the support struts, gradually corroding them to red metal skeleton legs. I shook myself and looked away. Reminders of our precarious position were never welcome. I knocked again, growing impatient.

There used to be a sign on Anathi's building. It had lost a number of the letters and read "W st Rand P blic wimm ng Pool". Over the boarded-up windows, some brave fools had stuck their own fliers. It must have taken considerable audacity on a competitor's part to advertise their supposed cures here. It was the usual: abortions, love charms, curses, money luck, Taint cures, penis enlargements. I lingered over the unlikely proportions the last one promised.

I was considering whether I should knock for a third time or simply abandon this venture altogether, when the door opened a crack. A pair of small, dark eyes peered up at me. The door opened wider and the little boy silently beckoned me inside. Anathi's butler.

As I passed through the door, I thought I saw something out of the corner of my eye. I turned around and looked back at the street. There was nothing there. The brief impression I had of the dark, hulking shape seemed to have no grounding in reality; the boy looked at me quizzically, but without comment. I shook my head and followed him, my back itching.

The foyer had probably once been a well-lit, bustling place, filled with eager children in colourful swimming costumes and water wings. Now it was grimy and moulding, grey plants hanging from the ceiling and moss dampening the sound of our footsteps. On the floor was a chipped mosaic of a school of dolphins cresting a wave. The smell of chlorine and salt had been replaced by the musty odour of earthy decay.

The turnstiles were stiff with age. The boy slipped beneath them, but I forced my way through a screech of unhappy metal—an effective doorbell. Anathi certainly knew someone was coming now.

We walked through the changing rooms to the swimming pool.

Light filtered through the glass ceiling. Some of the panels were cracked or shattered, and roosting birds darted in through the holes. The pool, drained years ago, was brimming with plants—hundreds of them, blooming and creeping and spreading greenly to fill the miniature arboretum. In a city where a pot plant was the crowning achievement of most people's gardening careers, this place was a strange kind of paradise. Despite my reservations, I could not help but be impressed.

Anathi was seated on the floor on the far side of the pool. She was a striking woman. Somewhat overweight, with a broad face and huge eyes that she had heavily accentuated with black liner, she was dressed in a long skirt that was spread out around her in a wide circle. She watched me approach, her face impassive.

"Molo, uMama," I said.

"Molweni, mtwana wam," she replied, indicating that I should sit in front of her.

"Unjani?"

"Ndiyaphila, enkosi. I get the impression you are more comfortable with English."

I flushed in embarrassment. "Whatever your preference is, I can understand you fine."

"Akukho ngxaki. Many of the younger generation have abandoned their language. Although I find it sad, I have no objection in speaking whatever my customers are familiar with." She straightened her skirt fastidiously. "What brings you here, my son?"

This was a ridiculous situation. For a moment, I was inexplicably ashamed. I felt like a hypocrite, as if I was turning my back on my religion of science and hospitals.

After a second of hesitation, I spoke. "Mama, my name is Khuselwa Miya. I think you may have known my aunt, Nokhanyo?"

"I did. I am sorry that I could not help her in the end."

I nodded. "It was the Taint. There was nothing to be done."

She inclined her head.

I continued, "Mama, I have a problem of my own." I paused again, not knowing how to express myself without sounding ludicrous.

"A problem of the body or the spirit?" Anathi asked.

"Er… spirit, I think. It is not something I could have spoken to doctors about." I pushed a neat roll of bank notes towards her. She picked them up and counted them carefully before she set them aside and looked at me expectantly.

I took a deep breath. "Mama, I think something is following me."

A disturbed expression passed over her face. "Did you not think seeing a sangoma would have been more appropriate? I am not much of a diviner. My speciality is herbs, not spirits."

"I could not find anyone reputable, but my aunt trusted you," I pressed. "I am sure you will be able to advise me."

"Well if you insist, my son, but I cannot promise to help you. Please tell me as much as you can."

"This… thing, I first saw it about a month ago. I have never been able to see it clearly, and I first believed I was imagining it. I can only catch glimpses of it."

"Where does it appear?"

"At first, it appeared mostly around the city hall down the street from my apartment, especially near the fountain. I saw it from my window. But for the last two weeks, it has been getting closer. Two days ago, I think it was inside my bathroom." I pushed back the fear that was rising in my throat.

"Has it tried to communicate with you?"

"No. It just watches me."

Anathi's face was purposefully impassive. "And can you describe it?"

I swallowed hard. "It is large, maybe twice my height, though it stoops. Very fast. It moves like an ape, on four limbs. Its body is dark, but somehow indistinct. Like smoke. But its face… It is beautiful. A woman's face, like an angel."

Anathi had remained silent and still all the while, but her hands were bunched up tightly on her skirt. She spoke with perfect composure. "Is there anything else, my son?"

"When I entered my bathroom that day, there was water all over the floor. All the taps were closed. This is not the first time."

Anathi was silent for a long while. I waited until I could tolerate it no longer.

"Mama, I am afraid. I am a grown man, but I am so afraid that I can scarcely function. Please, please, help me."

"Oh, mtwana wam." She signed and raised her eyes. "In this cursed world, there are two problems I have no power at all to fix. The first is the Taint. And the second is this." She reached out and clasped my hand.

"What is it? What is this thing?" I fought to keep my voice steady.

"I do not know. I know that it is very old. In the last twelve years, two others have come to me and described just this creature. One of them called it the Deepling, on account of the affinity it has with water."

"How did you help them?" I implored.

"I couldn't. They were both dead a week after they spoke to me. Drowned on dry land."

I sat there stunned. Anathi rubbed my hand beneath her cool fingers.

"Dead?" I asked.

She nodded.

"There is nothing I can do?" My voice had a curiously distant quality.

"There are some things." She thought for a moment. "These are merely ideas, but since as you are the third person I have encountered with this condition, I have some idea of how the creature operates."

"Please, anything."

Anathi nodded. "Firstly, stay away from water. All water. Arrange to have the water cut off from your apartment and stay inside. If it rains, seal the windows as best you can. Do not go outside unless you absolutely have to. Keep a bottle of water for drinking, but no more than two litres at a time should be in your proximity."

I absorbed this information eagerly, already making mental arrangements.

"Next, organise for someone to stay with you at all times. I have never heard of the creature getting too close when there are others around."

This would be more complicated, but I nodded.

"Finally, and this is very important, do *not* look at the creature. Especially not its face. Do not meet its eyes."

"How can I fight it?"

"As far as I am aware, you can't," she said grimly. "So I would suggest you try and stay out of reach and hope it loses interest in you."

Anathi arranged for her butler to walk me home. I felt guilty that the child would have to return to her on his own, but Anathi assured me he would be fine. No one laid a hand on what was known to be hers.

The fog had set in thick. The globed streetlights hung in the air, ephemeral as spirits, glowing diffusely.

The little boy led me forward by the hand; he did not seem in the least perturbed to be wandering around after dark. His small hand was warm and he held me firmly. He had still not said a single word, but something about his presence was curiously reassuring.

He left me at my door, refusing the money I tried to give him. A part of me wanted him to stay, but obviously this was not an option. As I closed the door, the room seemed to get colder.

I stood for a moment in the doorway, utterly exhausted and overwhelmed. Then I shook myself and set to work.

Terence, my landlord, had promised to turn my water off by the following morning. He was a little bemused by the request, but he and I went back a long time, so he obliged without too many questions. I was ruthlessly reliable with my rent, and we'd known each other since high school. He was prepared to cut me some slack.

The first thing I did was turn on my dehumidifier. With that working to suck moisture out of the air, I turned my attention to the kitchen and bathroom.

I figured that the Deepling wouldn't be able to use alcohol, fruit juice or soda to travel around, so I left that stuff alone. Also, I felt that I was probably going to need a strong drink sooner or later. Probably sooner. I tied a wad of dishcloths over the taps and stuck the plug firmly into the drain. I thoroughly cleaned the fridge and removed any frost. If there was a power failure, that stuff would melt and then there could be trouble.

I was more apprehensive of the bathroom. The Deepling had been here before. It took considerable nerve to push open the door. I wasn't quite sure what to do, so I decided I would wait for the water to go off before embarking on serious DIY projects. For now, I blocked the doorway with a mountain of towels and locked it. For good measure, I pushed my cupboard in front of it as a barricade.

That was the fun stuff complete. It was time to get onto the painful part.

I fished my cellphone out from between the couch cushions and flicked through my contacts. My finger hovered over dial. Then I took courage and pressed it.

My phone rang six long times before someone picked it up.

"Hey, Ela, I need you to come over."

It took several minutes for me to assure her that, no, I was not drunk and no, I did not think she was that kind of girl. Even then, my ex was far from pleased that I was interrupting her Friday night.

Nevertheless, fifteen minutes later, she was on my couch.

"A monster?" she asked, before taking a large gulp of beer.

"Yes."

"You want me to stay with you?"

"Yes."

"For how long?"

"Until it goes away."

"And you are following the advice of some kind of witchdoctor?"

"Don't be disrespectful."

She snorted. "You've changed your tune. Khul, this is weird."

"I know. I know. But I'm freaking out."

"And you really had no one else to call?"

"Please don't make me say that again."

She rolled onto her stomach and wormed her way into a more comfortable position. "Well, so long as you are feeding me and providing somewhere to sleep, I can deal with it. But this had better not be some kind of mind game. And no touching."

I breathed out in relief. "Ela…"

"Don't thank me. I'm sponging off you. Nothing more. I need the money. Also, I'm getting the bed. You are taking this flea-infested couch."

"You're the best."

"Easy on the compliments. Just remember that we are done, okay?"

"Very done. Completely and utterly done."

"Good. Now go make me a sandwich."

I retreated to the kitchen with more of my ego intact than I had initially anticipated. Ela turned on the television and sprawled out across the furniture like she owned it. I made her a sandwich out of reconstituted chicken (the expensive stuff) and mayonnaise substitute. I put on little flakes of dried chilli, the way she used to like it. I delivered this masterpiece to her, along with a second beer. She burped cheerfully.

"You know what, I think I like you when you're superstitious." She grinned evilly.

After innumerable episodes of *Soso's Fabulous Cruizin Life* and another two beers, Ela announced she was going to bed. This was near 2am and a great relief to me. My burst of renewed affection for her had not persisted past three hours of reality television. She staggered off to the bedroom, complaining that she couldn't brush her teeth. I settled down on my sofa with a spare blanket.

For second time that night, I felt acutely aware of my isolation. Although Ela had been annoying, it was difficult to feel fear in her boisterous, obnoxious and drunken company. Now that my apartment was silent and I was on my own, the gnawing paranoia crawled back into my brain.

I lay on my back, but I could not sleep. For a while I fidgeted. I was too cold and Ela might not have been wrong about the fleas. I could hear her breathing next door. It had been almost a year since we split, but she had not changed at all. A stupid, jealous part of me wanted to ask whether she had met anyone new. Not that I wanted to start all that nonsense again. She was right. We were done.

I rolled to my feet again with a groan and stretched. I was going to be tired the following day, but at least it would be Saturday. I opened the fridge and gulped down some milk, considering my options. Nothing sprung to mind that would improve my position at present.

On my way back to my bed, I paused outside the bedroom. The door was ajar. Ela was facing the window, her arm carelessly flung out over her head. She was half-falling out of the bed; only her torso remained under the covers. I hesitated for a moment and almost walked away. Then I stiffly pulled the duvet over her legs. She snuffled in her sleep and her fingers twitched.

I returned to the passage. The bathroom door was standing open.

It was strange, but I almost didn't notice. The cupboard was back in its usual position and everything simply looked ordinary to me. I had taken a few steps towards the couch before it even registered that something was wrong. Even then, I was not exactly scared. I suppose I assumed that Ela had something to do with it.

My hand was around the door handle to pull it closed when I saw the water on the floor. I traced it back to the source.

The bath was full, though I had not heard running water once that evening. While I stood there, a single drop fell from the faucet. Ripples spread out across the surface like a tremor of fear. The room was icy cold.

I stood perfectly still. I knew it was here. I could feel it watching me, but I was too afraid to turn around.

Another bead of water had formed on the lip of the faucet. It swelled slowly. Inside it, I could see my own inverted reflection and the rest of the bathroom. The reflection was tiny and compressed, but it was as if my vision had narrowed to this tiny little bubble. I watched it in fascination.

There was a patch of darkness behind my right shoulder. As I stared, it grew darker and closer. It moved languidly, like black smoke. Or fog. The impression of a face hovered beside my neck. I could have been wrong, but I thought it was smiling.

Then the drop fell and the spell was broken.

All the lights went out.

I stumbled forward with a strangled yell, spinning around to try to strike the creature that had been right behind me. My fist passed through air. I lost my footing as I slipped on the wet floor and cracked my head against the side of the bath.

The Deepling was still in the room; I could hear it moving towards me, breathing wetly. I struggled to rise, but I was too dizzy. I floundered on the floor and tried to crawl to the door. It slammed shut.

I think I was still shouting. I remember the blind panic and the pressure on my chest, the cold weight and the brush of its lips upon my own. I remember that I could not breathe.

Then the door burst open and the lights came on.

I was dazzled by the brightness. The Deepling relinquished its hold on my mouth and vanished into the shadows beneath the bath. I coughed up water and then vomited.

Ela was in the doorway, holding a carving knife with both hands. She threw it aside and dropped down next to me.

"Khul? Hey, stay with me here, honey." She lifted me by my shoulders into a sitting position.

I wiped bile out of the corner of my mouth. I was shaking so much my teeth were rattling. "Ela, I'm sorry—"

"Shhh. Your head is bleeding. Come on; let's get to the kitchen so I can patch you up. Can you stand?"

I made an attempt.

"Never mind, I've got you. Just lean on me, okay?" She got herself under my arm and hefted me upright.

"Did you see it?" I asked her.

"Don't worry about that now." She grunted. "Have you put on weight?"

I recognised her dismissive attitude. She did that when she was stressed. I squeezed her shoulder. "Maybe a little. Mostly muscle."

"Pssh. You wish."

She sat me down at the counter and took out the medi-kit from the cupboard above the fridge. I was shivering and soaked. Before she sorted through the antiseptics and healing agents on offer, she passed me a quart of brandy. I drank it straight from the bottle.

Whatever she applied to my head stung intensely. I bit my tongue and swallowed the pale green pills she handed to me. Within a few minutes, I was already beginning to feel better as the nanobots set to work on fixing the damage inflicted on my skull. Ela fetched the blanket from the couch and wrapped it around my shoulders.

"Why didn't we work things out?" I asked her.

"The brandy is talking," she said with a gently mocking smile.

"I was stupid to lose you. There was never anyone else."

"We aren't doing this again, Khul. I like you too much for that." She stood on tiptoes and kissed the top of my head. "You should lie down now. I'll keep watch."

She evaded my grasp and retrieved the knife from where she'd dropped it. I swallowed more brandy and put the bottle back down. The combination of the nanobots and the alcohol was doing strange things to me. My legs were not all that steady, but I made it back to the couch.

The world was spinning, but I was aware of Ela taking up station on the chair at my feet. The knife was in her hands. She adjusted the blanket over my legs and nodded encouragingly to me. I felt completely safe, but crushed.

"I never stopped loving you," I croaked.

She did not respond. I fell asleep.

I had not slept soundly for weeks, but after I passed out that night, I was dead to the world. I only woke around midday, when the smell of frying Baco-Mix revived me. Ela was at the stove, humming to herself.

The food was not for me. She was just raiding my freezer.

There were dark shadows under her eyes; she had not slept. Although she was her usual cheery self, the carving knife never strayed far from her reach. I noticed a tension in her jaw and the way her gaze darted towards the bathroom continually.

I had made a full recovery, though I was not healing from the humiliation of my grovelling behaviour any time soon. Ela had the good grace not to tease me about it. Perhaps it wouldn't have been so embarrassing if this had been the first time, but it was the third. I had nearly made it six months. I was ashamed and extremely grateful that she had not walked out the minute I re-declared my undying love.

Terence had turned off the water at last. Ela had arranged for a friend to deliver a week's worth of groceries, for which she was charging me. Her friend would also drop off a two-litre bottle of water every day. All in all, it seemed like things were getting nicely organised, but the thick bank of cloud outside the windows worried me. I did not want it to rain.

The Deepling did not bother me further during the day. I even, at times, began to doubt the veracity of my experiences of the previous night. I briefly managed to convince myself that it was all just a delusion brought on by Anathi's suggestions. Then I felt a ghost of the pressure on my chest, or the freezing touch of the monster's lips on my face and my shoddy justifications crumbled.

I watched TV and Ela slept next to me. I was beginning to perceive that this arrangement would not work for long. I was asking too much of her, but I put off these thoughts. I could see no other solution and did not want to face the Deepling alone again.

At six, she stirred and declared that she wanted pizza. It was some kind miracle that she did not get fat. The way she ate, Ela could expect to suffer from a heart attack by forty. She used to tell me her personality burnt up all her energy. I think she simply had a metabolism like no other.

It began to drizzle.

She ordered a Meat Mayhem with extra everything and graciously offered to share it with me. Given that it was on my account, I should probably not have been so thankful.

The pizza arrived at seven. The delivery guy mashed on the hooter of his souped-up scooter to save the airtime of calling Ela down. I offered to fetch the food, but she told me to stay put. The rain was coming down in earnest and I was jittery. We had sealed the windows as much as we could, but the flecks of water on the panes were enough to send chills down my back. Ela pulled on my windbreaker and locked the door behind her.

I felt stupid and childish, but hoped she would be quick. To stave off fear, I turned up the volume on the TV and set the table with mismatched crockery.

The bike gargled back to life outside. That meant Ela had received her pizza. I grabbed two beers and pushed aside the sentimental nostalgia that had risen warmly in my chest. It had been a long time since I had shared a pizza with anyone.

I hit mute on the TV. I shuffled the cutlery around on the table. I sat on the kitchen stool and got up again. Ela was slower than she used to be. In the old days, she jogged the stairs. The rain pattered against the glass, setting me on edge.

I pulled back the curtain and peered down to the street below. It was grey outside; the rain clouded my view. The edges of the buildings were blurred and my breath produced white fog on the cold windowpane, but I could not miss the bright yellow patch of my windbreaker.

Ela was standing in the rain. She was unmoving, staring at the fountain across the road. The hood of the windbreaker had blown off and her dark hair was drenched and flattened against her scalp. The pizza box was on the ground in front of her, growing soggy.

As I watched, she took a step forward into the road. She moved strangely, without her usual bouncing energy. Her progress was laboured; her feet dragged along and barely left the ground.

A movement beside the fountain caught my eye. A flash of darkness.

I was out of my apartment and halfway down the stairs before my brain even caught up with what my body was doing. It was not heroism; I did not have the time to consider being brave. If Ela reached that fountain, something terrible would happen. I had to stop her, Deepling or not.

I nearly broke my neck as I ran down the last flight of stairs. I rushed out into the pouring rain, throwing the doors of the lobby wide open.

"Ela!" I shouted.

It was too late. She had made it across the road and was stepping into the shallow pool. As she lowered her leg into the water, she turned. Her mouth was open in a scream, but she did not make a sound. It did not matter. I knew she was calling out to me.

Then her body crumpled and she disappeared into the water.

I sprinted across the road. Rain streamed down my face, falling in heavy sheets. The water in the fountain was black, infinitely and impossibly deep. I did not think. I dove into it headfirst.

Blackness. The darkness swallowed all sound. My eyes were open, but I could see nothing. I swam downwards, casting around for Ela. The water pressed against my skin like a sentient being, like it was trying to crush me. I forced my way forward. I would find her.

When the Deepling appeared before me, I initially mistook it for Ela. In the pitch darkness, the comparative lightness of its face misled me. It was smiling, beautiful and perfectly serene. The monster believed it had won.

I hated it with every fibre of my being.

It opened its arms to embrace me. I flew straight at it, propelling myself forward with as much force as I could muster, desperate to tear at its face, digging at the monster's eyes and clawing at its mouth. I did not care that it could hurt me. I only wanted to hurt it back. I was not afraid.

The pressure on my chest grew more intense, until I felt my lungs would explode. The Deepling's eyes bored into mine.

Then it disappeared beneath my hands.

I was so surprised that I accidentally let out the breath I had been holding. My mouth filled with water and I choked. I needed air. But I needed Ela more.

Lights were sparking over my vision when my hand found hers in the darkness. It was warm and she squeezed my fingers. I drew her into my arms and held her close. She clutched me. The blackness around us was lifting and I was no longer conscious of the pain in my chest.

Together, we swam towards the light.

Kerstin Hall was born in Cape Town in 1993. She currently attends Rhodes University in Grahamstown, where she studies English and journalism. She is the founder and chairperson of a student society called Ink, which encourages creative writing and provides support to other writers at the university. When she is not writing or studying, her interests include hiking, photography and culinary experimentation in the student residence microwave.

MOUSE TEETH

Cat Hellisen

At seventeen, Elsie de Jager suffered a gum infection and the dentist had to pull every single tooth out of her head, collapsing her mouth before it ever had the chance to bloom. Of course, Dokter Marais had said there was nothing else for it, that there was no saving the teeth, and everyone in Flora agreed that it was a terrible thing, a terrible thing to happen to a young girl, and she'd been so pretty before that, they said. But Elsie knew it wasn't disease that took her teeth.

When she was seven, she'd baited one of Ouma's wood-and-steel traps with a little ivory point of a baby tooth, like a tiny fat dagger, and placed it under her narrow bed. When the crack had come, deep in the middle of the Free State night, she'd heard the scream as it died—a thin, vicious squeal.

Elsie had buried the dead tooth mouse. Not in Ma's barren yard, where the red-brown dust was swept smooth every morning under the sawing teeth of the outside broom. Instead she'd carried the little body wrapped in an old cotton handkerchief of her father's, and taken it out of the town, to where those English sisters lived, and buried it under a wiry tussock by their mailbox. It was a game the children played—primitive wardings to keep the English witches' eyes from them, to keep them safe.

One of the boys in her class claimed to have buried a stillborn sheep by the box, but Elsie didn't believe him. Her fingers turned the hard red dirt, easing a space between the grass roots for the little body. There was nothing buried there that she could see. No cats' bones or fragile corpses. She patted the soil down, and felt a tremor under her palms. Elsie pulled her hands away and glanced fearfully at the cottage. The air hummed around her as the bees from the sisters' hive watched, and Elsie had hurried back home as quickly as she could.

In Flora, everyone spoke Afrikaans, even the black labourers. When Elsie did hear the sisters speak in town sometimes, it made her prick her ears—such a slippery, trickster language, full of stolen sounds and mismatched vowels. And, of course, the English were evil. They'd stolen the land, and the gold and the freedom. They'd built concentration camps for women and children, and put glass in the porridge of infants. It made complete sense to Elsie that English was the language of witchcraft. Of evil. What else would it be?

But now she was eighteen, and she'd been to boarding school and she could speak accented English through her neat and painful vulcanite teeth, and give people neat and painful smiles. It was almost like she was English herself. The man she'd married wasn't. Elsie wondered if she'd been cursed. Living in a town with an English name, when the dusty, empty Orange Free State was loosely scattered with towns with real names, proper names, commemorating the fallen dead. Strong names, farmer's names, where they had slowed their wagons and loosed their oxen.

It was a trial then, to grow up in Flora and to be almost-but-not-quite Afrikaans, and be married at eighteen with no teeth to an almost-but-not-quite farmer. Elsie knew this, and at night, after wiping herself clean of her husband's needs, she fumbled her dentures out in the tiny bathroom and cleaned them with her special brush and paste then left them in a clear tumbler, where they grinned at her like imbecilic reminders of her ill-luck.

She would wake every morning at four so that she could set her teeth back in and make strong black coffee on the stove, and drink two cups before the man woke. Elsie was bleary-eyed, jaw-aching as the teeth settled (they never did, truly.) Instead they remained a constant vice-like ache, biting into her gums in punishment for that broken back, that last gasp of *merde!*)

Or perhaps the mouse had screamed *murder*. Elsie didn't know anymore. Perhaps the mouse had never screamed at all. The sun was just beginning to drizzle through the net curtains and, in the dawn light, Elsie saw there was still blood on the kitchen floor, caught in the little channels between the big raw-red tiles.

She looked to the closed kitchen door; it hadn't moved, so Gideon was still asleep. She had time. With a damp rag clutched in her bony fingers, Elsie got down on her knees and scrubbed at the flaking dried blood. Here and there little beads of it had gathered stickily in the corners, but soon they were also washed away, and the night's offering vanished.

If her kitchen floor had become the altar where nightly Gideon bled himself for his god, Elsie was no priestess. The kitchen was a violated shrine. It should have been offerings of malva-pudding and steaming maize porridge with cream and butter, or tripe cooked slow with beans and tomatoes, for some fat and happy goddess.

Not human blood. Not Gideon screaming and crying and telling her that they would starve, that he was going to lose this job too.

The god of Kerkstraat wasn't listening. Last night had been worse than normal—Gideon asking her what would she do without him. That if he went, there would be no one to take care of her. Cutting his arms to show how he suffered, like a glimpse into the hell the dominee told them was waiting for them if they strayed from godliness to sin.

One day, Elsie thought, one day he would cut too deep, and when they took his corpse, everyone would know that he wasn't fit for Heaven. Elsie rolled the kitchen knives away in a chequered dishcloth, and put them in her outside bag. Then she went to the bathroom, and took the Mercurochrome bottle from the medicine cabinet and made sure its lid was screwed on tight, before adding that to her bag. Gideon's razor was resting on one of the narrow glass shelves in the cabinet, next to his shaving brush and his shaving bowl with its sliver of soap cradled like a natal scrap. She could have taken the razor too, of course, but that would have pointed a mocking finger at his terror. Elsie had grown up knowing that men did not like to have their flaws recognised, especially the flaws they thought were womanly and hysterical, bloody like monthly flow and filled with salt-sick tears.

The coffee Elsie left for him on the stove.

Her heart was fluttering with something that veered between fear and excitement. She was turning her back on God, she knew, by going to witches. They were abominations, they should be stones, be beaten and burned. But they were women, and they were fat with women's secrets, like spiders in their webs. It didn't take long to reach the English sisters' house. Flora was a small town, neatly bisected by Kerkstraat, dividing the godly from the ungodly. The sisters lived on the side of sin, with the shops and the butchers and the women who sewed all through the night.

Elsie walked with her head held high, though it was early, and only a few old ladies had ventured out to sweep their empty front yards emptier in case the dominee should pass. It was a Sunday, so people would be getting ready to eat a full breakfast and suit themselves into their smart clothes. Then, with heads bowed and pious faces empty and barren as their dirt yards, they would walk down to the end of Kerkstraat, file into that dark building and begin to pray.

Elsie surprised a small flock of scavenging bosveldfisant, and the francolins ran off ahead of her, *kraaaing* like fat old ladies shocked by something vulgar. The air was clear and cold, morning air before morning had fully woken, and Elsie breathed in deep with each swing of her arms. She wanted her lungs to be full, as if she was about to hold her head underwater.

The sisters' house came into view. It was smaller than she remembered as a child, a little tin-roof box with a garden kept clipped and green. Waste of water, Elsie thought. There were roses, fat-headed and drooping, and they smelled like Tannie Issie's perfumed Sunday best, and Elsie felt a prick in the corners of her eyes, like bees had stung her blind. It took her a moment before she could walk on, past the little chicken-fence gate. More flowers were growing between the rose bushes. Elsie didn't know what they were called, most of them.

She stood on their stoep, assaulted by the sweetness of the English garden, and covered her mouth with one hand, her tongue pressing at the backs of her dentures, until she was certain everything was straight, before she knocked at the door. Her shoes were small and pointed, and made her feet hurt, church best against the ragged stoep paint, and Elsie stared at them until the door creaked open, and a round-faced woman peered blearily out at her. Elsie wasn't sure which one this was, Catherine or Elizabeth.

When Elsie was seven, the sisters had seemed severe and ancient. Now, at eighteen, she realised this one, at least, was small and soft, and only about fifteen years older than she was.

"Elsie de Jager," the woman said without surprise, as if she were used to strangers arriving unannounced on her stoep at five on a Sunday morning.

"Snyman," Elsie said automatically. "It's Elsie Snyman now. I married Hendrik Snyman's son."

"Gideon or Theunis?" the woman asked. Then she closed her eyes. "What does it matter, Elizabeth? Stop talking nonsense and let the poor girl in." She opened her eyes again, wide and startled like a little witkoluil, and stepped back to beckon Elsie into her house. Even the way she bobbed her head reminded Elsie of an owl.

Elsie murmured her thanks, and put one foot firmly over the threshold. She wasn't sure what she expected in a house of English witches, but the sisters' little cottage was neat and simple, and there were handmade doilies on the small couch, just like in her own house. Elsie felt a little disappointed. A round-bellied black stove sulked in the corner, but it was too small to burn a child in, unless perhaps they squeezed a newborn into that little mouth. Perhaps there were tiny bones in the ash they scraped out. They had a wall full of books, so that at least was different.

"Catherine, dear," Elizabeth called. "We've a visitor." She turned back to Elsie. "Sit down, Miss de Jager, and I'll bring you some tea."

She wanted to point out (again) that she was married now, with a married woman's stamp of authority, and that she preferred coffee, because that was a real drink. It put hairs on your chest. Elsie swallowed the words like a mouthful of bees, and surprisingly, she felt better for it. They warmed up her stomach.

The other sister appeared from the back of the house. She was older and taller than Elizabeth, and it gave her a more stately look—a goshawk to her sister's owl. Her hair was greying and pinned back neatly in careful curves. It looked like she'd been up and dressed since before the moon had set, and Elsie wondered if they'd been awake all night, chanting and dancing, leaving sacrifices to English gods they'd brought with them in their trunks. Celtic goddesses they'd wrapped in the broken wings of fairies, garlanded with flowers that wouldn't grow here in this arid place.

"It's not often we get visitors," said Catherine, coolly. "To what do we owe such an honour?"

"Oh for heaven's sake, Catherine, stop being such an immense drip. It's obvious the poor girl's been shaken up by something. And she wouldn't come to us unless it were a secret." Elizabeth bustled back into the front room, and set out a tray of pretty little cups and saucers, and a steaming pot of tea clad in a voluminous cosy. "You can tell us, dear," she said to Elsie. "We're used to it. We hear it all. The little secrets and the big ones."

Elsie swallowed. "What do you mean?" She'd thought her English remarkably good, but now here, against their shatter-bright tones, her words felt clipped at the edges, so that they came out the wrong shape, flattened and dull.

"They wouldn't be secrets if we told you," snapped Catherine, who Elsie was beginning to dislike in a fearful sort of way—the kind of dislike that was gilded with guilty admiration. She wanted to be sharp and snippy too. A falcon instead of a little dog with no teeth.

Elizabeth poured tea and milk for her, and stirred in sugar when Elsie asked. Finally, when all the three women had their porcelain shields in place, Elizabeth smiled at her, sipped once, and said, "You may begin. Elsie, dear."

Where did she start, Elsie thought. What could she say that didn't make a small thing sound bigger than it was? And it was a small thing, really, in the grand scheme of the world and the universe. "I think my husband is going to murder himself," she said.

Elizabeth set down her tea, and glanced at her older sister.

Catherine sighed. Finally she spoke. "Why do you think that?" Her voice had changed from beak and talon sharp. It was a careful voice now, one that was unpicking knots in silk.

Elsie cleared her throat with an embarrassed cough, and fumbled in her bag for the kitchen knives. She unrolled the dishcloth, and displayed the knives on the sisters' ornate table. "He uses these," she said, without looking up. The blades were old, but sharp. They had been her ouma's, given to her after the funeral. Some were so well used that the blades had become sickle smiles, almost thin enough to see through. "He uses these," she said to the grinning silver. "Nightly, in the kitchen, and he cries for the Lord, but I do not think the Lord is listening."

A very long silence was punctuated by the long slow tick of the clock on the wall, and the faint drone of the bees as they worked the flowers outside the window.

"He will kill himself, eventually, yes," said Catherine. "And he will blame you for it, like men always blame their weaknesses on women. You will try stop him, playing your part of dutiful wife, and he will leave scars on your arms, and guilt in your heart."

Elsie shivered and bowed her head closer to her chest, trying not to cry in front of these Englishwomen. They were witches, seeing her future laid out like a poor man's feast—gristle and bone and empty dishes.

"What do you want us to do?" Elizabeth said kindly. "We cannot stop him."

"No," said Catherine, and Elsie looked up into her amber eyes. "I'm afraid that we cannot change what must be. We cannot avert the deaths to come, or change the shape of the heart."

Elizabeth nodded. "We cannot make love grow, and we cannot rip death out by the root. We cannot change one flower into another, not forever, anyway."

"Then what can you do?" said Elsie. "What use are you?"

Catherine stood. "We can save you from wasted time." She went to the long bookcase, and opened one of the leaded-glass doors to take out a small box, like a cigar case. She brought the little case back to the table and handed it to Elsie, who took it, her eyebrows raised. "What is this thing?"

"Open it," said Catherine.

The box was small enough to balance easily on the palm of her hand. Faded lettering was inked on the top. It was tin, the corners rusted, brown earth dry as old breadcrumbs caught in the hinges. Elsie struggled to open it, but finally the lid snapped back, and inside was small roll of cotton, carefully wrapped around a desiccated bundle of bones and skin.

"You left it for us," said Elizabeth, from the couch. She blinked once, slowly. "A powerful token. You must have had some natural skill. Oh, what we could have done with you if you'd been ours. What we could have taught you."

The mouse was ten years dead, held together by dust. Elsie pressed her tongue against her false teeth and swallowed. She closed the tin carefully. "What—what must I do with this?"

"Your man eats, doesn't he?" said Elizabeth, and Elsie was reminded then that as round-faced and owl-eyed as she was, owls were still killers, breakers of bones, silent hunters. "Gideon or Theunis or whatever son he is, they all eat.

125

They never cook. Cooking is the witchcraft of women." She leaned forward and tapped the edge of the tin with one oval nail. "Grind it into his food."

B ack at the house, Gideon was awake, drinking his coffee sweetened with condensed milk. "Where were you?" he said.

Elsie's heart shivered like a mouse before a cat pounced, and she smiled her neat and painful smile, her gums aching. "I needed antiseptic. We'd run out." She fished in her bag, careful not to touch the wrapped blades or the little tin mouse coffin, and drew out a glass bottle. "I got some Mercurochrome from Sanet—"

"You didn't say what it was for," he said, his voice hard and scared and angry.

"No." Elsie set the small dark glass bottle down on the table, her hands shaking. "Of course not. I'll just get some bandages and we can clean you up properly before church. You don't want infection setting in." As though the cuts along his arms were accidents, a slip, *it could happen to anyone.*

When he was stained and covered, Elsie made breakfast. Porridge, milky and sweet, the oats soaked overnight, heated slow and sticky, smoothed out with salted butter and the cream from the top of the milk. The mouse she ground down in her herb mortar, and Elsie stirred the dust of its bones into his bowl, before sprinkling a crust of brown sugar over. She brought him his breakfast in the dining room, and they ate in silence, heads bowed before the grace of God.

That night, after Elsie had taken out her teeth and polished them and scoured every line and dip, and drowned them in cold water, she tiptoed to bed in the dark, her mouth sunken and soft. She lay straight as a new sapling next to Gideon, and listened to him sleep. The sounds he made were soft and furry, and Elsie put one hand to her breast and felt her heart beating under her palm, until the sound of it filled her ears and her skull and pulsed her bones like a drum. She wanted to dance to that beat, to shake off her nightdress and run naked through the night, taste the stars like white bees. Swallow mouthfuls of them until she was stung back to life. Instead, she kept stiller than still, and fell asleep, her skin shrouded in thick flannel.

In her dreams, she walked the passage of the house Gideon Snyman had bought her with his share of the Snyman inheritance. He'd given up his claim to the farm in order to have a share of the money early. He'd wanted to impress his bride, the most beautiful girl in Flora—or she would have been, if her teeth hadn't all been pulled out.

The floors were dark beneath her bare feet, and Elsie looked down at the smooth, silky wood in surprise. She never walked barefoot, that freedom lost to childhood. But there were her feet, white and plain. She'd never had pretty feet, just solid, peasant ones. Boere-feet. Feet that could walk for miles, feet that were narrowed by shoes so that they would look neater, adult and proper. Her toes lengthened, the nails turning into sharp claws that tacked along the wood. Elsie the dog with no teeth. She growled, and the dreaming Elsie turned over in her sleep and pressed one hand against her husband's spine.

Head down, Elsie sniffed along the edges of the passage, nosing the trail of twisting scents that zipped and zagged and jumped and popped along the skirting boards. Mice. The house had never had mice before, and the little terrier wagged the stump of its tail in delight, ready for a hunt.

It didn't take long for the trail to lead her to the mouse. It sat on its back legs, blatant and uncaring, on the dinner table, stuffing its bewhiskered face with food. There were dishes all over the table, left uncleared, the food half-eaten, and the gravy congealing in oily lumps. Elsie leapt up onto one of the chairs, and placed her front paws on the table.

The mouse paused, and looked once at the terrier, before resuming its gluttony.

"You should be scared of me," Elsie said.

"Scared?" The mouse threw down the maize kernel it had been nibbling. "Of a little dog with no teeth? I don't think so."

And Elsie knew it was right, could feel the useless slobbery gums that were all she had. She couldn't eat the softest food without pain. How was she to snap up this little intruder?

She whined softly and sunk her head onto the table.

Her jaw ached.

In her marital bed, Elsie twisted, turned away from her husband and curled up, her knees against her stomach. She pressed her hands against her empty mouth and wept in her sleep, soaking the pillows with salt.

On the dining room table, the terrier ground its jaws, feeling the splinter sharp pain as new teeth, fat and pointed, tore through the soft gums.

The mouse froze.

Upstairs, Elsie overslept. She slept through the rising sun and the bells from the distant station. She slept through the milk van, and the clatter of hooves as one of the labourers drove his cart through the town main road.

She slept curled up around herself, while at her back, her husband cooled.

It was near noon when she woke. Gideon didn't stir, though Elsie watched him for a long time. In a daze, she dressed, and walked to the police station, her tongue pressed against the tiny ivory pegs in her mouth. She spoke to the constable dully.

"I overslept."

"He was like that when I woke."

"No, I don't know what happened."

When she got back home, late, so late in the afternoon that the sun was turning the few trees on the road into red sentinels, Elsie stared at her reflection in the bathroom mirror. They had taken the body away, made notes of the cuts on his arms.

"Woodworking accident," Elsie had told them.

Her vulcanite dentures grinned at her from their tumbler, like exhibits in a museum.

Elsie de Jager bared her teeth in the mirror. They were small and fat and new. Children's teeth.

Tomorrow she would catch a train to Bloemfontein, and from there to Cape Town. She would learn English properly, and to play tennis, and to drink lemon-tea and gin, and the names of flowers, and how to use mouse bones for magic, and she would call herself Elizabeth.

Cat Hellisen lives in Cape Town. She's the author of the novels When the Sea is Rising Red, House of Sand and Secrets, *and* Beastkeeper. *Previous short fiction has appeared in* Something Wicked, Tor.com, Apex, *and* The Magazine of Fantasy and Science Fiction. *She likes Bloody Marys and long walks in the nuclear fall-out.*

SPIRITS OF THE DEAD KEEP WATCH

Mishka Hoosen

Never had I seen her so beautiful, so tremulously beautiful... How could
I know what at that moment I might seem to her? Might she not with my
frightened face take me for one of the demons and specters, one of the
Tupapaüs, with which the legends of her race people sleepless nights? Did
I really know who in truth she was herself?

> – Paul Gauguin, on the genesis of his painting, *The Spirits*
> *of the Dead Keep Watch*, Noa Noa, 1919.

When she arrived, she was so tired she slept for three days on the sofa in the study. She has grown to a woman during the past ten years. The same long, dark hair, the same hands, but the breasts are fuller, the hips and waist more shapely. She appeared on Friday morning, ten o'clock, after I'd come back into the study from breakfast.

Sprawled on the sofa, she wears a plain black dress. It suits her, like the dresses women wore when I was young. Others her age might consider the style old-fashioned, but I like it on her. Only her face disturbs me; it has a blankness to it. Still lovely, if somewhat coarse in its prettiness, the lips too red, still bitten (how, after ten years?), a kind of dark campesina prettiness, too generous to be refined, or elegant.

Any other twenty-three-year-old woman would have some kind of mark, some sign of time or experience on her features, and even a worldly turn at the corner of the mouth. Her face is empty and blithe as a renaissance Madonna's. Of course it makes sense—she hasn't done the living that would have given her the signs of age—but it unsettles me. I am afraid for her to wake, to see that blank child's face on a grown woman move and talk. It disturbs me more than her coming back.

I cannot lie and say that I have not been expecting her for years now.

I wake and he's there, old—older now, and dozing in the chair at the desk. The room is lit by the glass lampshade, stained with thick, blazing roses. It makes the shadows honeyed, heavy. Outside the night drops soft on the sweeping lawns, the hundreds of little English flowers nodding, little ghosts. There's ivy crept closer around the windows but otherwise nothing else has changed.

The sight of him sets things tilting. My head is sore and thick, my throat rough. I don't know where anything is, only that I've been gone—a long time I think now, looking at him. I remember nothing about it and feel cheated. Perhaps I really don't deserve Heaven at all, and this is Hell.

If so, I want him awake even less, and I lie still, breathe slow and small through my nose. My breath hitches when I realise I don't know if I'm wearing any underwear; it seems stupid, but there's no way to check without moving enough to wake him. I don't know why it matters to me so much. I don't understand why I'm here or why I'm wearing this old black dress. The room surges and I lie back again, and close my eyes to make everything settle. The shapes of the stained glass roses burn through my lashes.

When I was small, I wore a dress with blue roses on it and never any underwear. I'd never seen blue roses in real life. These were dark and tangled. They looked like the impossible flowers in nightmares. I liked that the dress never flew up in the wind.

When I was bigger and went to the primary school in Newclare, they used to say Pinkie-Pinkie was in the girls' toilets, and that if you wore pink underwear, you would be raped. I saw him once, sliding eyes, pale and sickly, grabbing amphibian hands. I saw him in the mirror right at the end of the row, where the water and piss leaked across the floor and the lists of everyone who'd had sex were written up in chalk. He let me go. He knew I never wore underwear. I was proud my name was never put up on the wall.

It's strange seeing him doze in his chair like that, to see him grown old. He seems vulnerable, like afterwards, that quiet spent look, his eyes closed. But never for this long. I'm embarrassed looking at him like this, and I'm afraid of him waking to see me staring. This is the first time I've ever seen him sleep. Strange, when you think about it. There was a time I thought we were lovers or something. Don't they see each other sleep? Sometimes I'd go so quiet and close my eyes so he thought I was sleeping, but I wasn't.

The first time, he hated the way I stared at him. He seemed embarrassed. He pushed the hair from my forehead, held it too tight so my face tilted up to him. He looked at me for a long moment before his mouth twisted, almost a smile. "Your eyes are too big," he muttered.

I closed them after that.

I knew the degrees of closeness, the highest being skin to skin. Often I told myself I was special, that he picked me. It was me he chose to tutor for the scholarship exams, the English Olympiads, the Eisteddfods. It was me he read to, talked to about music. And then there was this, the highest closeness, even if it hurt, even if it was dirty and I shook for hours afterward, not understanding why. I thought, to see him with his eyes closed, spent and helpless for a second. That was love, and I reached up to him, to touch his face or hold onto his shirt to bring him down to me.

He pushed my hand away. My hands were probably dirty and his shirt was clean and expensive. I didn't know where to put them, what to hold onto. That became the main thing I thought about. I didn't like grabbing onto the sheets. I couldn't let my hands lie beside me like dead things. I hoped he never noticed them. Anyway, it kept me occupied while it happened.

Sometimes he'd look at me almost as if he were scared. That was only when I stared at him, though his mouth clenched when I made a noise, once, because it hurt. But I learned to fix my breathing and bite my lips so I wouldn't make a sound. Sometimes I looked at him, with his eyes closed and his breathing heavy and him hurting me but needing it, I thought, like a little boy. And my job was not to let him know it was hurting because that might hurt him. Not to have him feel hurt. That was when I loved him. I tried very hard to love him. I thought, this is what women do. I reached up for him and thought, I am a woman now.

I wake and God help me, there are those black eyes gleaming at me. Blank and dark, and like a bird's. You think, surely it's not thinking much, behind those eyes, but what if it is?

I am getting away from myself, it's the uncanniness of it that shakes me, but I know what must be done. She's come for me, for retribution of some kind, and I must be the one who wins. If I keep my head about me, if I am calm and rational, I will. I know I will.

So I sit upright. I clear my throat. I smile. "Hello, Antoinette."

There's that quick birdish flash. She's been waiting, I think. How like her. "Hello, sir," she says.

Somehow obscene, coming from a grown woman, especially as she lies there, propped up on an elbow, watching me, eyes intent. What do I say now? It seems grotesque to ask how she is, why she's here, even. She'd throw it back in my face, insolent and accusing. I use her own tactic against her: simply watch.

She stretches and rises to sit up properly. Her gaze never leaves my face. There is a precision to her movements, the stiff-backed way she sits, folding her hands just so in her lap. She might be mocking me. Or else she hasn't lost that knack she's always had for adapting, and has picked up again, like back then, on the precision and elegance I value. Is it terrible of me to feel a stab of gladness, that some things don't change, that the quick-eyed, willing child is not completely gone? Don't think for a moment that I didn't mourn her deeply.

"You're older. How long has it been?" She rasps as she says it. I won't let the vulgarity of the question throw me.

"Ten years, but I thought you'd know that."

She's shocked, blinks deliberately as if that will help. I hadn't expected her to look so lost. I'm almost disappointed, thrown myself, but I won't let her see that. I must stand my ground. The best way with her has always been gentleness, when she least expects it. I will smile kindly. "Were you in Heaven then, Antoinette? What was it like?"

My throat feels raw, I can feel my blood pulsing there, saying run, run, run or play dead. Be dead again. I can't let him know. Once I shook and shook and he said to me, be calm. Be calm and it will be fine. Of course it hurts when you get hysterical, but if you're calm you can do anything. So I am calm, or pretend to be. Now he leans in his chair again, and smiles. I never could tell what he thinks when he smiles like that, asking what Heaven was like.

I did not know. I was there for ten years, and I remember nothing. I breathe slowly and tell him lies: "It is very quiet. There are many hibiscus flowers and a thick sweet smell of rain. There are crumbling French façades and bougainvillea. Jacaranda blossoms crushed by rain. The old people—some of the angels are kindly old people, grandmothers and grandfathers—are very beautiful. The light is soft. Like old pictures. It's very quiet, but full. Like a beehive just been smoked. All the bees dreaming a little aloud at once."

Quickly I remember something—I am sick with the shame of it—a man saying to me, in that strange city, saying it was all right that I had been whoring myself on its streets. Was that really Heaven, I asked? And he said yes, but that it had its rules too, its customs. And I cried a long time in his arms. He wore a clean white shirt and I felt bad for spoiling it. I said I was sorry. He said it was all right, that I had been gone a long time with the Devil, that I'd been in Hell. Why could I not remember it, I asked. He said I would in time, but that I must not rush those things.

By the time the memories come back you will have learned the customs of Heaven and nothing of Hell will hurt you. You will carry Hell safe back with you but it will not touch you.

I wanted to know what he meant but my throat clenched—to have Hell with me, on me like a smell. How could it not hurt me? He walked me to a hammock on the stoep of a grand, crumbling old house where a tall black woman with long, golden earrings was singing to a guitar. She put flowers on my eyes, jacaranda blossoms soft as shadows, and said sleep now, baby, thula. And I did.

That memory comes so quick I'm sick with it, and the room spins again. I stay upright, though. I have a knack for it. I don't talk for a minute. I'm afraid if I do I will be sick. Can I be sick?

I will admit: I was shaken when I heard her speak. Don't think there was no love in me for her. Looking at her now, the old tenderness comes back. She was a promising girl, pretty, very clever. I am not one of those sickly creatures abusing themselves in the dark over sticky pictures, nor am I a sociopathic pervert abducting little girls from playgrounds to do horrible things to them. I am as outraged as you when I read these horrible stories in the paper. I am, all considered, a decent person.

When I got the news, a terse letter from the mother, an invitation to the funeral I never attended (I sent a hundred white orchids instead—I wonder if the family realised how much those were worth), things slowed and drooped around me like a neglected hothouse. I did nothing to stop it. I did not so much as look at another girl again. I'd dream, yes, but she'd always walk in, somehow, or the girl would have her eyes or waist or voice. Eventually, even the dreams stopped, and I left everything to stop around me with all the grace and courtesy of which I am capable. I hope at the end it might mean something.

We can agree, as intelligent adults, that human affairs are not predictable, black and white. We know there are exceptions to everything, and she was—really I mean this sincerely—astute for her age. In its way, strange and difficult as it was for both of us, it was love.

Beyond all this—without getting carried away by sentimentality—shall we say, that the definitions applied are a little extreme. A couple of years ago I read a column by some rabid feminist saying that she realised in adulthood that every man—note: every man she had ever slept with (quite willingly, she admits freely) in her teenage years, was a paedophile. Now, I ask you, considering the fact that, as I mentioned, she states she engaged in sexual acts with these men of her own volition (she was not forced, she was not threatened, she found them attractive) is it fair to condemn them? They may have even had the most tender feelings for her after all; is it fair to label them, paedophiles, perverts and criminals, just because she happened to be below the legally defined age of consent? How do we measure maturity in any case? How do we say she was excused from her sexual behaviour because she was legally defined as a minor in that country? I know of schoolchildren aged eleven—two years younger than my Antoinette when we first slept together—who do filthier things together in their school breaks, for God's sake.

Still, there was a fair share of hell in it. It was almost too easy, with her, a few months of talking—she came for the tutoring. When I asked her to come look at the artwork in the bedroom, a fine reproduction of one of Gauguin's Tahiti paintings, she stepped after me, quiet and blithe.

That first afternoon was too bright, the difference in light between the bedroom and the study too marked. Going into the bedroom for a moment, I was blinded. Coming out I was blinded again. The day, and all the days after, seemed to come unhinged. Maybe it was the heat. It was a strange summer, full of exasperating insects that died in droves on the windowsills, full of crushed flowers finding their way under one's shoe heels to make the rooms drunk with scent.

Her hair, perfumed and dark, was shot through with shafts of copper that startled when they caught light.

She felt so small sometimes, a bundle of delicate bones shaped into a woman. But she was never quite untouched. She had smudges of red dust on her socks, her hair smelled of dust, and that other, low, rich smell, and her waist and breasts were formed and ready. Not a child, not by a long way. Other than her clumsy earnestness and big eyes, she was almost preternaturally grown up. You'd bury your face in her hair, in the copper and the dark, and you were aware of not wanting to crush her, of holding back from too much roughness, but a moment comes when every man forgets. She didn't make a sound, much of the time. It was like a fever dream, like dying for a small time, and surfacing. Addictive and exhausting.

When you're done, there is that spent moment when your face is lowered into her hair, eyes closed. Then the scent is cloying, almost drowns you, and because it clings, it seems cheap. You pull out of her, get up, zip up your trousers. Don't meet her eye. When she looks at you afterwards, she's clinging to you like that scent. What does she use in her hair? Some kind of oil. No wonder the scent never seems to fade. Too much of it might ruin a shirt.

I smiled again, said, "And here I've been, in the same old house. I've missed you, Antoinette."

But she seems to have drawn strength from talking, even if it makes her dizzy. She laughs, leans forward almost drunkenly. "You know, walking to your house I hated you. With every single step I cursed you. I hated everything about your street, about that whole part of town. The green, the oaks, the beautiful houses with their wrought iron gates, the lawns, the little white roses nodding.

I hated them all like poison 'til I felt sick with hating it. Can you believe it? I actually felt sick with hate. I hated the beauty and the grace and the loveliness."

I hadn't expected this. When she was angry or afraid, she would lapse into that coarse common accent; it was an accent that made the speaker seem more stupid, somehow. Stupid and sometimes worryingly emotional, volatile. Once even, can you believe it, she said huh-uh and shook her head. Stoppit, suh. It set my teeth on edge. Saying it's soh—instead of "it hurts".

The music in her was gone, her fine grasp of language, her capacity for beauty. It's heartbreaking to see that gone in a bright person, to see them replaced by something common, something really below them.

You know just what I mean too. I know you do.

I was thankful she didn't lapse into it now. She was eloquent, impassioned, and had a good turn of phrase. I'm glad I had given her something, and if she must hate me for all the rest of it, at least she could explain herself adequately. I choose not to show any annoyance.

She leans again, continues, "Wasn't always like that—first time I saw your house, when I walked over from the bus stop, feeling so proud you'd picked me, and all the other girls had a crush on you and thought you so brilliant, and finally there I was in your study, with all these books, and the paintings, the piano in the lounge. I thought, people live like this. Imagine." She's almost bent double, almost spitting as she talks, half-laughing and coughing.

I'm not accustomed to this much emotion expressed so shamelessly. It seems melodramatic, somehow insincere.

I must intervene, before this gets out of hand.

The room seems too bright, the memories are coming back, and more than that. Here his mind is bare, laid out like a chessboard. This man I loved once. I did love him. Here is his mind sprawled in the red light, in front of me: There are orchids, thick flowers like in a hothouse, a sheen on everything like smoked glass. I see the bed, and when the child goes to the bathroom he goes to the stereo, smoking a Sobranie, and plays Schubert until she has collected herself and comes out.

He checks his watch to make sure there is enough time for the cleaner to come in to change the linen. The timing must be precise so that it is before the cleaner comes in. Just before. There's a pair of red shoes at the foot of the bed, the shoes I bought with the prize money for the poetry contest he told me to enter.

When I wore them at home, my aunt said, you know what those mean, and even though I did, I smiled sweet and said no, Auntie… what do they mean? She tutted and huffed. What do they mean? I asked her again, sweet. I wanted her to say it. I wanted her to say it, the word slut out loud, but she shook her head and blew through her lips and said, no, girl, you too young to know… It'll make you shy. And I laughed. I'll wear them in Heaven, Auntie, I said, and she smacked me on the mouth.

I'm laughing now—he gets nervous, and seeing him there, old and white-haired and his fine face and pale eyes paler and worn turns this laugh hitching in my throat to a sob until I double with it. The look on his face is almost kind.

All at once, seeing her hysterical there, I know just what she's come for. This is a place of ghosts, after all. Every story tells you ghosts must be quieted if they're to have any peace. It almost hurts, the tenderness I feel at that, knowing I've always been able to soothe her, quiet her, until she closes her big eyes and goes sweet and still to that other place. This isn't retribution; this is a request. Of course.

"Antoinette, my dear," I say, "calm down."

The morning is thickening and the sky paling over the hedges of the garden. I venture the ritual question: "Why did you do it, at last?"

Her mouth falls, as if I've hit her. She heaves a breath through her nose, shakes her head, and smiles. Her eyes are half-lidded and she sways—from remembering or from tiredness, I can't tell.

"A little while, maybe two weeks after the seventh time, I went to Evangeline's fourteenth birthday party. We were going to her uncle's pool after the school fête. I bought her red lipstick at one of the stalls for R5 and she put it on everyone at the party: five girls. She had her hair up in a ponytail and her mum had done it with henna so it glowed. We went to her uncle's house in Florida—a double-storey house with a big garden and a pool. It was wonderful, and I just sat there watching everything. I didn't want to swim, like the others. I don't know why. I just didn't like getting undressed, swimming with them. Didn't feel right."

She rubs her hand against her forehead. The sound of me clearing my throat, the words, "Go on," never making it from my mouth, seem deafening to me. She doesn't notice, rushes, "They were splashing around, showing off. The twins were lying on the warm bricks next to the water, sunning themselves. Evvie was sitting on the edge of the pool with lipstick on, kicking her feet in the water. Pa used to say that was bad luck, to swing your legs like that. He'd say you're kicking your luck away. She was singing this song. Stupid blêddy—" She winces. "Stupid song. It was playing on the radio all the time. All about like—"

She looks at me, wary as a rabbit, as if waiting for me to laugh, or hit her. She swallows. "About someone going away, and just saying you gonna miss me, you know? You gonna miss everything about me. And you'll know, you'll know I'm gone. And—" Her voice catches. "You'll miss me."

Her throat trembles, holding it back, the tears and this inane song sung by some brat at a pool party.

"It was just—she sang it like she meant it, you know, like she knew, like she just knew. Like she was this gorgeous thing—just drop-dead gorgeous thing, precious thing…" She clears her throat. "And she was tilting her head so her ponytail shone bright. Cheap lipstick mouth. Voice high and singing, ja, even with that accent you fuckin' hate, her voice like loose change and I loved her so much for who she was right then. Singing by the bright pool water in the sun. I loved her and loved her like my own sister right that moment, even though she called me a play-white slut, even though she only invited me so they could gossip. I loved her so much it hurt. I can't explain why—"

When she's serious her eyes get even bigger and fixed, but her mouth trembles. She leans forward and stares at you but that trembling mouth, the way she repeats herself, that fixed stare—she wants so desperately to be believed that she looks as if she's lying. Other adults were always a little suspicious of her, especially the women—put most of it down to histrionics. I found it charming at first, that earnestness. It's such a rare thing in a child nowadays. Maybe that's why no one trusted it.

She looks at me then, seeing how I can't understand, can only sit there nodding blandly, as if I always did.

"And I knew all of a sudden what you'd done to me—I'd forgiven and forgiven you and loved you even—but I knew all of a sudden everything you took away from me, everything for always. I didn't even hate you then, I was just sore—like after—just sore, here." She presses her fist into her belly. "I was just sad and sore. I couldn't take it anymore. I smiled at her and when they went inside to change I got up and walked to the oleander tree hanging over the water, and picked up one of the big rocks that ringed the yard, and I jumped into the pool. No one could get it away from me."

She says it with something like pride. That far-off smile as she sways and says, "Nobody could get me away from it or grab it from me. I held it in the water and it held me down."

Every so often I'd be overcome with tenderness for her, her memory. I will say that now without hesitation. The sight of a schoolgirl sleeping in a car outside of Pick n Pay while her mother darted for groceries—the girl's neck tilted, wisp of hair from her ponytail at the little hollow of her throat where her school tie lies loosened and askew. The late afternoon sunlight slanting across her mouth and neck. The picture was too perfect, so poignant somehow that it physically hurt me, and I would have to stop a moment to breathe again, to loosen the knot in my chest.

I don't want you to think I didn't suffer too—horribly.

I gather every part of that suffering and tenderness and say, "Oh, my dear. My dear, I am so sorry. Forgive me, Antoinette. Please forgive me."

She's silent, staring with those big eyes. I never know if she's afraid or hating me. She doubts everything. Nothing is ever quite wholly fact to her. It means she doubts herself too, and with her rather obvious, sometimes vulgar need to be loved she drinks in anything said with kindness. I must quiet her one last time, have her close her eyes and sleep, forever this time. I still have life left to me, and we both need the peace from this at last. She sways, stunned.

"Go to bed, my dear. You're exhausted. Sleep some more. We'll talk about it all when you wake up. And Antoinette—" I say it before I can stop myself "I did miss you."

She laughs a little. "Do you remember how once, afterwards, I wanted to fall asleep? I curled up and you took the edge of the sheet and shook it, and said the maid would be coming in at any moment?"

I choke on the words but manage to say, "I remember."

"Good," she says. Then furrows her eyebrows, a small child puzzling over something, overtired, "Good," she mutters. And lies back.

She has been here for weeks, has not disappeared, and only lies perfect and sleeping, warm and breathing on that blue sofa. I must be quiet, all the time. I cannot even risk the creak of the opening door in case of waking her. I cannot risk a sound on of the floorboard in case of waking her. The days go round her and she lies warm and still at the centre, while my breathing catches from being kept so quiet so long, while I wait and watch and cannot move for fear of her eyes opening again. Why has she not left or faded, a ghost as she should be? Ghosts fade when laid to rest, but she lies a woman grown and lovely and alive but sleeping for weeks now. I have not moved. I cannot move. If her eyes open, who knows what she will see.

Mishka Hoosen is the result of an unorthodox education by blacklisted revolutionaries, mad poets, and a cigar-smoking river shaman. Her writing has appeared or is forthcoming in Ons Klyntji, South African Rolling Stone, Chimurenga, New Coin, Bare Fiction, and Hunger Mountain.

Her nonfiction book, Hollow the Bones, deals with narratives of madness and is forthcoming in 2015 from Deep South Books.

Her preferred work spaces have been the tattoo parlour in Grahamstown, boats on the Mekong Delta, army hangouts in Jeddah, Fermoy and Dublin pubs, Eastern Cape farms, university attics, and rooftops. She mainly cares about Cohiba cigars and not getting caught

STATIONS

Nick Mulgrew

I

I was alive. I was dead. That's as much as I knew.

I want to tell you I woke, but I don't think I was ever asleep. I had passed through. Or something. There's no way to explain it, unless it were to happen to you.

I was disappointed at first that I couldn't walk through things; that I wasn't a ghost. I could still feel the brush of fynbos beneath me, the grit of rock against my skin. I expected to see blood, to see a crater or an outline of dust around where I landed. I expected to see a rope halfway up the cliff, worn through, probably, in frays, dangling in the wind; or a cracked helmet someplace, and a chalk bag somewhere else. I looked to my hands, no longer callused, left with no trace of chalk. I had no bruises, no bones protruding from my skin.

The sky was blue, but not a blue I had ever known before, hanging over the careering vista of Silvermine, with the green and the scrub and the haze and the ocean, unfolding and gathering and foaming and all of it—just the same as it was before. Then I turned around. The cellphone tower was gone. The buildings were in different configurations, but in which ways, I couldn't quite be sure.

Eagles circled above me. Jet streams were scarred on the firmament. The world was silent and full. In that moment, I was glad to be dead.

II

The road down was still there, although the substation it led to wasn't. At that moment, I felt no pain, no hunger. My legs felt light, healthy with muscle—just as they had been before, but as if all their cells had been generated anew.

Animals and plants poked through the scrub that lined the track. I'd spent a lot of time here before—but here were things I'd never seen. These flowers—crimson ericas, three metres high. An arm-length lizard gleamed purple and green on a rock by my feet. Things that had been long dead were here, alive. My nose itched with strange pollen.

I figured I was invincible. The road led to a knot of hairpins halfway down: a waste of walking if one could jump down a short section of cliff. My heart raced at this; at doing things without the promise of harm. A platform of sandstone jutted out about three metres down. I savoured the air on my skin as I dropped.

The soles of my feet tore as I landed. I slipped backwards, impaling my arms on the rocks, grabbing for any hold that would stop me careering down the rest of the cliff. I scrabbled and keeled over near the edge of the platform, with the air and the valley expectant before me. I rubbed myself over with my hands, finding new marks and scars on this body. I fingered a wound, fresh, a half-inch thick, in the side of my abdomen, throbbing and bleeding fast down my hip and thigh. I pressed my hand to it, feeling the quick heaving of my chest and the waves of pain washing through me. I panted. I breathed in dust. I thought about infection, about bacteria unknown to me.

Sitting back, holding my knees to my chest, I could feel the chill of the wind. I saw now that I was uncircumcised. I hunched over. I yelled.

There was no echo.

III

The pain subsided as the sun began its downward turn. I climbed from the platform to where the road resumed—ten metres, perhaps. Nothing large, but harder to climb without rubber-soled boots, chalk or clothes, even, to shield and stem the weepings of my flesh.

Only then, for the first time in years, I thought about my shade. When I was a child, my mother told me about how the spirits of the dead had to be led home so they could be put to rest. I had taken it for granted that was how things worked; when I died, sometime far in the future, I—disembodied, ethereal—would be led back to my birthplace, by whoever my wife or my children would be, and I would—well, I would rest.

But the living weren't here. Sal wasn't there—on the mountain, holding the belay rope—when I realised I had fallen. What Sal would be left with wasn't me, but only what would have been left of me. Something to piece back together. Something to bury someplace where someone thought I'd like to be. Home, perhaps. But there—wherever home is—isn't where I was.

On the road down, I looked across the valley to the parklands and the buildings, all of them thatch-roofed and spread out in grids. I thought about how Mother died, about how Yia died, about how everyone I knew who had died had died: all far from home. All had needed to be carried back, to be led. How strange these thoughts felt, as the road levelled and I could see what lay before me.

IV

M other, wanderer: now I know what you know. We are our own shades.

V

A t first I thought it was strange how everything was so familiar, but not familiar enough to be a comfort.

I had found a pair of white running shorts discarded on the hard shoulder. They seemed clean enough to wear, although even a rag would have done—anything to shield my nakedness from the stream of motorists on Ou Kaapse Weg or whatever it was called here. My wounds had begun to clog. I was limping. I tried to meet the eyes of the motorists who passed me; ostensibly to try catch someone's expression, to let a smile or a frown soothe me; to let me know that this was all normal and that I would adjust. But, really, all I needed was a lift.

No one looked. No one stopped.

I was dazed, from loss of blood or vertigo or both. The suburbs below looked as though they had been built from memory—a dreamworld, something hazy and inexact, where the streets and the skylines were not quite in the right proportions or configurations. The buildings were smaller, taller, more densely packed. The golf course had been taken over by houses with hearths and chimneys and gardens. I could see no prisons, no consulates, no malls.

Halfway down I came across a white cross leaning on a barrier by the side of the road. Someone had placed a bunch of puce azaleas under it, wilting in the sun. I tried to read the card someone had attached to the stems, but it was written with words I couldn't understand.

VI

There were people at the train station: cotton-shirted women and men wearing beads like my mother would. Children stood with adults speaking as equals—in Xhosa, in English, in tongues I'd never heard before. The boys gesticulated and the men listened solemnly: here, I realised, an adult and a child might be the same age.

I didn't know where the trains on this platform would go. The train I would have caught yesterday would have taken me from here towards Cape Town, passing Retreat. Plumstead and Observatory, and everywhere else I had lived. The stations here were likely different, the routes circuitous and strange. I turned to the couple standing nearest to me—a sun-spotted elder with buttermilk skin and a teenager in slacks and a T-shirt.

"Excuse me, sir," I said to the old man, "but where is this train going exactly?"

He looked at me, wordless.

"Ah, uxolo baba," I tried again. "Uloliwe... er, zayaphi?"

The man stared at the wound in my side and tilted his head, his eyes widening. He said something with words like dozens of fingers clicking.

The teenager chuckled. "You're new around here. Aren't you?"

"You could say that."

The man was pointing at my side, raising his voice. His fingers were gnarled with growths like bark. I asked the teenager what he was saying.

"He says you should get that cut looked at." He laughed.

I didn't.

He cleared his throat. "Look, this train goes lots of places. *Lots.*"

"I just want to go to town," I said.

"Town?"

"Cape Town. The CBD—you know? I want to look for people."

"CBD?" He paused for a moment. "Oh right—*right*. Ja, this train goes there. It's a nice ride along the ocean."

"Yeah, cool," I said. "Thanks."

The pair began walk away, resuming their conversation. "Wait," I said. "Wait, just a second, please?"

"Ja, what?"

"What about tickets?"

The teenager laughed. "You don't need *tickets*, man. It's a train. Just get on."

"You don't have to pay?"

"No," he said, turning from me again. "Things are paid for in other ways here."

VII

He was right—the view was nice. The air was clear, the sky abundant. The land heading north was about the same as I remembered it, littered with houses, complexes, apartment blocks.

I had somehow expected more.

The carriage was made of wood and plastic—musty, high-ceilinged and jiggering with the camber of the tracks. I had a bench to myself, away from the people who spoke softly in odd-matched pairs, about the weather and other things I couldn't decipher. A dark man—darker than me—was walking down the aisle, selling boiled sweets from a woven basket.

Despite what the teenager said, I couldn't see the ocean. And it figured. Surely one would only see the ocean heading in the direction of Simon's Town or whatever was there now. But in this direction? The stations we came to had no signs, only numerals, descending as we went towards the end of the line. A voice on an intercom spoke alien names as we arrived at each. I oriented myself by tracking the rotation of the mountain through the opposite window.

When we stopped somewhere near where I thought Rosebank would be—

VII—the voice said "Khayelitsha". My heart went cold. This was nowhere near Khayelitsha. I peeled myself off the bench and limped for the window. This was nowhere near home.

I stared out the glass but could see nothing but the station, built three storeys high from stone and pine, with a quilt work of flags hanging from poles on the eaves. To the left and the right were subways, heading underneath a road, flanked by a frontier of willows. I saw my face in the glass. I looked the same.

The carriage jolted and sent me sprawling on the floor. I felt the wound pulse under my ribs. I was surprised no one laughed.

Maybe the name for this new place was apt, I thought, retaking my bench. Maybe it was a different kind of new home. Maybe it was one that was better.

VIII

I had sat on the opposite side of the carriage, trying to look around the bank of trees as we coasted out of Rosebank, or Khayelitsha, or whatever it was. I was picking at a scab on my foot when the trees began to thin, somewhere near Mowbray, and the most incredible things opened up to me. Blocks of flats, towers of stone and mortar, all among the slopes and folds of Devil's Peak. Colonies of concrete favelas, houses with pitched roofs all hanging off the rock, connected by poles with wires like spider web. Funiculars climbed the slope, humming all around and across the mountain, all pulsing with movement. Neighbourhoods unimaginable and strange—people were living not around, but *on* Table Mountain.

Columns of Woodstock townhouses ran parallel from the peaks to the tracks—the most disorienting parallax, opening and closing like accordion bellows. District Six, a garden city in miniature, in octagon and pentagon, lush and glowing in the sun. In every neighbourhood rose dozens of statues on plinths, piercing and needling the pink-edged sky.

Just as suddenly, the train entered a tunnel, and I peeled my eyes from the window. The carriage was now empty, save for a pair of men, shirtless in slacks, with leather backpacks on their laps. They looked like they were Khoi. Or San. Khoisan. I'd never seen any Khoisan person in the flesh before, only in books and movies, worshipping Coke bottles and tracking kudu. One mimed the action of rolling dice. The other clapped hysterically.

The tunnel echoed the clacks of the wheels and the tracks and the engine. A minute passed in the darkness, the carriage lit by a single bulb suspended from a cable bound in rope, which cast harsh shadow of amber and orange. The men were laughing, and I caught myself staring at them, trying to decipher their rasps and clicks. And they stared back, furrowing their brows, stone silent—until I looked away again and waited for us to emerge.

IX

B ut the ocean. The ocean, cellophane blue, crashing and crinking on itself. And empty. There was no harbour, the cresting shoreline naked of concrete or metal. Highways and high-rises had cut off the city as I knew it from the ocean; from the shelter the bay gave from the squalls and the waves and the deluges of winter; from the entire reason of its existence. How naked it seemed now.

We followed the shore into the city bowl—except I could see there was no city. Just small neighbourhoods, like everywhere else on the flatland, interspersed with the towers and the spires and the statues. Smoke billowed from the top of the mountain like clouds. Signal Hill festered with strange trees.

My heart dropped. This place had a geography that had to be relearned.

X

L ater I found that the spires and the minarets I had seen from the train were just that: there were still churches and mosques here, teaching the same things they always had—forgiveness, piety, fear; with scriptures ret-conned into interpretations that would explain this afterlife.

Although this wasn't the afterlife. This was life. Death was nothing to be feared, for this was death. What was unknowable was plainly knowable; experience, plain experience, unavoidable. And experience was knowledge. As was memory—all of it. Every iteration. Every variance.

Remember this. Number your lives like mysteries on beads.

Every station is numbered. No station can be named.

XI

I got off the train in town because that's where the train terminated. Tracks extended past the station, towards what would be the Atlantic seaboard. I was curious to see what would be there too, but there was no rush, I figured. I had the time.

The station was cavernous, an arcade with open timber struts running its length. I left through an archway, turned left and, after a few steps, found myself on a belvedere looking over a beach. The Foreshore was gone. It had not been rebuilt, not the ground, its streets nor anything built to replace it. No moors or docks or even a pier. I supposed the slaves who had built those things during their past lives weren't in the mood to build them again.

The wind picked up. The water lapped against a stone wall below. The sun began to dip behind the forests on the hills. Clouds gathered over the mountain. My skin grew taut.

Out the corner of my eye I saw the Khoisan men behind me, sauntering over Strand Street, towards a park where the Grand Parade used to be. I followed them.

XII

Cecil Rhodes was sat on a taxidermied horse in a cage on a plinth in the middle of the parade. I wouldn't have known who he was if they hadn't left a sign. Old men were slinging stones at him disinterestedly from a few metres away. Blood dripped and foamed out his mouth. His chest heaved.

He was alive. He couldn't die.

There were dozens of them, men and women, caged and shackled on pillars throughout the parade, some neglected and bored, tenderly stroking wounds, some bearing injuries that would have meant death under other circumstances.

Truthfully they spoiled the view. The park was beautiful, filled with sage and yellowwood and unknown shrubs, all filled with the sunset chatter of animals I'd never heard before. Families walked down the lanes. Children sat on benches and ate apples and drank from water bottles, enjoying the last sun of the day. Some of the pillars holding the cages were encrusted with the most exquisite flowers, glowing gold and fuchsia and grey, growing over dried and drying blood, their growth obscuring the gore.

I realised then that all the plinths I had seen from the train were supporting these living statues. I realised too that, if I concentrated hard enough, I could begin to ignore the groans.

XIII

This city was too saturated with memory. Perhaps that's why they never rebuilt it, letting this park to do all the remembering for them.

I left the park and took a right down a lane flanked with townhouses. Buitenkant, I thought. I tried to anchor myself with memories of this place. I tried to think about the days at the bookshops and theatres on the intersections, about the parties I had stocked from the bottle store, about the nights I had spent at the tavern further up the hill.

The statues were on every corner—supplicating people, begging to be stared at, begging to be pitied. No doubt they deserved their suffering, otherwise then why would they be there?

I asked a man marked with the name of a settler why he was trapped upon his plinth.

"Wat dink jy?" he asked me. His teeth were chipped and yellow. "Dit is net wat jy sien."

"Jy was 'n slegte persoon in 'n vorige lewe," I accused him.

"Maar wat beteken 'slegte'?" he mumbled. "Julle mense vra al dieselfde vrae. Die wêreld bereik ewewig uiteindelik. Dit is net wat jy sien."

The decades had reduced him to platitudes. I asked him if he wanted to die.

"Maar ek's alreeds dood."

I asked him if he wanted to die again. He was silent.

I asked a passing man why the settler was up there, forced to live his life in pain and resignation. He hunched his shoulders, although I'm not sure he understood the question.

XIV

The foghorns began like calls to prayer. The lights of the buildings of the new villages shimmered up the mountain. The cloudbank had settled, and the flashes of streetlights and the pulsing of the electricity and fire came to me in waves, unrelenting, unsettling.

This was no CBD. This was no town. No wonder the teenager had laughed at me. I walked up the entire length of Buitenkant, between the truncated high-rises and the duplexes. On every block was a different living statue, in various poses of torture, with various inscriptions of sins and the pains they had visited on the people with whom they had shared the world before, and with whom they were forced to share the world again. It was as if the people had moved from this place, from the idea of this city, and from this city that had itself been a monument to so much pain—to so much ruin, even in its beauty. Something that had been built on bodies and bones. As if this place was a monument to everything that had come before; to the people that had destroyed their past lives, in the hope they could have the lives they wanted now.

I tried to make my way up to the mountain, to see all the new things, to see what people had remade of themselves, to find someplace to stay. I could start looking for family, for friends tomorrow. I could find them in a phonebook, maybe, if phonebooks were a thing.

I could see the funiculars in the distance; their stations beginning on the edge of Gardens. The foghorns rang loud and true. The streets had emptied, apart from the statues. I felt this creeping inside my chest, this electricity, constricting and hammering at me. I quickened my step.

On the corner of Mill Street, under a bridge, I came across a man—a black man, in a suit—on his haunches, checking his watch. I said hello to him. He smiled at me and spoke in Xhosa. I felt myself smiling back at him. Tears gathered in my eyes—for what, I couldn't be certain. I asked the man what he was doing. He said he was waiting. I asked him what he was waiting for. He said he liked to hear the music. I asked which music, and that's when they started to sing.

All the men, all the women, all the statues, all on their plinths, all in their cages. A thin trail of voices rising from the streets nearby, punctuated by the foghorns, softened by the noise of the night. They began a hymn. They sang, well-practised, well-routined, mournful:

> Genade onbeskryflik groot
> het U aan my bewys
> verlore seun 'n wegloopkind
> weer in die vaderhuis

They do this every night, the man said to me, and he came out every day to listen to them. He said he liked it. He found it soothing.

I asked him why they sang.

"Why would anyone sing?"

> Maar U sien ver, oneindig ver.
> U sien my honger, dors.

The man started singing along, softly, to himself. The streetlights flickered on, glowing blue.

I spotted a man not far away, sitting in regalia and shackled astride a stuffed horse. He was set on a wide plinth, flanked by jacarandas in bloom. He led those around him in a monstrous baritone, with his eyes closed and his eyebrows furrowed handsomely. A great thicket of beard moved with his words.

I crouched to the suited man. "Uxolo baba," I said in a hushed voice, somehow not willing to disturb the sanctity of the hymn, no matter how grotesque its performance. "Ngubani na lo?"

He looked me in the eye and whispered. "Ningazazi?"

"Hayi."

He grabbed my hand, scarred and bloody, and said solemnly: "uBotha ligama lakhe."

"Louis?"

"Ja."

> *Want toe ek kom, my skuld bely,*
> *druk U my aan die bors.*

I stared at Louis Botha, in the same position I'd always known him, as a statue outside Parliament, although Parliament wasn't there anymore. I wanted to say I felt comfort, but maybe comfort isn't the word.

I felt an itch on my side. I inspected the wound. A fly had landed on it. I flicked it away with a fingernail. The wound started bleeding again. The man beside me told me I should get it looked at, then continued singing. I nodded and bid him goodbye.

I turned to the mountain and walked.

Nick Mulgrew was born in Durban, South Africa in 1990. He is an associate editor of Prufrock, *the editor of* uHlanga, *and a columnist for the* Sunday Times. *He has won national awards for his fiction and journalism – most recently the 2014 National Arts Festival Short Sharp Stories Award. He lives in Cape Town.*

EDITÖNGÖ

Mary Okon Ononokpono

K'editöngö, Abasi akanam Enyong ye Isong.
In the beginning, God created the heavens and the earth.

There is a veil that separates this world from the world of the spirits. This veil is invisible to all but the few who know where to look. In the oldest parts of this world, there are points where the veil is worn thin, like a skin stretched taut over the mouth of a drum, and traces of what might be described as magic dance in the rays of sunlight. If you were to stand in such a place and were sensitive, after the fashion, to these things, you would be afforded a glimpse into a time when the veil was rent open and the first spirits cloaked themselves in the fabric of the earth.

For these are the magic places of the world, where eternal echoes of words of power, long forgotten, linger, suspended as clouds of memory scattered throughout the atmosphere by an invisible hand. Here, the air is dense with the presence of the watchful ones, their enchantments imbuing the land with an iridescent glow that illuminates the soul.

Many are the numinous places of the world, filled with portals long traversed by spirits, doors concealed within the atmosphere, hidden in plain sight; with no region containing as many portals as the first landmass, that prehistoric centre, drawn forth by the Mother herself from her primordial ocean. The world has been broken and remade several times since that day before days, yet this landmass remains at the core. She has been called by many names over the course of time, but her true name has long remained hidden, deep within her bowels, lest her magic be usurped and misused.

This land is the cradle of life. It is the origin of civilisations, of gods and monsters, of sprites of wood, air and water. This is the birthplace of nymphs, of faeries, of guardians great and small. It is the source of pools, of waterfalls, of mist and rainbows, of worship, of mystery and of magic. This is the abode of the face of the Nameless, most sacred of all, Eka Abasi. She is the Mother, supreme giver of life, source of abundance and bringer of sun and moon. Her essence can be found within all living things. She is the heart, the soul, the Word made manifest. Her melody can be heard in the song of the sunbird and in the tinkle of cascading water.

Bearer of light and shadow, she is one, though her faces are many. Split a log and you will find her, cleave the rock and there she dwells. She is Abasi Isong, the earth, and Abasi Offiong, the moon. She it is who spoke the word that gave rise to an eternally unfolding saga. She is the Mysterious, the Unknowable, that which is unseen, but felt as a gentle whisper. She is not as the others, for she is the one who has her dwelling place beyond the veil. Nor can she be counted among lesser gods, for it is she who drew them forth from her womb. Between them is fixed a gulf so vast, which cannot be negotiated, lest she herself wills it to be.

She it is who birthed her son and consort, Abasi Obumo, the Thunderer, commanding him to split the sky with his rod of lightning, thereby separating night from day. She it is who commanded him to raise the holy mountains and rent valleys from which the living would spring. She it is who imparted her essence into the guttural word, ushering the spirits to come into being. For within her word is contained the divine spark, the source of all life, that peculiar element that gives rise to animation. She is the water, the void, the womb from which all things spring. Weaver of fates, author of stories, she alone composed the constellations.

In the silence of the void the Nameless sought to become aware of herself that she might increase in wisdom and understanding, and in order to expand her capacity to love, intuits that she must replicate through separation. For consciousness cannot know itself through a fixed angle, to have knowledge of the whole it must perceive itself through a spectrum of gazes. Long before humanity discovered how to split the atom, she gave rise to herself, spoke the Word and split the divine atom, thereby pulling out new forms of being. From her singularity many emerge, and in a twinkle, a myriad awakens.

Through sound these forms are made visible, and dancing, pass through the veil into the void. Within each form she imparts a name, the unique vehicle through which their power issues. These names are entrusted to Obumo, who is commanded to speak them in the correct order, thereby drawing the personas into the world. And he calls them individually by their rightful names, and they issue forth through the veil, cloaking themselves in the raiment prepared by the Unknowable.

They emerge, slowly at first, one by one according to their rank they come, inhaling the new air and delighting in their surroundings. From the oceans and the mountains they appear, spirits at once magnificent and terrible to behold. The invisible is made manifest and their magic fills the viscous void. The guardians take their forms, issuing forth tree, and rock and fire. They begin a great work, undertaking the will of the Nameless, preparing the world for the pleasure of her offspring.

The weavers of destiny are the first to appear, chief of these being Atai, Lady of the Fates, who on looms of enigma and paradox weaves with nimble fingers the tapestry of time. All fates are decreed by her, there is none that is not known by her, for she alone knows where the story is birthed and where it goes to die. Next are the elementals. Imbued with superior intelligence, these beings are the building blocks from which all others are made. Born of the dazzling darkness, they dance a great dance, giving rise to collision and calamity wondrous to behold, and in their wake the heavenly bodies are formed.

They ascend from the heights and from the deep, these ancient mothers of all creatures great and small, higher and lower spirits materialising, each one following the former in order of rank. Sprites of fire populate the void, with sprites of liquid, earth, metal and air, in vast numbers and in order of rank.

From the skies they appear, spirits cloaked as dragons spewing flames imperishable. From the swamps they arise, crocodile, panthera, eagle and leviathan. They issue forth through the veil into the void. Minotaurs, chimeras, mermaids, faeries, spirits of mysterious gifting and strange proportions. All will play their part in the great unfolding. They take their rightful places, and the void is filled with a holy sound.

They celebrate, and they watch, and they wait. They wait for that sacred hour, the hour which has long been appointed in the mind of the Mother. It is in this hour that the Unknowable rises from her throne and fills the void with the enchanting sound of her heart song. Her song is like the rush of many waters, a living tapestry that causes every knee to bow. As she sings, all that she has birthed joins as one, weaving notes forged of unearthly light in worship of her glory and her mystery.

But the voice of the Nameless comes as mighty drops imbued with such power, and beauty, and bliss and melancholy, her chords at once profound and deep, that as one, all of creation falls as dead. And of the song she sang, only fragments of shadows now remain, for there are none now living who remember.

Yet memories linger, for the land is but a storehouse of memory and the heavens ring with echoes of that eternally unfolding song, a fragmented vision of a fading dream, its spectral fingers unfurling wide and long. These ghostly appendages conceal harmonies suffused with hidden power, a force unstoppable, suspending dreams in place, a splendid symphony of all uncharted hours. And if one pauses for a moment and listens with ears unseen, the concealed will be revealed, for the powers speak ceaselessly, in urgent speech, awaiting an open vessel.

They were there, the earth and her breath, on that, the most hallowed of days. Co-creators, ancient witnesses to a remarkable thing, a souvenir of which they retain. For in this sacred hour, encircled by celestial chords, the Nameless fashions a thing exceedingly strange and marvellous to behold. From breath of Enyong and flesh of Isong she forms a living nephish into which she sings life, and her song is the sweetest kiss, and sending forth her soul she awakens, Adia-ha, Mother of humanity, sung into being from darkness into light.

She is breathtaking, a babe defenceless in her purity, rousing from long slumber into blissful paradise that she herself has created. Her obsidian skin sparkles after the manner of the depths of the deep; for from darkness is born all that was, is and will be. She is black and comely, a wonder above wonders, forged in splendid perfection, fat, rolling and healthy, the rarest specimen of divine beauty, for within her is set the very universe in motion.

It is with laughter, that she who is called Adiaha opens new eyes filled with astonishment beneath the watchful gaze of the lady of the night. Inhaling deeply, she drinks air yet untouched by mortal kind as she rests in the most sacred spot on earth, buried deep within mouth of Ubong Obot, the holy mount. Here she frolics with butterflies and brown-limbed faeries, their wings, spry, delicate things, hued in colours that have long passed out of living memory. For the guardians have cloaked themselves in a manner that will be pleasing to the babe while they prepare to guide her in the ways of the world.

Here the powers converge, higher and lower orders, they minister unto her, swaddling the infant in a cloth woven of threads of light, coloured by Atai herself. Awestruck, they bless this exceptionally strange and exquisite creature, this miracle that glitters as a living coal beneath the glow of the first light. In their hordes they come, a multitude without number, sprites of purity and protection, sprites both winsome and ferocious, gently they approach her, for she speaks without words to the core of their innocence, and she knows no fear, for fear has not yet passed through the veil.

This is the holiest of nights, a night like no other, filled with all manner of wonderment and elegant dreams of enchantment. In this moment unparalleled, all lives are entwined, dreams and legends intersect and the earth hums with burgeoning promise. All powers bow before the feet of the blessed babe with minds of one accord. Guardians of forest and of mountain, stewards of river, of grass, of sky, they jealously guard the babe in her infancy, smiling as she frolics with the birds, sprites and all creatures of delight. They look upon her and they love her, singing as she drifts into euphoric sleep, sprinkling her dreams with prayers that caress her, imbuing her thought with images woven of laughter.

As she wakes, her sight is filled with unquantified discoveries and smiling, she absorbs the majestic scenery wild eyed. All is new to the babe, for the mantle of flesh has banished her memory beyond the furthest recesses of the most distant stars. It is in this state of forgetfulness that the child is nourished, for she imbibes living waters supplied by river sprites. The air still rings with unbridled potency, causing the bowels of Isong to swell with a bounty of fruits that murmur of forgotten charms. These are harvested by guardians of flora, tree nymphs that make ready the yield for the infant to consume. So the child eats and is strengthened, and turning her mind to thoughts of abandon, she has no limit to her playful diversions, delighting in the innumerable gifts bestowed at her feet.

Cavorting with butterflies, she is watched by the powers, who tenderly pre-empt all her needs. They walk beside her, she that draws them into being, instructing her in their arts, divulging the secrets of the stars, thrilling her with displays of skin changing, and she imprints herself within their hearts. All are smitten by this intoxicating marvel and vigilantly guard her path.

So she grows. Deliberately, solidly. The magic of the new morning infused with a tonic for uninhibited growth, for all are giants in these days, as enlargement has not yet been barred with restraint. First the babe is sitting, then she is standing then crawling, now she is walking, and as she walks, all bow, for all that she touches is greatly blessed, where her shadow falls new things waken, and flowers instantly sprout in grassy indentations left by her tiny feet. Her smile is a thing of uncommon beauty, filling the heavens with rainbows and a heady mood of magic. When she laughs, it is as though the whole universe erupts into song, causing streams to bubble where before the earth was barren.

So walks Adiaha, first daughter, beloved and cherished of life and her days are filled with bliss and plenty. Growing and learning, she converses with guardians and companions in silent thought until the moment she conceives of a new design. The powers watch as she fashions the first repository of speech, a living bough gifted by a gnarled Iroko and covered with the gift of a sheath from Asabo. In amazement, they listen as she forges audible speech, words erupting as an unrestrained mighty river from a source deep within her belly. They stand awestruck as she converses with the drum, marvelling as her words explode into living, breathing things that unfurl into songs of their own.

How she grows, this rarest of diamonds, waxing in wisdom, beauty and grandeur. She is glorious, a being without blemish, the pinnacle of unfathomable design. And how the guardians cherish her, this curious phenomenon, this enigma they perceive to be larger than revealed.

They are with her by the waters as she speaks words into the glass, setting in motion songs and stories that will take on life and breathe millennia after her present form has passed. They stand poised and guarded as she discovers portals into parallel worlds, guiding her as she travels, leading her to doorways that return her to her abode. Revelling in her exploits, the powers expand with her, responding to moods corresponding with the melodies from which they were called.

But as the new day lengthens it brings with it subtle changes. It begins with the withering of desire, slowly, vaguely, a gentle erosion of the longing for flights of fancy. No longer content to dance with nymphs and converse with merpeople by hallowed creeks, all thought of wild roaming to distant galaxies fills her heart now with sorrow. Her disposition becomes melancholic, for she is filled with a quiet yearning, and searches for something she cannot yet name. Driven to aloofness, increasingly she evades those charged with her keep, for she intuits that the answer to her riddle must be solved by her and her alone.

From a respectful distance, the powers observe as she wanders long and far, consumed by a familiar sweet forgetfulness, oblivious to all but her gnawing need. Discovering liquid leaking from her eyes, she ponders upon it, a strange occurrence to one who has never known the sting of tears. Immersing herself fully in the alien sensation, she savours the salty taste of the large, glassy drops that now run freely down her face, and calling out a name she does yet know she stumbles. As she weeps, the wind looks upon her and is moved to pity, and whispering words of comfort to ease her distressed soul, increases her gentle dance and begins to grow.

The wind rises, disturbing the peace of all that obstruct her path, her gentle whistles transforming to forceful howls. As flower sprites flee, nymphs of wood return to their boughs and mermaids slink into watery chasms to shield themselves from the unlooked-for spectacle. Obumo speaks. Fire sprites answer. Still the maiden weeps, yet the wind's arms surround her, a typhoon that veils the girl from sight. Blinded by her tears, the wind transports her, carrying her gently to a concealed place.

She is deposited at the entrance to a narrow corridor, a path leading to a hidden vale and slowly pries open blurred eyes. Whispering words of strength and kissing her brow, the wind departs, for she is not permitted to enter the vale. There is something peculiar about this place and it is noted by the girl who stares now, drawn always forward by an unseen magnetic charge.

She knows this place, she is sure of it, yet her feet have never trodden this path. The walls are made of the smoothest rock, black, sheer and glittering, mirroring the girl's flawless skin—a picture of ebony liquid frozen to stone. Silken to the touch, the walls ring with a strange fire, murmuring of forgotten spells. These are pillars that stretch for miles above ground, towering precipices reaching unto the heavens, lending the sky the appearance of a distant sapphire serpent who watches the girl with a smile.

With each step she is drawn ever closer to waters that mutter of a deep magic unknown to the powers. This is a strange place, a secret place, a place of lightness of being, easing the girl of her unnamed sorrow. She walks through the passage with a heart that is gladdened, her tears now nothing more than a dismembered memory. With newfound purpose, she moves steadily towards a coloured refraction, a spectrum of light that is not of this world. It draws her onwards, curving and bending until she is greeted by the voice of a stream. Its words are a thing of delight, chattering and playful, its excited chortle giving way to rivulets of rumbling speech.

Onwards she walks, listening to the river, remembrance roused by words uttered from the deep. The river speaks of a dream, a dream of beginnings, of words of power and a song of awakening. The road by the river twists and writhes and suddenly leads to an open creek. A perplexing enigma, this a place of raw might, guarded at the mouth by higher incarnations of Ekpe, Asabo and the hawk-eyed fish eagle who watches from above. These guardians of land, sky and water fiercely protect the place from unwelcome, prying eyes.

This is a place deceptively small yet with a sense other than sight, she perceives that this place is veiled. Its apparent smallness merely serves to add to its alluring mystique; it is a land laced with the remnant of world-forming utterances, hinting at a brilliance sweltering with secrets, which if divulged would destroy all but the purest who gaze upon it. It lies as if at the bottom of a great well, an unlikely bowl deftly hewn by an unknown entity. Encircled by high banks of obsidian, a natural vessel whose bottom is cloaked in a grassy vale girdled by the great river. All is enclosed, save for the narrow neck through which the child has entered.

The banks of the vale slope upwards and at its centre stands a single palm whose branches reach high into the clouds. Here Enyong, Isong and Inyang meet, for this is a place where worlds converge. Lifting up her gaze, the child is met by an uncommon spectacle, a thing strange and never before glimpsed by mortal kind.

Hugging the island on the opposing bank, the waters flow into a great fall, the current moving upwards instead of down, defying universal laws of gravitational pull. Momentarily pondering the strange marvel, the child's gaze soon flits to absorb more sights which perplex.

She stands at the mouth of a garden whose opaque, coloured waters are strewn with myriad twinkling lights. The surface is scattered with innumerable flowers, great lilies, milk white with cores of solid gold. The voice of the river has grown into a chorus, a cacophony of thought arising from liquid glass teeming with life. These are the whispers of trillions of souls, housed in sacred kingfish that are the source of the mysterious glow. Here they dance in a ghostly circle, awaiting a time they will be reclothed.

Tentatively and trembling, the child wades into the water, entering the holy of holies, her footfall drawing a effervescent dew that falls as gentle flakes from a breach in the heavens. Time does not exist in this place. As the girl walks forward, a presence rises, a voice cloaked in a dense mist and adorned in fat, rolling clouds. As it walks forward to meet her, it surrounds her. Enveloping, cooling, warming, brightening. All thoughts of longing are banished to the shadows, for she has found what she did not know that she sought. This is a being crowned in splendour, wreathed in rainbows, lightning and sparkling flame, Eka Abasi, Isu Mma, her Mother. Herself. Her higher incarnation.

"Adiaha. My child. My self," utters the voice in a guttural rumble, causing lava to dance and Isong to tremble. None are privy to the communion that unfolds, save the guardians of the abode and the souls that swim in the great river of forgetfulness. They converse long and deep as far from this place stewards drift into fresh dreams.

Night falls and Offiong rises, bringing with her a blossoming. As the Nameless divulges creation's deep secrets, so Adiaha blossoms into an exceptionally beguiling creature, the like of whom will never again be seen on the face of the earth. It is here that her first moon blood is borne into the teeming waters, a living sacrifice for the purification of generations to come. Here she grows in grace and in stature, glowing as a vessel housing the first light.

The woman eventually emerges from the sweetest communion irrevocably altered. As a being wrought in fire she returns changed to her abode. All shield their eyes from her newfound brilliance for it appears to the powers that a star has fallen from the skies.

With newfound authority she speaks a word and draws life into being within her own womb. As her belly begins to swell with a light, the guardians watch over her, until travailing, she pulls him forth, reversing within him her genitalia after divine blueprint. They are there at his birth, he that is called Akpan, her opposing mirror image. They bear witness to a wonder of wonders, as Woman and Man are created in one vessel, and separated through song that they might multiply and populate the world.

Vigilantly they watch their charge and her new babe, nurturing him as they nurtured her, watching as the two wax in strength as they forge a story of love that will last through ages unnumbered. For the new babe grows quickly, and as the shoot from young plants overtake their sires in stature, soon he overtakes his mother and embraces her, so they appear as one, though they are now two. To each is given power and authority to govern their environment in equilibrium, in accordance with their stature. But to the woman, Adiaha, the greater power is given, as she is created mother after the fashion of the Nameless.

Theirs is a sacred love that will outlive time. It is a pure love, wholly incorruptible, a love that spans distant galaxies and far-flung worlds. Of all she has discovered she teaches him tenderly, save the secrets divulged to her by Isu Mma, for woman is of the order of creator. Of the secrets concerning the guarding of words of power, man is not permitted to know, for in foresight the Nameless knew that the day would come when her sons would desecrate and attempt to erase her.

And as the child Akpan grows, he is aware of the long disappearance of Adiaha and resentment blossoms in his heart but he skilfully conceals it. Thus, the seed of enmity is planted between the woman and the man she birthed, and as the seed germinates and grows within the womb of the world, so the silent seed of enmity bides its time, taking root within the hearts of men.

Soon the two venture down from Ubong Obot, and copulating at the foot of the great mound, bring forth twin daughters, Ima and Idara, one spirit in two vessels, of whose like has never before been seen on the earth. The hallowed family are in an eternal dream, from which there is no awakening save through a thing not yet conceived, but even this is no end, merely a return to recurring beginnings.

This is a tale passed through generations without number, a story existing beyond the confines of space and time. It has known many endings and borne many versions, yet beneath the variation lies a truth eternal and unchanging. For there is only one story, one desire that seeks fulfilment of a designated end. An ending which is in truth a beginning. For the world is much older than is supposed, and all that is, it has already been, and what is human life if not anguished arpeggios of a recurring dream?

But what is one story to a face that has lived many lives? What is this dream to one summoned repeatedly over the course of time? One fated to be summoned ever at greatest need, and need again calls me, coaxing me gently from sweet clutches of sleep.

This is my story, my unfinished melody and she summons me now, disturbing my peace. Once more I am called to breathe into my dream by bloodied steps repeating the pattern of the Iroko's first speech. I see her now, this child that I shall soon call my mother. The girl with fire in her face, the moon in her belly and wild midnight for hair. She flees through conical pyramids, testaments to lost civilisations of unsurpassed grandeur, wrought and perished in days long forgotten. Her way is cleared by guardians not yet known to her, for if she knew what hunted and protected her she would be driven to the brink of an abyss from which there is no return.

It has grown too large. This thing that pursues her. A madness wanders here, a thing utterly wretched and without redemption, its very presence marring the land which for all beauty retained, lies now darkened, blighted by the offspring of this foulest of creatures, fell beasts that brood and creep among both living and unborn. Where it passes, it poisons even the most righteous of thought, rendering all words and deeds indelibly corrupted.

Even lesser guardians cower from its great shadow, for it is wreathed in vile incantations loosed at the great splintering so long ago, that the memory of its origins are but a whisper in the oldest of legends. This is a relic of a time when the word was besmirched and its potency tarred. The Egbo has grown. It has long consumed those that wrested the protective cults from the first daughters, their tortured souls now forming his profane cloak. He is a law unto none but his own self, a spirit ravenous with unnatural terror, desperate to feast on all that is sacred and pure. Where he treads, far below in the womb of Isong, even the bones of the dead cower.

As he passes town after town he cries a terrible cry, alerting the townsfolk to his malevolent intent. All twins are left this night by the edge of the once-sacred forest, the ultimate sacrifice. How the sprites of purity weep, a great cry that erupts in the firmament, for the greatest affliction is borne upon them. Yet this night is unlike any other. A strange magic is afoot and guardians and witnesses once more walk abroad. All must conspire together for this very hour. They move to protect her, the powers have woken, they wrestle to bring her to that sacred place that countless lives ago I once called home.

I have worn many faces, returned many times, but few have insight to glimpse beneath my veiled disguise. Others go before me. Spirit children, ordained before birth as my living oracles. At times the people hearken to them but this is a rarity. Mostly they are shunned and driven to live as outcasts. Their gifts manifest in different ways; they have the power to speak and effect change, but do not always know their power.

Some are driven to dreams of madness by this spirit, this frightful masquerade that nets their steps, for it will do anything to prevent the emergence of a rogue element, an agent of change that will alter its ghastly steps. They speak in strange tongues of dreams of rivers and oceans blood, of the death of an old world and the birth of a new. They speak of the advent of gods of industry and of trade, gods of metal, of steel and war.

As I prepare to be once more reborn, I recall the story of my beginnings. This time I shall not forget. I will be born into a new vessel full of knowing, full of remembrance and regret. Some will look at me ats some sort of prodigy, but others shall accuse me of sorcery. I will know great suffering for I am the solace for pain. When they ask me who I am I will tell them. I am the voice of one who long ago fell silent, and my silence has lasted an age and an age.

Mary Okon Ononokpono is a writer, artist and illustrator. Born in Calabar, Nigeria, Mary moved to the United Kingdom as a baby and has lived there ever since. Mary has a passion for African arts, culture and history. With a background in design and journalism, Mary has been featured in numerous Pan-African publications. Following a brief return home to Nigeria in December 2012, Mary turned her hand towards creative writing. Mary has recently completed her first work of children's fiction and is currently working on her debut novel.

CJ

Chinelo Onwualu

There are no direct flights from Lagos to the small towns of the middle belt. So, on the morning of Vi's wedding, I stepped off the train at Miango in Plateau State. Normally, I would have hired a car and an AI, but I was trying to keep a low profile.

It was dawn and the platform was deserted. Even the ticket conductor had yet to arrive. The porter was probably sleeping in a warm corner swaddled against the harmattan cold. Outside, I was struck by the curiously dream-like quality rural Nigeria possessed. The colours were somehow more authentic. The tidy brick houses that lined the dusty road were a deeper red brown; the rows of cacti that acted as their fences were a more vibrant shade of green. Shops were designated by hand-lettered signs. Fat cotton-ball clouds drifted lazily in an unbelievably cerulean sky that was quickly brightening.

While I waited by the bench that marked the station's bus stop, I was engulfed by a feeling of utter desolation. Without the close press of tall buildings above my head, everything stretched into infinity around me, and I imagined I could float up and be lost in that terrible blue horizon. The world felt empty, and I was reminded why I hadn't been back here in so long, even though it was where I had grown up. I gripped the bench to steady myself and the feeling soon passed, but I could not calm the dread that had lodged itself at the bottom of my belly.

An old-fashioned red pick-up truck barrelled down the main road, and a woman was waving frantically out of the driver's side window. Vi and her fiancé, Olamide, were here to meet me. I could not conceive how they had managed to get away from their hectic pre-wedding schedule, but I was glad they had. I was relieved to see a familiar face.

"Em!" squealed Vi as she launched herself out of the cab.

I caught her easily and wrapped her in a bear hug.

"Emeka Okafor, put me down!" She tried to sound indignant, but she was laughing too hard. "You bully." She mock-punched my arm when I put her back on her feet. "You haven't changed at all."

Once she regained her composure, Violet Parker—soon to be Ogundare— took charge. She was still as tall as she had been in secondary school, but her body, which had once been fat and lumpy, had smoothed into sleek curves. Her olive skin and curly black hair spoke of her multiracial heritage—her mom had been Lebanese-Nigerian.

Olamide—"call me Ola"—and I shook hands as we were formally introduced. He was a rotund little man with an unruly Afro. His round head seemed to grow directly out of his shoulders, and his bulbous nose gave him the impression of a cheerful snowman.

"We got you a room at the rest home on Mission Drive," Vi said as Ola bundled my luggage into the truck. She still moved impatiently, as if she needed to be somewhere more important, but love had softened her. Gone were the tight Victorian buns into which she used to trap her hair; now a simple ponytail sufficed. She'd opted for gene therapy for her myopia, and had abandoned her horn-rimmed glasses.

"We wanted to have you stay at the farm, but with both our parents in town, we thought we should spare your sanity," said Ola with a wry smile.

As he fired up the engine, Vi and I shared a look. The man had a sense of humour. I approved.

"So how's the new man?" Vi asked me, never one for subtlety.

"He's great," I said. Kevin's musty smell still lingered on my shirt from when he had he dropped me off at the airport the night before. We had argued again that morning, and his kiss had been perfunctory. The last I saw of him, he had been waving goodbye, his dark hair catching the neon lights while he scanned the oncoming traffic. "Just great."

Vi eyed me quizzically.

"And what about you? How's work?" I asked before she could question me further. She worked for some big lab in Abuja, but I had only a vague idea what she actually did.

"Well, my project's in limbo right now. The company had wanted me to divert our research into this new thing they're doing—meta-human targeting," said Vi. "I won't bore you with the science, but there are more of them popping up every year and nobody's quite sure why. It used to be just people who could play the piano with their feet. Now you've got people who can change their skin colour or walk through walls."

"Oh, like this guy in Lagos," I said, remembering something that had popped up on my news feed a few days ago. "They say he's incredibly strong, fast and, apparently, bulletproof. Runs around in a mask and black leotard, beating up area boys and rescuing people from burning buildings."

"Eh-heh, like that," Vi said. "Except most of them are using their abilities to rob banks and do wayo."

"I see…" was all I could say. It was one thing to have such stories in one's feed—they were usually data traps to lure one into giving up one's metrics—but to have it confirmed by one of the most level-headed people I knew was something entirely different.

"Anyway, the company wants to figure out a way to track and identify these people, and they want to use our bio-genetic research to do it. Well, I told them to go fuck themselves, so they put me on indefinite suspension. With pay, of course. Ola and I bought the Yangs' old farm."

"The one with all the horses?"

"Yes, but those are all gone now," said Ola. "They went bankrupt in two thousand and twenty-five. We're going to fix it up and see if we can get anything to grow out there."

"Imagine me a farmer." Vi sighed comically. "Just the thought of collecting eggs again gives me the creeps." I could see her in a pair of overalls and a Fulani straw hat—like the ones my mother used to wear—weeding the vegetable garden. Except Vi hated weeding.

"You're right. You won't last a week."

She mock-punched me again as I laughed.

That evening, after a good, long nap, I met up with Vi at the Falling Meteor Bar. Named after some long-forgotten celestial event, the bar had once been a popular snack spot. Though the new owners called it something else, it would always be The Meteor to us. Ola was at the only club in town, attending his bachelor party, and would not be joining us. We found a table in a fairly quiet corner, away from the speakers which were blaring the latest Afro-pop, and ordered our drinks.

We were deep in conversation when we heard a crash from across the room. A tall man in an old-fashioned plaid jacket was helping a young waitress to her feet. He had possibly caused her to drop her tray of drinks, though I could not figure out how. The woman brushed off his attempts to help and began clearing the mess. The man stood uncertainly after she'd gone and scanned the room. Then CJ spotted us and waved.

Maybe it was because I hadn't seen him in such a long time—not since his father's funeral—that it struck me: I had forgotten how he moved. CJ wove through the crowded bar with an odd combination of a schoolboy's awkwardness and a dancer's grace. Eyes downcast, his bearing as stiff as a cornstalk, he would throw his hands up, palms out, like crisp military salutes, apologising to everyone in front of him. Yet, for all this, he never actually hit anyone—never even touched them. Without his constant apologies, I doubted any of the weekend crowd would have noticed him go by.

"H-h-hi g-guysss," said CJ as he reached our table. "H-how'sss... everyone doing?" CJ spoke as if he was dragging the speech out of himself in uneven loads. Sometimes words would spill out, tumbling over themselves in their eagerness to be heard. Other times, a short phrase or gesture seemed to be all he could manage.

"Ceej!" Vi threw her arms out and CJ leaned down awkwardly to hug her. He and I exchanged the complex handshake and half-hug-with-brief-back-slap thing that straight men give each other. He had filled out quite a bit since I last saw him—almost as big as me, and I had a personal trainer. Seeing him up close made my heart yammer; I hadn't realised how much he looked like Kevin. They had the same fair skin and glossy black hair, but where Kevin's eyes were a sharp green, CJ's were as blue as a dry season sky.

He smiled shyly as he sat—his smiles were always shy, as if he wasn't sure it was fully appropriate. Indeed, he always seemed slightly bewildered by everything around him. Simple questions seemed to catch him off guard. CJ couldn't always tell people how he felt from one moment to the next, but ask him about the stars, and he would come alive.

CJ knew the name of every star, nebula and constellation in the night sky. His parents had saved up for a year to get him the powerful telescope that had been his prized possession growing up. Back then, the three of us would spend the evenings of our long vac on the roof of his parents' house, spinning tales about our futures. I never had much of an idea of what I was going to do beyond leaving this town, but Vi was going to become a mad scientist who would cook up the cure for cancer in some basement lab, and CJ would be Nigeria's first Euro astronaut, hopping from star to star. That's why we were so surprised to hear he had gone into the newsies, writing stories for the feeds.

After graduation, I had taken off for Nollywood, while Vi had gone to ABU Zaria on a full scholarship. CJ had stayed behind to help his parents on their farm, as his father's health had been failing. I didn't hear much from him during those years. Vi was the bond that held the three of us together; she was the one who called me when CJ's father died.

At the funeral, CJ's eyes had been glazed and he'd worn a strange, lopsided smile. He looked like he was on another planet entirely. I should have gone to him then, but I had just come out, and was dealing with my own issues. CJ left for Lagos soon after that, and even Vi lost contact with him. This was the first time we had all been together in more than ten years.

"There's something different about you, Ceej," said Vi, after ordering us a round of beers.

"Oh, really! W-w-well—I mean… What do you mean?" He blinked and used his forefinger to push his thick, old-fashioned glasses up the bridge of his nose. It was a gentle, careful movement, as if he was afraid he would break them. *When had he started wearing those?*

"I don't know," she said. "I can't put my finger on it, but it's something."

"W-w-well, Vi… I-I don't know about that," CJ said.

Vi leaned back and stretched out her hands, surveying him through a square she made with her thumbs and forefingers. She turned to me for support. "There's definitely something, isn't there, Em?"

Vi was right. There was a certain solidness about CJ, an assurance that was new. For Vi and I, it had been the childhood taunts that had bound us together, the name-calling that echoed with the odd prescience of children, but what drew CJ to us was subtler. He never played any sports, though he had the physique for it. He didn't call attention to himself with stellar grades like Vi did or a flamboyant persona like me. Yet, there was something not quite right about him. Maybe it was the way he would stare at people, as if he was studying their movements, or how it would take him a few minutes to react to things, as if he was struggling to remember what the appropriate response should be. Back then, it had been as if he was lost and trying to understand where he was. Now, that was gone.

I looked at CJ and we locked gazes for a moment. I knew that look too well; I saw it in the mirror every day.

"Seems like the same old CJ to me," I lied. Before Vi could protest, I called for another round.

The next morning I awoke in the clutches of a crushing hangover. I stumbled to antiseptic toilet in my room at the rest home and promptly threw up. Then, for fifteen minutes, I burbled under a cold shower. When I emerged, I was almost myself again. I sat on the edge of the bed, my skin drying and tightening between my shoulder blades, and tried to remember the events of the night before. I didn't know whether to trust my memories, because they seemed more the stuff of my adolescent imagination. Surely the CJ I knew, the strange boy with the faraway eyes, who could stand perfectly still for hours, who walked in pin-drop silence, would never have done what I think he had.

Vi and I had gotten into some mock argument about why we had never dated in high school—I was sure that my sexuality had been a well-kept secret; she assured me it hadn't. When the bar closed, she had returned home and CJ and I had ended up on a rooftop somewhere—must have been a building on the grounds of the rest home. Whose idea had that been? Mine? His? It didn't really matter. Above us, a bright constellation had shimmered like a universe of possibility.

"So why the newsies?" I had asked him. "Weren't you supposed to be up there among the stars? You should have at least joined the Nigerian Space Agency."

CJ had shrugged, a bemused smile on his face.

"There are enough Nigerians in space," he had said. His stutter was gone—just like when he would speak about astronomy. "Besides, why be up there when you can stay down here and change things?"

"I don't know about that. This country has more problems than one man can fix."

"That's true, but if we all work to the best of our abilities, we can make a difference."

"You sound like your dad when you say that."

CJ's expression had grown sad. "My father tried to teach me a lot of things. I just wished I had been a better student. You know, I didn't understand what he was trying to tell me until I moved to that metropolis of ours and started hearing people's stories. So many times all they needed was someone to listen to them or to step in at one critical moment—"

"Someone to save them, you mean?" I had said. I too lived in the city and, making my way through the movie industry, I'd heard my own tales of woe. Stories of thwarted ambition, greed and self-destruction, usually. "Look, our people are always looking for someone to swoop in and rescue them from the problems of their own making. We need to start saving ourselves, if you ask me."

"So, what would you do if you saw someone in need and you knew you had the power to help?" He had turned his gaze to me. There had been a look in his eyes then, something I could not immediately place. For a moment he had appeared unutterably alien. "Would you stand by and watch them suffer?"

"It's not that simple, CJ."

"Yes, it is." He had turned back to gaze at the stars. "We all have unique abilities that could change the world; sometimes people just need to be reminded of their own power."

We'd lapsed into a thoughtful silence, each occupied with our own musings. It occurred to me then that CJ and I had never spent much time alone together, without Vi to anchor us. It felt as if I was getting to know him all over again.

"Come, what is a walz?" CJ had turned back to me. "Vi said I would have to do a walz tomorrow."

"It's a *waltz*," I had said, laughing. "You mean to tell me you still haven't learned to dance like a Euro? You sure say you be oyinbo true-true?"

CJ had blushed deeply and ducked his head.

I had risen and offered him a hand.

"Oya, let me teach you some moves. I don't want you to disgrace yourself tomorrow."

He waved my hand away and stood facing me. CJ was nearly a head taller than me, but something of his old awkwardness had returned, stirring long-forgotten memories. I had snaked one of his arms around my waist, while I draped my arm across his shoulders, my other hand in his. The feel of him had been almost familiar. Strong and solid, yet gentle, holding me with the lightest of touches.

We had danced for a little, I remember that much. I had pulled in closer, breathing in his smell—a mix of beer, aftershave and something indefinable. Then, nuzzling his impossibly smooth cheek, I had kissed him. Softly at first, tasting the skin in the hollow between his jaw and neck, moving to his mouth. His lips were almost girlishly soft. He did not resist—at least I don't remember that he did.

Try as I might, I could not remember exactly what happened after that. Images and impressions slid through my mind, slippery as a bar of soap. There had been a sensation of air against my face and body, as if I was falling or flying, and then… nothing. I couldn't even remember how I got into bed.

Wait.

I was naked when I woke.

I never slept naked.

I stood, ignoring the surge of pain in my head, filled with desperate hope. I tugged frantically at the covers on the bed, flinging pillows aside until I found it. Yes. That smell—a sharp sting I could not identify. He had been here. What must his body have felt like? What might he have whispered or screamed? God, how could I have gotten so drunk? I was usually much better at holding my liquor.

I folded the bed sheet carefully and sealed it in the vacuum bag in which I normally kept my underwear. I shaved, dressed and packed, since I would be leaving right after the reception.

In the lobby, I searched the pimply, teenaged desk clerk for signs of disapproval. I used to get them all the time from the landlord of my apartment building in Lagos whenever I had a "friend" stay overnight.

"Good morning, sir," he greeted me with an eager smile. Perhaps he hadn't been the one on duty the night before. "Your guest left something for you this morning."

"My guest?" I asked cautiously.

"Yes, the oyinbo man who stayed with you yesterday night. He left this with me." The boy handed me an old-fashioned e-reader. It was CJ's diary. He had carried it everywhere with him throughout secondary school.

"Thank you." I took the tablet.

"Oga, I like your shades," he said. "They make you look just like that actor, Max Power."

"Really? Everyone tells me that."

I looked at him closely. He was a skinny country boy with slightly buck teeth, awestruck by the big city guy in front of him. He reminded me a lot of myself at that age. On a whim, I fished out my extra sunglasses and threw them to him. He caught them deftly and beamed at me.

Just then, the driverless limo pulled up. I was Vi's "maid" of honour, and it was time to attend to the bride.

The ceremony was a modest affair on the lawn of the old Yang farm. Despite Vi's suspension, her employer had provided a lovely stage with a canopy garlanded in blue-and-white roses. Clearly, they still wanted her back.

Vi wore a cream, medieval-style gown that flattered her ample curves. Bucking tradition, she had left her hair loose, with only a simple coronet of white roses circling her head. I wore a pale blue suit that matched the other bridesmaids' gowns, while the groom and his men wore cream suits with back shirts and white ties.

As the judge spoke, I looked about, pleased with the arrangements. The guests were seated below the dais and I spotted CJ immediately.

He looked distant, as if he were listening for something only he could hear. His black hair was brushed back, an attempt to control his unruly curls, but one lock had escaped to fall over his forehead. He must have felt my stare, because his eyes focused and he turned to me. Grinning widely, he gave me a cheesy thumbs-up. Typical CJ.

When it was time for the couple's first dance, CJ came up to where I was sitting at the high table.

"W-wanna dance?" he asked.

"I don't think that's a good idea," I said. Times may have changed, but I was still a gay man, and this was still Nigeria.

CJ laughed. "Oh come on." He urged me to my feet. CJ was surprisingly strong, yet I sensed this had required hardly any effort on his part. "Wouldn't want our practice to go to waste, would you?"

"Aren't you scared people will think you're gay too?" I asked as we started to dance.

He shrugged. "Human sexuality is such a wide continuum. Can you imagine what it might be like for a non-human?"

I gave him a quizzical look. For a moment I thought I caught a glimpse of secret knowledge in his expression, as if another person entirely were hidden beneath the man I knew. Then he grinned.

I left soon after that. My part was finished and I had no desire to mingle further with the denizens of my home town.

Once on the plane, I booted up CJ's e-reader. The entries stretched back decades. Many were cryptic poems of loss and alienation, but most were stories, fantastic tales of men and women who could fly or run at speeds faster than sound or lift tractors with one hand. They were good too. The mystery of CJ's career had finally been explained. The most recent entry, though, had been added just last year. It was a movie script.

I patched my agent on my com feed.

"Max, where have you been?" She sounded hysterical, but then Maggie Yuen always came across that way. "You were supposed to be on set in Hong Kong two days ago."

"Relax. I had to see some old friends. Besides, that movie is so behind schedule, two days won't kill anyone."

"Well, the studio is probably going to try and knock down our fees now," she said sourly. "I hope it was worth it."

I thought about it for a moment before answering. "I have my memories. Mags, you know how you've been disturbing me about opening my own studio?"

"Of course, you're a hot commodity. Why should you let these studio boys be dragging you up and down?"

"Well, I think I'm going to do it." I turned down the volume just in time or I would have been deafened by her cries of delight.

"Okay! You need a script for your first vehicle." She'd already called up a list of writers and was highlighting names. "Let me get hold of Chuks…"

"No need. I've already found one." I peered at the e-reader. "What do you think of this title: *The Super Man*?"

Chinelo Onwualu is a writer, editor, journalist and dog person living in Abuja, Nigeria. She is a graduate of the 2014 Clarion West Writers Workshop which she attended as the recipient of the Octavia E. Butler Scholarship. Her writing has appeared in Ideomancer, *the* Kalahari Review, Saraba, Sentinel Nigeria, Jungle Jim, *and the anthologies* AfroSF: African Science Fiction by African Writers *and* Mothership: Tales of Afrofuturism and Beyond.

THERE IS SOMETHING THAT OGBU-OJAH DIDN'T TELL US

Jekwu Ozoemene

Sometimes I wish my grandmother had had the time to tell us Ojahdili the great wrestler's tragic story from the point of view of Ogbu-Ojah, his legendary flautist. For this praise singer it was who, once he wet his pursed lips and hunched his shoulders in a crouch (as flautists were wont to do), would unleash an intoxicating melody that buoyed his master's spirit, waking in massive convulsive ripples the most tired, injured or atrophied muscle and sinews. It was said that even birds paused in mid-flight upon hearing this tune, several dropping right out of the sky to their utter astonishment. It was also said that it tended to rain birds (not cats and dogs), whenever Ogbu-Ojah let loose his:

Ojahdili!

Ngolo di golo di gongongo!

So it was little wonder that Ojahdili soon ran out of men who could defeat him in a wrestling bout, and stumbled upon the idea of travelling to the spirit world. For was it not common knowledge that no man had been known to defeat the spirits? Was this even Ojahdili's idea in the first place? I must have been too awestruck or frightened at the prospect of wrestling with a spirit to broach this important question to Grandma.

So we were told that it was Ogbu-Ojah's magic sweet melody that, despite the reservations and admonishment of Ojahdili's parents and friends, ferried his master through mmiri na asaa, agu na asaa, forded seven great rivers, across seven dangerous forests, to Iton-Kom. That mythical land, situated smack between the land of living and the land of the dead, was where the dead freely interacted with the living, and animals were known to mingle and talk with both man and spirits.

It was still this same Ogbu-Ojah's sweet melody that saw Ojahdili through the first victory with the one-headed spirit, and through to his legendary defeat of the spirit world's wrestling champion, the much-dreaded ten-headed spirit.

With the benefit of hindsight, I would have loved to ask my grandmother why Ogbu-Ojah and Ojahdili did not stop after the legendary defeat of the ten-headed wrestling champion of the spirit world. Didn't they notice the conspiratorial look between the spirit lords? Didn't they hear the lull, and feel the chill when the spirits demanded one last fight? Were they not puzzled when the new challenger produced by the spirit lords was a puny-looking, emaciated spirit that stumbled into the wrestling arena with a drunken gait?

Though Ojahdili must have been inebriated by his recent victories, for some reason I have always believed that Ogbu-Ojah knew that this was it, that this was that moment when a man would be finally and irredeemably broken. So why didn't he stop his master? Why did he have to unleash his melody once again? For he must have known that even this would be of no use.

He had barely gotten to the second stanza when, in a blur, his master was whizzed through the air, and landed spread-eagled on his back in a deafening thud. When the dust settled, Ogbu-Ojah's eyes were tortured with the strangest of sights—the uncanny image of the puny-looking spirit straddling his master's muscular chest, pinning both his massive arms with what looked like thin air. In the ultimate humiliation, he had stuffed the once-great Ojahdili's mouth with clods of dirt, dry leaves and what appeared to be maggot-filled faeces...

I remember the expression on my grandmother's face when I asked who the puny-looking spirit was, mouth agape and in awe, the whispered question barely escaping my lips. The look she gave me was as if to say, was it not evident? It was his chi, she responded with a sigh, his personal god. For no man, however great or strong, can defeat his personal god... no man.

Somehow I was left with an inkling, this feeling that Ogbu-Ojah knew, as soon as he set eyes on the puny spirit, that it was Ojahdili's personal god. So why didn't he stop him? Why did he have to play the flute that one last time? Had he become tired of Ojahdili's belligerence, his quest to conquer? I doubt this, because without his rousing melody, Ojahdili would never go into battle—never. Or was this pure and simple envy, anya ufu? Did he want to see Ojahdili fail, his master humiliated. Did he? Hmmnnn... there was something that Ogbu-Ojah wasn't telling us.

Things only became clearer when grandmother told us the story about Udene the vulture and his affair.

I never really understood how a vulture could have an affair with a human being. How? That is, assuming that ili enyi meant having such an affair.

Growing up in the village, there were so many euphemisms to mask what adults got up to behind closed doors. One of the things I noted quite early in life was that these dysphemism helped to differentiate between what sex meant to adults and to children. So, while for the older ones, sex or an affair was referred to as ili enyi, as different from ime enyi (enjoying friendship as opposed to being friends), for us children it was represented by just one sufficiently ominous dark phrase, ife alulu ani, implying a bad, dark, terrible and dirty activity. Thus if during the monthly egwu onwa moonlight games a boy was caught wriggling on top of a girl, it would earn the erring child a visit from the neighbourhood disciplinarian, Nne Godi.

Godwin's septuagenarian mother had racked up quite a reputation for herself due to her legendary leg-lock or ipa. Long before Americans invented water boarding, Nne Godi would imprison an erring child between her legs and smear hot chilli pepper on or into their privates, depending on the sex. Suffice to say that Nne Godi's visitations were enough to deter all but the lion-hearted neighbourhood child from exploring ife alulu ani.

So how could I, under these Guantanamo Bay-like, life-threatening circumstances seek clarification for the meaning of ili enyi from any of the adults without incurring the wrath of Nne Godi? How? Unless I asked the slightly older children during the next 'egwu onwa session. Unfortunately, the next session coincided with my preparations for the annual Federal Government College Common Entrance examination into the country's unity schools.

So, that moonlight-bathed night, when a horde of neighbourhood children came calling at my heavily fortified home's, padlocked and chained wrought iron gate, it was my stern-voiced father who bellowed, "Rapu nu ya. O na agu akwukwu." Leave him alone. He is studying.

Of course that didn't deter the bellicose children from composing a spur-of-the-moment derisive song for me:

Jekwu puta egwu onwa!

Kpom kpom!

Okuku aka anabara ina alaru ula!

Kpom kpom!

"Jekwu come out and play! How come you have gone to bed long before the chickens have come home to roost?"

All I could do was to bury my head in shame (and my Larcombs mathematics textbook) as I struggled to figure out the square root of five and six. I couldn't recall which one was more devastating, the shame of the mockery from my friends or the fear of not having a clue to the required square root.

Grandma came to my rescue the very next day, as providence forced my father off to Lagos for an emergency business meeting—a trip that at the minimum, would typically last one week. However a concession had to be made in order not to incur his wrath. I studied up until the time for the egwu onwa games, but rather than release me to go play with the neighbourhood children (and possibly earn me an opportunity to sneak into Nne Onyewe's cocoyam farm and get up to no good under the canopy of swaying broad luxuriant cocoyam leafs), she brought out and spread her ute raffia mat on the cemented courtyard and invited us all to come join her for another session of akuko iro.

For those who don't know, Grandma was a repository of, what appeared to me at the time to be, thousands of folklores, oral tradition akuko iros that had been handed down from generation to generation. It was acknowledged that if she ever invited you to listen to an iro, you had better put your butt down on that raffia mat and listen attentively, for you were most likely never again going to have the opportunity to hear that story from a storyteller as gifted as her.

It was said that Ogbu-Ojah slunk back home from Iton-kom, that mythical land situated smack between the land of living and the land of the dead. It was known that Ogbu-Ojah's magical sweet melody had ferried the town's champion wrestler Ojahdili to the land of the spirits, to challenge the spirit champions to a wrestling match. It was also known that Ogbu-Ojah's sweet melody had seen Ojahdili through the first victory with the one-headed spirit and through to his ultimate demise at the hand of his personal god, his chi. Defeat in the land of spirits meant death in the land of the living, so it was only Ogbu-Ojah who was allowed home through the portal that separated the land of the living and that of the dead.

No one of age, inclusive of the pubescent, would ever forget the day that Ogbu-Ojah returned from Iton-Kom. For the first time in living memory, the town crier beat his wooden gong in broad daylight, summoning all village elders and Ozo titleholders to an emergency meeting at the home of the oldest living citizen in the village. The outcome of their deliberations was a tightly held secret.

What the rest of the village recalled was that early the next morning, long before the first cock's crow, roughly at the time the first guinea fowl awakens, a scuffle was heard in Ogbu-Ojah's compound. Ogbu-Ojah's proclamations of "kedu ife me?" (What did I do?) rang through the early dawn air, followed by grunts and moans of what appeared to be a struggle between Ogbu-Ojah and several men.

It was later known that Ndi Ichie, the village elders and Ozo titleholders, had decreed that Ogbu-Ojah be ostracised for oso-ochu, manslaughter-related exile, for actions capable of or leading to the death of a brother… a ten-year sojourn in a foreign land or ajo-ofia, the evil forest. His mystical flute was to be hurled into the Ori Ngene, the local river deity, never to be played or touched again by man, for it was believed to be from the spirit world. His name was to be proscribed, and his very existence was to be represented by the name of the foulest of beasts.

It is said that when one of the emissaries sent to carry out Ogbu-Ojah's sentence threw the flute into Ori Ngene, a hand was thrust forth from the depths of the river just before it could hit the river's surface. With what sounded like a sonic boom, the flute was caught, and the Ojah was slowly and delicately lowered into the river's depths. As the flute sank, it let loose one of the most beautiful melodies ever heard by man. The young men stood transfixed by the bank of the river and until today have refused to talk about other eerie activities they observed that night. Two of them were known to have become mad a short while after this mission.

All assumed it was to be the last to be heard of Ogbu-Ojah.

Prior to his death, Ojahdili had four male children, named after the four market days in the igbo commercial calendar: Eke, Afo, Orie, and Nkwo. It was no surprise that none of his children took up wrestling. In fact, the town council proscribed wrestling after Ojahdili's death, for what other profession could intoxicate a man to the point of challenging his chi? His beautiful wife, Oso-di-eme, was inconsolable. After the death of her husband, she began to take long trips into the forest, abandoning her four children to their fate. Sometimes she spent months on end before returning to her matrimonial home. It was rumoured that she had gone stark raving mad. Others speculated that she constantly journeyed to the borders of Iton-Kom, out of grief and hoping against hope that she would be allowed through to the land of the spirits to bring back her husband.

So, when she became pregnant two years after the death of Ojahdili, the village gossip ecosystem exploded in a flurry of hypothesis. However, nobody was willing to incur the wrath of the spirits, for was it not common knowledge that Oso-di-eme constantly visited the land of the spirits? And, by extension, was it not logical that she had been impregnated by a spirit, or by her dead husband who, by the very fact that he was dead was a spirit as well? So, though the gossips and speculations boiled and bubbled over, no one ever dared challenge Oso-di-eme to her face.

Oso-di-eme had a baby girl and named her Ifesinachi, a child bestowed by a personal god. The villagers were not that accommodating, and preferred the more mundane and vindictive Nwa ajilija, a child born of gravel and dust, of unknown parentage, and in essence a bastard.

It was said that Nwa ajilija grew to be a beautiful young girl with the most melodious voice known to anyone, living or dead. By the time she was three, her voice would be heard by the horde of women doing their laundry at the banks of Ori Ngene, her tunes hummed to by the sweating men working in Oma-agwu (the fertile farms situated far within the forest), and skipped to by her fellow children as they played in the dirt in the village obodo-ezi playground.

All this while, Oso-di-eme continued her regular forays into the forest. This time she was forced to always strap Nwa ajilija to her back, as there was no one with whom to leave her, since her industrious elder children spent the whole day at the farm.

Perhaps Oso-di-eme should have listened to the villagers, who all believed that Nwa ajilija was a child from the spirit world. One day, upon their return from one of the regular forays into the forest, Nwa ajilija asked her mother, "Mama, who is this man that you go to visit in the forest?"

Oso-di-eme stopped dead in her tracks, her hand frozen in mid-air. The raffia fan she was using to whip up the flames in the hearth for the evening meal was suspended like the wing of a bird transfixed by Ogbu-Ojah's enchanting melody. Oso-di-eme swept the kitchen with her gaze, looking for the source of the adult voice, the source of her query.

Her attention barely rested on Nwa ajilija until the child angrily barked, "What are you looking for? Can't you see the person talking to you?"

There was an eternity of silence as Oso-di-eme stared at Nwa ajilija, a stare that was returned defiantly. In that moment, Oso-di-eme realised how old Nwa ajilija's eyes were—far older than her three years, far older than her mother and even older than the oji tree in the village square, that was alleged to be older than the oldest man in the village.

No one knew at what point the idea occurred to Oso-di-eme but what everyone seemed to concur to was that she should have known that the little girl could see through her actions and read her innermost thoughts. Oso-di-eme flung Nwa ajilija on her back and took off in the direction of the Ori Ngene River. What happened next was never heard of or seen in the village, and it was confirmed that it never happened again. From the child strapped to Oso-di-eme's back emerged the most melodious and sonorous of songs, a call for help to her brothers working in the faraway Oma-agwu farms. It was said that even birds paused in mid-flight upon hearing this tune, several dropping right out of the sky to their utter astonishment:

Oh Ori Ngene!

Eke, my dear brother!

Oh Ori Ngene!

She wants to drown me in Ori Ngene!

Oh Ori Ngene!

A despicable wild beast is dating our mother!

Oh Ori Ngene!

Nwa ajilija kept on singing, drawing on all her strength to call on her siblings. It was said that the birds of the forest took up this song. The trees gustily sang its refrain, the blades of grass, even the grasscutters and guinea fowl were not left out, until the song reached the ears of her brothers in their far away farm.

It was said that upon hearing Nwa ajilija's plea ferried on the very wind itself, her able-bodied siblings, Eke, Afo, Orie and Nkwo, threw down their hoes and cutlasses, and immediately raced towards the banks of Ori Ngene. They barely made it in time to see a wild-eyed, clearly delirious Oso-di-eme on the verge of throwing Nwa ajilija into the turbulent depths of Ori Ngene.

"She is having an affair with Udene the vulture!" screamed Nwa ajilija. "Ya na Udene na elie enyi," an allegation that Oso-di-eme did not bother denying, aside from an almost involuntary shaking of her head.

It was also said that given that Ori Ngene, was usually the final arbiter in matters such as this this, Nwa ajilija's siblings took the unanimous decision to request the river deity to determine whether it was right for their mother to have an affair with the despicable wild beast Udene. As soon as this question was put to the river, Afo cast both Oso-di-eme and Nwa ajilija into the roaring currents of the river. Just before both of them could hit the river's surface, a hand was thrust forth from Ori Ngene's depths, pulling down a screaming Oso-di-eme into the bowels of the river and throwing Nwa ajilija back on shore. It was a jubilant Nwa ajilija who was carried home shoulder high by her siblings.

I remember the look on my grandmother's face when I finally summoned the courage to ask her the question, "Mama, but how could Oso-di-eme have an affair with the despicable Udene the wild beast? How can a human and a vulture have an affair?"

I also remember the look she gave me as if to say, was it not evident? Ndi Ichie decreed that Ogbu-Ojah be ostracised for oso-ochu, his name to never to be mentioned again and his very existence to be represented by the name of the foulest and most despicable of beasts, the vulture. Oso-di-eme's affair had been with the man who had led her husband to his death and as for Ojahdili, she mused, no man, however strong, can challenge his chi to a wrestling match.

Jekwu Ozoemene holds a Bachelor of Arts from the University of Lagos and a Master of Business Administration in Finance from the University of Leicester. He is currently studying for a Doctorate of Business Administration in Banking and Finance at the University of Zambia / Binary University College, Malaysia.

He is the author of Shadows of Existence: An Anthology of Poetry *(2009), and a collection of plays,* The Anger of Unfulfillment: Three Plays Out of Nigeria *(2011). One of his poems appeared in the recently released* Poems for a Century: An Anthology on Nigeria, *edited by Tope Omoniyi.*

APE SHIT

Sylvia Schlettwein

He is waiting for you, not just anywhere. He is seated on *your* chair on the veranda. You have named him Jonny, despite your intention to shoot him He is the leader of the pack, he is fearless, and he deserves a name. You suppress the urge to wave a fist at him out of the car window as you pull into your parking spot under the big bush willow next to the veranda. You will not ridicule yourself in front of a baboon. Opapi is watching from his room—the curtain was pushed aside with a bony finger as you drove onto the yard. You get out of the bakkie and, as you slam the door, Jonny leaps from the chair to the table, onto the bonnet of the car, then flies past you, so close you catch a whiff of him: faeces meets the scent of scorched hair. Is that Opapi's chuckle you hear or the bloody baboon's?

You walk around the house to see where the rest of Jonny's pack is—all gone, just the high-pitched silence of midday heat reflecting from the walls and roof of your house. As you walk around the corner, you fumble in your pocket for the key to the kitchen door. You always enter here when you come home from a trip to town. Urea stench lets your hand stall a few millimetres before the keyhole. Your eyes try to follow your sense of smell in first an upward then a sideways movement. The wall around the kitchen door is not whitewashed anymore. It is streaky brown; it is smeared with shit—baboon shit. They have taken over. No, how can you think like that? They have not. You will not let them. You are the human and they are the animals. It is your house, your yard, your farm, and your decision when and how you will put an end to the harassment by a horde of obnoxious baboons. You will have to show them.

In the beginning, their antics outside your garden fence were entertaining. You still thought it was funny when they one day clambered over into your garden. They climbed the deserted anthill next to your scrap yard. You were impressed by their agility and their interest in the rusty car parts and tools. You sniggered when one of the females got her hand stuck in an empty can and sent it flying against another's head as she shook it off in frenzied panic. Watching them pick nits from each other's hairy backs made you feel a sense of companionship with them. It reminded you of yourself wiping the flakes of dry skin off the coarsely knitted jumper that covered Opapi's bony shoulders.

When they ventured too close to where you sat at your plastic table under the corrugated iron roof of the veranda, you threw your empty Tafel Lager can at them. You laughed as they scrambled in all directions and fled over the fence. They eventually assembled under the big ana tree next to the gate, from where Jonny bellowed to his troop.

"General Jonny, get your soldiers off my land," you screamed in mock declaration of war. "I have cannons. You don't!"

"Bohum, hu-hu-hu-hu!" Jonny answered and hammered his heaving chest with his bristly, dark grey fists. His troops scrambled around him. You could have sworn he had flashed you a triumphant look before he gave orders to his mostly female and child army to follow him into the veld.

"Bohu-hu-hu-hum! I have an army, you don't!"

This is not funny anymore. You push the key into the keyhole, you turn the key, and put it back into the pocket of your cut-off jeans. You open the door and stare into Opapi's rifle barrel, shaking in skeletal hands. How has the old man with his gun reached the kitchen so quickly? Does your own father want to kill you? Is he finally going crazy? Does he want to show you that he is still the man he used to be—the hunter, who could hold a gun with his steady hand and shoot straight to kill a trophy animal, no matter whether he was sitting on a nervous horse or on a shaky stance. You don't know what you find more repulsive. Is it the trembling, mottled hands of death that must have once touched your mother's breasts in the act of planting the seed that became you? Or is it the mental image of hairy primate hands smearing your wall with the brown stink from a bright red anus embedded in swollen grey bulges of flesh? Sweet-sour vomit clogs your oesophagus.

"There you are. I have guarded the door. The baboons are coming. In fact, they're not coming. They were here. No joke, my son, no joke. You must take action, otherwise they'll take over. I might be an old man in a wheelchair, but I know when a baboon wants to take over."

"Opapi, put down the gun, and don't lie to me. You were in your room when I came. I saw you pushing aside the curtain."

Opapi obediently rests the gun in his lap. He grins like a schoolboy caught reading *Playboy* under his desk.

"Observant you are, my son, indeed. Yes, I was frightened and hid in my room 'til you came. I wouldn't want that baboon to take my rifle."

"Which baboon?"

"The one you call Jonny."

"How do you know his name?"

"I heard you calling 'You're dead meat, Jonny, you're dead meat!' the other day."

Your ears burn. He can still humiliate you—the residue of skin and bones that was once your muscular father, who made you take cold showers to "toughen you up"; who made you gorge on oatmeal slime for two weeks to "purge your spoilt intestines". The problem is his able mind that refuses to follow suit to bodily decay. Sometimes you fear he will survive you, just because his brain refuses to die. He has always thought for you and beyond you. Grey matter swallows your every move, producing the soft-spoken porridge sentences of an elder, who has one foot in the grave and the other firmly rooted in the here and now.

You make him take a cold shower, and you put him to bed without dinner.

He smiles as he says: "Good night, my boy. Pray that they don't return tonight."

You don't pray, and they don't return during the night. They don't need to. They are present in their stink that creeps from the smeared wall through the kitchen, into the empty dining room, past Opapi's room and through the slit under the door of your bedroom into your bed. You turn the duvet. You shake your pillow. You open the windows. You close them again. You even try not to breathe. It doesn't help; it is like somebody painted a moustache on your upper lip with baboon shit. Not somebody—Jonny himself.

You try to shave off the smell the next morning. It only vanishes when your upper lip starts bleeding because you've shaved off the skin. You try to lick away the blood, but it only becomes more. At first it tastes sweet, then salty, then bitter. After frantic searching, you find a plaster hidden in a dusty washbag. You don't really overnight in the city anymore. You retrenched all your workers, whom you were not able to pay anymore. You cannot leave the farm and Opapi alone for too long. Your sisters say you got the farm for nothing and they have husbands and children to look after, so you can look after the old man for nothing. You stick the plaster on your lip. It at least stops the blood from flowing into your mouth. When you bring Opapi his morning tea, he cannot stop his whooping cough laugh and spurts tea all over his bedding.

"Stop behaving like a child!" you scream.

"I can't help it. You look like Hitler. That should scare Jonny all right."

You have to get the shit off the wall. You know they are watching you while you stand on a wobbly ladder and scrub at their anal graffiti with a wire brush and Sunlight soap. The sweet-sour vomit of yesterday returns. You swallow it. You will not give them the satisfaction of seeing you throw up. You scrub the whole day, and your sweat dissolves the stickiness of the plaster, which falls off. A crust forms on your upper lip; you feel it crack, but resist the temptation to lick it, even when the salt of your sweat stings through the cracks. By sunset, you are ready to wash away the vile taste of it all with a Tafel Lager.

With the swish and plop of the cap of the beer bottle, they appear from where they were hiding under bushes, behind stones and tree trunks. They clamber over the fence and settle on the patch of lawn you have managed to cultivate. The females and children start grooming and teasing each other. Jonny sits aside with his favourite female and lets her pick nits from his matted mantle. When she pinches him too hard, he gives a yellow-toothed bark and pushes her aside. She squeaks and starts picking herself. Jonny jumps onto a dead tree trunk and fixates on you.

"Wifeless, childless, you are, alone with the sack of bone and flesh that you have to call a father. Jealous, that's what you are. You'd swap lives with me anytime, hairy enough you are, ha-ha-hum bohum!"

"Al dra 'n aap 'n goue ring, hy is en bly 'n lelike ding!" you retort with an Afrikaans proverb.

"What? Thing is, I don't need a golden ring to be what I am—an ugly thing that has what you don't have. Wives, children, power, the power to irritate the shit out of you on your own land that can be repossessed any minute. Then I will still be here, while you have to look for a place to eke out an existence, with your father attached to your apron strings. Here, you want her? Just once? To relieve you? You can have her. Right here and now. Like this!"

Jonny grabs the female and forces himself into her from behind. She squeaks and squeals, but lies still, while he jumps and thrusts, grabs her neck fur, bites her neck. She first closes her eyes then the lids open to reveal only the white of her up-turned eyes. Her lips spasm into a grin. Jonny stops, without withdrawing, holds her by the buttocks with one hand and waves at you with the other.

"Come! Stop watching. Join the fun. She can take more. Her name is Johanna. Sound familiar? Oh yes, now I remember. Your mother was also a Johanna, Jo-ha-ha-na-ha-hum bohum! Your father had his way with a Johanna. I can do the same. You can do the same. It's only a name. Ha-ha-hum bohum!"

Enough is enough. Not your mother. You grab your rifle, and you aim. The dust settles after the dry bang and the scurry and screams. Your bullet has turned her into a hairy hillock with scarlet rivulets making their way to the sand waiting to swallow the thick meal of blood. Johanna will no longer produce little Jonnies to carry on her back. You decide to let her cadaver rot right where it fell, even if it spoils the lawn, and if Jonny comes back to hold the vigil by the body, you will get him too.

"What was that noise?" Opapi's voice scratches the back of your neck.

"What are you doing here? Go back to your room. How many times have I told you not to sneak up on me like that?"

"Works every time. This wheelchair is well oiled." Opapi's chuckle sounds a bit like a staccato version of *ha-ha-hum bohum*.

"Was that a shot I heard? And it sounded like a hit. Did you assassinate Jonny?"

"No, I killed his female."

Opapi attempts a whistle through his teeth. "Changing the rules of the game, eh? Trying to hurt him where you think it hurts most? Johanna, eh?"

"How do you know her name?"

"Oh, Jonny and I, we speak. I mean, that's as good as it gets when you're not around. If you can't beat them, join them."

"They're baboons, not people, Opapi."

"Exactly, my son, exactly. Don't you forget that now."

"Go to your room," you say.

Opapi shrugs and circles his hands over the wheels in mock helplessness. "This thing is not very modern. Too heavy to manoeuvre for an old man. I can drive here, but I can't turn it around."

You sigh and get up. Time for his cold shower anyway. You usually get a rush when the jet of cold water hits the naked folded skin and bones in the wheelchair under the shower. Opapi never cries like you cried, but you can see how he shivers. It makes you smile. Revenge is a dish best eaten cold, but today no rush kicks in. Today you feel the spray of the cold water as if it hits your own skin. You shiver with Opapi. You quickly turn off the shower and dry him faster than usual. When you help him onto his bed and into his pyjama pants, you take care not to hurt him a bit like you usually do.

"I can't find my gun," Opapi informs you while he closes the buttons of his pyjama shirt over the wiry hair on his chest.

"What do you mean?"

"You know I keep it in my wardrobe and next to my bed at night, and now I can't find it anymore. I've looked in the wardrobe and you can see it's not next to my bed."

You look under the bed. It is not there. You go through the wardrobe—nothing except dead clothes.

"Did you take it to your room after you had it in the kitchen when you were scared of the baboons?"

"I think so, or did you take it from me, son?"

"No, why would I?"

"Because you think I cannot handle it anymore?"

"You have a point there, but, no, I didn't take it. Sleep now."

"I'll try. I'm a bit afraid Jonny will come back. Can't I sleep with you in your bed?"

"No, you can't. You never let me sleep in your bed when I was afraid at night."

"Good night, son. Sweet dreams." He chuckles and again it sounds like a croaky ha-ha-hum bohum.

As you draw Opapi's bedroom door closed behind you and enter the living room, you slowly remember how Opapi put the rifle on his lap, how you took it from him, put on the safety catch and rested it on the couch next to the gauze door leading out to the veranda. You check the couch; there is no rifle. The old man probably found it there the next day while you were out hunting and misplaced it. But where? You are too tired to look for it now.

"The house doesn't lose anything," your mother used to say when you were looking for something you were sure you had left *right here*. "Tomorrow is another day," she would say. "We'll find it, don't you worry. You go to sleep now and dream of where it is hiding." She would ruffle your hair and stroke your forehead. Her sandpaper skin tickled you. Underneath the roughness of her skin her fingertips hid like soft little pillows. The tickle and the softness made you sleepy. You would drift off to sleep and, even though you would not remember your dream of your lost thing's hiding place, you would invariably find the missing item under your bed the next morning.

Your own rifle is still lying on the table at which you were sitting when you shot Johanna. You go outside to get it. Before you go back inside, you aim at her dead body on the lawn. "Boom," you whisper. A wry laugh stays lodged in your throat. You peer into the dark to check for baboon silhouettes. Nothing. You listen whether you can hear any baboon noises. They could be hiding. Nothing. "Rest in peace," you say in direction of Johanna's body. "Looks like Jonny is not coming back for you."

In your room you slide your gun under your bed like you always do. You slump into bed without undressing, washing or brushing your teeth. This time it is the sweet smell of the decaying flesh of Jonny's dead companion that seems to envelop you. You like it. You breathe it in deeply; it makes you fall asleep.

It is the first time in ages that you dream of your mother. She sits on the couch that still stands in the living room and is knitting with brown wool—probably a jersey for Opapi. She puts down her knitting and looks at you. She smiles at you while waving a reprimanding finger. Her lips move, but there is no sound. You ask her to tell you where Opapi has put his rifle. She shrugs, still smiling. You try to read her lips and, for the first time, you notice that she has large, yellow teeth, not small, pearly white ones like you always thought.

You are pretty sure that she is saying, "The house doesn't lose anything." She reaches out a hand to stroke your cheek then carefully touches the wound on your upper lip. The bits of rough skin on her fingertips hook into the cracks of the scab and you jerk awake into an upright position. The room is filled with the greyness of dawn, which weighs on your lids like thick paste and clogs your ears. A slamming from the bedroom window sluggishly works its way through the greyness.

You turn your head towards the window. Jonny's yellow grin shifts in and out of focus in the window frame as he keeps slamming the windowpane, not with his dark grey fist, but with the shaft of Opapi's gun.

Sylvia Schlettwein was born on 16 November 1975 in Omaruru, Namibia. She studied German language and literature and Romance studies at the University of Cape Town, The University of Stuttgart and the Ecole Normale Supérieure de Lettres et Sciences Humaines in Lyon. After completing her Master's degree, she returned to Windhoek in 2003 where she now heads the Department of Languages and Communication at the International University of Management and lectures German, French and Communication.

Sylvia writes, translates and edits short fiction and poetry in English, German and Afrikaans. In July 2012 her short stories were published in the collection Bullies, Beasts and Beauties. *She co-authored and co-edited the German language anthology of poetry and short stories* Hauptsache Windhoek *published in 2013.*

Sylvia lives, loves and works in Windhoek where she is involved in various literary projects.

WHAT IF YOU SLEPT?

Jason Mykl Snyman

"What if you slept?
And what if, in your sleep, you dreamed?
And what if, in your dream, you went to Heaven
And there plucked a strange and beautiful flower?
And what if, when you awoke, you had the flower in your hand?"
    – Samuel Taylor Coleridge, "What if you slept?"

In his dreams, at least in the beginning, Hugh Heller could fly, drive a luxury car or bed the most exotic, beautiful women.

In the waking world, however, he could do none of those things, and as the years swiftly fell away into oblivion, could no longer dream of doing them either.

On a frigid, miserable morning, he awoke unpleasantly in his wheelchair as it rolled over a stretch of bumpy cobblestones. To both sides, his waking vision swam with the luminous pinks, greens and bright blues of square houses. Consistently oblivious to all of time and place, he had no idea for how long he had been out or where he was headed on this brain-jarring road.

"Swan," he murmured drowsily. "Is this now?"

The plump lady behind him gave him a brief pat of assurance on the shoulder.

"Yes, Mr Heller, sir. This is now."

The wheelchair rattled on over the cobblestoned streets of the Bo-Kaap, and Hugh's bloated old body vibrated in the leather seat.

"I say, where are you taking me, woman?"

Miss Swan had been his nurse, his minder and, indeed, his only friend, for many years. As his disease grew progressively cruel and began to rob him of everything that made him a capable human, he found it necessary to have somebody of her excellence by his side.

"I'm taking you home, Mr Heller."

Hugh looked about them in bewilderment. His teeth rattled together as Miss Swan pressed onwards down the path towards the warm house awaiting them.

He craned his neck backwards to look up at her. A slow smile crept out between her two fat, rosy cheeks.

He narrowed his eyes at her. "Are you sure this is now, Swan?"

She shook her head and chuckled.

Upon arrival at their home at 1865 Grappenhall Street, as he had it written on the front page of his pocket notebook, Hugh Heller lifted himself cautiously from the wheelchair and walked through the open front door.

In the kitchen, he found his blue helmet on the table and had begun strapping it on when he heard Miss Swan close the heavy front door. She came in shortly after and stored the folded wheelchair behind the kitchen door. She checked his helmet straps carefully and gave him a tap on the head.

"Your nose is red, Swan," said Hugh. "Should we make a fire?"

Swan toddled away towards the oven and joked, "If you'd be so kind to chop the wood."

"Very funny," he replied and skulked off towards the living room to put a little fire together while she prepared their supper.

The logs had already been chopped for him, into kindling of all sizes. The thought of him being allowed to wield an axe was preposterous. He placed the shards into the firebox in a teepee-like structure around small cubes of firelighter.

Upon the first thrilling sight of flames, Hugh Heller lost consciousness and hit his helmet against the fireplace where, as he fell before it, a shooting spark set fire to one of his eyebrows.

From the tender age of five, Hugh had begun displaying symptoms of severe narcolepsy and cataplexy, which grew gradually more brutal over the years, and which no medicine seemed to remedy.

Sixty years later, it had become so that neither simple frown nor smirk occurred without punishment. He would frequently doze at the slightest emotion and at the most inconvenient of times or places.

Hugh Heller, it was gossiped, had woken in more gutters not knowing who or where he was than the most awful vagrant drunks and tik-fiends of the inner city.

When he roused this time, he lay beneath a large Brabejum wild almond tree, which grew upon the slopes of Signal Hill behind his home. He had been here before, as he found the Brabejum both captivating and mysterious, but still it took a few moments to conclude where he was.

The tree was magnificent, boasting whorls of beautiful leathery leaves and an abundance of splendid, radiating flowers—and was admired by the entire neighbourhood as it stood in solitary grandeur upon the hilltop.

Despite the shade, the day was warm. Hugh's clothing had changed—this wasn't what Swan had laid out for him in the morning. At least, not that he could remember.

"Swan!" he cried, his calm abandoning him. "Is this now?"

He was all alone, and only the small white flowers of the wild almond were there to answer him, as they broke apart in the light breeze and drifted slowly to ground.

"Is this now?"

Hugh crawled from the shade and hurtled down the hill towards his home, which he never reached, of course. So overcome with anxiety as he was, he sprawled into the grass somewhere halfway downhill, and slept deeply, with the intoxicatingly sweet scent of the Brabejum clinging to his nostrils.

Miss Swan ran a cool, damp cloth over his forehead and singed eyebrow, and he blinked his drowsiness away. She offered him a warm smile.

"Swan..." he began.

"Yes, Mr Heller. This is now."

He sighed with relief and allowed his fluttering eye-lids to fall—like heavy theatre curtains—and upon the darkened stage he sat quite still, listening to the firewood crackle and hiss from somewhere beyond the drapes, and breathing in the perfume of wood-smoke.

"I made soup, you should eat. Took another nasty knock you did."

But the bloated, balding old man was already gone.

Gently, she cast a woollen blanket over his body and removed his shoes from worn feet. She tucked him in on the couch and left him there at peace, then returned to the kitchen for a bowl of warm butternut soup. Something, she thought, smelled strongly of wild almond flowers.

Hugh sat at the kitchen table wearing his helmet. His chair was of his own design, and had a seat belt harness not at all dissimilar to that found in a racing car. Miss Swan strapped him in and returned to the stove to warm some soup.

"You know, Swan, I'm not an invalid. I can strap myself in!"

She gave no response at all, only kept her back to him and stirred the simmering, golden contents of the pot.

"I'm narcoleptic, not a bloody child," he mumbled, all brimstone and fuming. Still, she gave no reply.

Hugh folded his arms across his bony chest then fell asleep with a deafening thud as his head collided with the table.

When he awoke, he found himself once more on the couch by the fireplace. Swan had put a woollen blanket over him, one she'd knitted herself in his favourite colours, and she sat beside him on the rocking chair reading a novel by firelight.

Hugh sighed audibly, staring into the flames as they licked at the firebox walls.

"Something the matter, Mr Heller?" asked Miss Swan.

He lay silent, sulking. She waited a while for him to respond then returned to her book, rocking in a gentle, soundless rhythm.

After a few more moments he sighed again, louder this time.

Miss Swan put her book down and stared at him. "Are you going to tell me what's on your mind?"

"You were ignoring me earlier," he mumbled. "Didn't do my straps properly either. Made me pass out and I hit my head."

Miss Swan stared at him, her eyebrows stitched together with confusion. "When was this?"

"Just now, you daft woman," he snapped. "In the kitchen, while you warmed the soup."

Miss Swan shook her head in disbelief. "Silly man. You've been asleep since you hit your head on the fireplace. You haven't moved from the couch at all."

Hugh stared at her with scepticism, not entirely sure of what was happening.

Evil dreams and evil waking were blended into a long, nightmarish cocktail of bewilderment and terror. His colours had spilled and run together, mixing on the canvas—terror of never knowing for sure where he was or when he was or what ill fate had befallen him; the terror of no longer being capable of differentiating between the waking world and the sleeping one, where his dreams had become so insipid they had come to resemble his true world in almost every conceivable way.

Day after day and night following night he would live the same lives in both worlds. Doing the same things again and again, and repeating himself over and over. He saw new places before he'd ever been there. He suffered double the indignities and lived twice the disgrace and public shaming.

Forced to drink of this dreadful cocktail, he could never be sure which way was up or which road led where. Which actions were truly his own? On which accomplishments could he put his true name? How exactly came all these dreadful scars and dents upon his head?

He rolled over in the couch and, for a long, agonising time, could not slumber.

The fire died to glowing embers, Swan snored from her rocking chair, and all Hugh could hear was the gathering rumble of the thunder outside, echoing down into the beatings of his own tired heart.

Hugh awoke in his wheelchair, being shunted over the rutted paving of Adderley Street, past the oldest Christian church in the country. The street children ran and sang and played in traffic and Miss Swan reprimanded them loudly and firmly. He fell asleep listening to the great church bell swing in its ancient tower.

He woke and was in the bathtub, where he wasn't allowed to be. Bored to tears, he read the back of shampoo bottles then dozed off and swallowed too much lukewarm soap water.

He awoke urinating in his bed and Miss Swan scolded him soundly. He fell asleep fleeing the room and hit his head on a doorframe marked with the heights of forgotten children.

He awoke in the same bed, but cleaner now and it smelled fresh and crisp, like the smell of rain on a dusty Karoo road. His head ached, his mouth tasted foul and he dozed off scribbling hastily in his pocket notebook.

He awoke slurping soup from a rusty spoon, several times, again and again and again until soup became unbearable and he pledged suicide if Swan ever gave that awful swill to him again. Sometimes she answered him. Sometimes she behaved as if he wasn't even there at all, just a rocking, muttering ghost. Hugh pulled what was left of his thinning hair and fell asleep screaming.

He awoke under the wild almond tree and laid his notebook open in his lap.

I don't remember writing this.

And the clouds were shaped like pixies, fairies and sprites who had come to carry his sane mind away into the sky and over the African horizon. The smell of the lance-shaped leaves anaesthetised him and whisked him away down dark, slippery slopes and into the outstretched arms of yawning Mother Sleep.

He awoke again on the couch and listened to Miss Swan rock and snore. The coals had died and grown cold. He screamed at her for not strapping him in and he drifted off before she could say anything.

He awoke in his bed with a throbbing face and surreptitiously wondered if Swan had been hitting him while he slept. He lay there for hours, calling her name, and she never answered.

He shuffled around his abode like a grey, swollen spectre eating handfuls of Provigil, Ritalin, Dextroamphetamine and Modafinil. He drank one bottle of superb red wine and, when it was empty, he sobbed loudly and sought comfort in another. He dozed, foaming at the mouth.

What was real and what was reverie, when everything was of the same stone, the same ground, and the same flesh and blood; when nothing he did in one place made any variation at all in the other?

He shambled to the rhythms upon which the universe was constructed, from one world to the next and to the next. Fits of sleep and fits of waking. For all he knew, it could all be one long, atrocious stretch of deliria.

"Swan," he asked. "Is this now?"

He had just woken on the couch covered in sheets of stained old newspapers. She perched in her rocking chair like a fat owl, with her little beak buried in the pages of her book.

"Yes, Mr Heller. This is now."

How could he be sure at all? He had to take her word for it, time after time, day after day. How long had it really been? How far was the distance between one absolute day and the next? How far did time surge between every hour's vanishing and rebirth?

The sky overflowed with dark, sinister clouds. God's cup runneth over sullenly. What once was green was browning. What once had leaves stood naked and grey. It was cold, it was winter and the world had fallen into slumber.

"What's this all over me?" He turned over and the newspaper rustled loudly.

"Pages from last week's Argus, it seems," answered Miss Swan. "You got up a while ago and covered yourself in it."

He felt like reprimanding her for not stopping his foolish sleepwalking escapades, but thought it better not to. "What time is it?"

Miss Swan folded a dog-ear into the page she was reading and shut her book, placing it down on the small table next to the chair.

"Time for your shower." She stood up with some difficulty.

Hugh silently speculated how often the fat woman rocked herself to sleep trying to get up from that ghastly old chair.

"Fine," he said, rising in a cascading mess of newspaper and sweaty clothing. "I don't appreciate you trying to hide the time from me like that, that's all I'm saying."

He stretched and ancient bones creaked and clicked like rusty springs.

Miss Swan sighed and took him by the hand. "Come along, Mr Heller. You ridiculous, paranoid man."

"This is still a better gig than your last," he reminded her, as he did every day like clockwork. She had spent the better part of her youth working the gloomy halls of Helen Joseph Hospital and trying to keep ill, incoherent men on foam mattress beds from dying.

She led him gently through the house towards the staircase. Hugh had come close to drowning on his own soapy, dirty bathwater in the tub on a number of occasions and, since then, had been obligated to use the shower instead, where he could sit down on a small plastic chair and wash in relative safety.

The problem with this, of course, was that the only shower in the house was located upstairs—a climb Hugh would begrudgingly complete once a day and complain all the way up and often well into the second lathering of shampoo.

He frequently feared falling asleep halfway up the long staircase and tumbling into a dream from which he would possibly never wake.

For this reason, he would begin the ascent to the second floor and the great Miss Swan would follow. From time to time she would put her hands on his shoulders and he would berate her for treating him like a "helpless old cripple".

"You're just a safety net, Swan! I don't need help lifting my own two feet up a couple of stairs!"

Miss Swan moved a chubby hand to Hugh's lower back, which he swatted away angrily. The infinitely tolerant woman sighed and clung to the wooden banister, using it to pull herself up.

"Leave me, I say, insufferable woman!"

"Leave you to fall then, that's what I'll do!" she scolded, pointing a sausage-sized finger at him.

Halfway up the stairs, Hugh paused and oscillated like a pendulum in a grandfather clock.

Miss Swan immediately seized him by the shoulders and braced for the weight of his body, but it never came.

"I'm fine, I'm fine," he said. "Just a bit light headed." He brushed her hands from his shoulders and pushed onwards. "Leave me then," he grumbled under his breath. "Better to plunge to my death and end this misery once and for all than be treated like a feeble imbecile."

Miss Swan ignored him and followed steadily. Nearer to the summit of the narrow staircase, Hugh once again came to an abrupt halt and swayed from side to side.

Again, Miss Swan grabbed a firm hold of him.

Aggravated, Hugh swung round and swatted at her. "Leave me!" he shrieked, flailing his arms about wildly.

His bony elbow collided with the side of her head with a sickening thud and the kindly Miss Swan keeled over backwards, wide-eyed with horror.

The wooden staircase gave a groan like the roots of an ancient tree being torn from the earth, and like that tree, Miss Swan toppled with a hideous shriek and crashed down into the stairs.

Too late, Hugh grabbed at empty air and watched in dread as she tumbled and careened down into wall and wood, and hit the bottom of the staircase with a stomach-turning crack.

Her large body lay bent and broken; it shivered for the briefest of moments, and then mercifully came to a halt. Her silver-blond hair splayed out in a pool of dark blood flooding into an expanding puddle. Tiny fragments of skull rolled in the gore.

Hugh yelped and fell to his haunches on the step, urging himself not to flee across her broken body and gallop screaming into the night.

Slow and low, a stuttering moan grew and grew within his throat, the sound a deranged animal would make, emanating from deep within the yawning rumbles of the belly and vibrating up to the mouth, where he spat it out and sobbed uncontrollably, rocking against the wall.

His howls were of dissent and distrust, staring down at the unmoving mass of woman who was once a living, breathing Miss Swan.

For a long while he sat upon the step wailing, waiting, and praying for sleep to carry him away to wake someplace else, far from this hellish nightmare. No sleep came and the pool of blood grew greater.

Hours had dragged by, minute by excruciating minute spent gnawing his fingernails down to the flesh, and still no sleep came to Hugh Heller. Still, the large body of Miss Swan lay crumpled at the foot of the staircase, and the massive pool of blood around her had grown cold and dark in the carpet.

The unforgiving sun crashed into the golden horizon and resigned the world to a bottomless darkness. In those final moments of light, as it crawled across the ruined carpet, it almost seemed to Hugh that Miss Swan could be raising her arms, throwing them up in despair…

But soon the sun fell, and so too did her lifeless, flabby arms, and Hugh was left to swallow down ruthless sickness, misty and vacant-eyed.

Rigidly, he stood, and made his slow way down the stairs to where her body lay.

"Swan?" he whispered as he drew nearer to the bottom.

He reached the final step and tried to peer over the large mound of a body to see her face. Barefoot, he stepped into her congealing blood and prodded her in the back with his fingers.

"Swan?"

He circled her body and the blood squelched between his toes. Hugh looked into her wide, lifeless eyes. The warmth and joy he had always known in those eyes were gone, snuffed out, extinguished in a series of savage, crashing blows. In despair and fright, he screamed like a waylaid creature and dashed away into the kitchen, leaving a scattered trail of bloody, smudged footprints all the way. He crashed noisily into the kitchen table and collapsed among the table legs, cloth and shattered crockery, where he finally slept.

When he awoke, Hugh sat once more at the very table he had just upturned in a deafening collision. His head pounded and pale sunlight gleamed through the window blinds across the entirety of the kitchen, making everything feel eerie and blue.

He tried to stand and found himself strapped into chair and helmet.

Miss Swan stood by the stove with her round back to him, stirring a pot of soup.

"Swan…" he croaked.

His dry lips trembled and the frantic drumming in his head grew greater and unsteadier.

Miss Swan turned from the stove and gave him a cheerful smile. "Yes, Mr Heller. It is now," she answered before turning back to the soup.

"N-n-no…" stammered Hugh. "I mean… Yes. But… Are you sure?" He stared at her, running a nervous tongue over his arid lips.

"Well…" she said with a giggle. "It's now to me?"

Hugh chuckled hoarsely. *Now to me.*

Now washed in and out like a rolling wave, a hypnagogic tide dragging him all the way down along a jagged shore. He could feel the ebb of that tide even now, always, tugging at his ankles.

"I had the most awful dream, Swan…." He leaned his head back against the chair and sighed, his entire body trembling with relief. "The most awful dream I've ever had."

What sordid chicanery was this that his mind now played on him? What evil dreams now plagued Hugh, flooding him with shadow and doubt and disorder?

"I don't know what's real anymore, Swan," he mumbled sleepily.

Miss Swan dished a bowl of warm butternut soup and brought it to him with a spoon. She put it down in front of him with a smile. "Well, Mr Heller," she began.

But Hugh had dozed off again, his hands clasped neatly over his lap and a single tear rolling down his cheek.

The sun rose above the hilltop and set fire to the clouds, and Hugh Heller awoke once more beneath the great wild almond tree. His clothing was dirty, torn and damp, and a serious ache worked its way around the inside of his face to settle behind his heavy eyes.

Beside him in the earth was a massive hole and beside that, a colossal mound of dark, wet earth. A shovel leaned against the mottled grey trunk of the tree.

Hugh, on all fours, peered into the deep hole and, in it, found the half-buried body of Miss Swan. His head pulsated horribly and he vomited into the hole and onto the body.

Crying, he wiped his mouth on his shirt and picked himself up. With the shovel he scooped and pushed the mound of earth into the hole until it was filled.

He flattened Miss Swan's grave, painstakingly patting down the soil. Stepping out from under the Brabejum, Hugh looked up into the sky.

The pinks and blues and fiery oranges of the dawn sky stretched as far as the eye could see and it was indeed quite beautiful—perhaps, the most painfully beautiful thing he had seen in a long while.

While walking home barefoot, with the shovel slung over a bruised shoulder, he wept, often hysterically, and the people who encountered him spoke of him all day long, unable to put such a heart-breaking and peculiar sight from their minds.

Hugh went home that day to get down on bended knee to scrub blood from the carpet and stairway. He soon gave up, though, and dozed right there in the soap and blood, contemplating drowning himself in the bathtub.

He was merely a passenger on this hopeless, ill-fated voyage, doomed to cast anchor into stupor and oblivion and spend forever seeking in a world of searchers, the difference between the faux world and the real.

When he awoke, he sat before a great fire in the hearth, leaning against the couch, warming his feet. Miss Swan sat beside him in her rocking chair, gently swaying.

For a long while, he sat quite still, so motionless, in fact, that Miss Swan still thought him asleep until he spoke.

"Swan..." he said, hypnotised by the flickering flames. "Swan, do you know what a swan song is?"

He turned to look up at her. She lowered her book into her lap. Her round face had a festive glow in the firelight.

"I've heard the phrase, Mr Heller. Can't say I know what it means, though."

He gave her a sad smile. His eyes felt swollen and heavy, brimming like storm clouds. Slowly, he turned back to the fire and sighed.

"They say," he began, "that the mute swan is entirely silent during its lifetime until the moment just before death, when it sings one astounding final song." He turned again to look up at her. "They say nothing on earth is more beautiful than the ultimate lament of the swan."

"Have you ever heard a swan die, Mr Heller?"

Hugh thought this over and then nodded wretchedly. "I'm afraid so."

"And?" asked the large woman. "Was it as beautiful as they say it is?"

He turned back to the fire, and soon his mind had gone adrift among the fervent dancing of the blues, oranges and yellows as they twirled to the hissing and the crackling of the burning wood.

Was it beautiful? Had she ended swan-like? Had she faded to a stirring death-hymn as she plummeted to her demise? Had it taken his very soul by the shoulders and viciously shaken it?

"No," he said, at last. "No, it was quite awful."

Miss Swan sighed, leaned back and returned to her book…

Hugh stared into the glowing flames and embers until they turned bitter and dark, and Miss Swan was snoring behind him.

Slowly, he lifted himself from the warm floor and fetched a blanket from the hallway closet. He cast it gently over her and kissed her tenderly upon her forehead.

"Goodnight, my Swan," he whispered to the darkness.

For the first time in as far back as his memory could stretch, Hugh Heller walked himself to bed that night, where he fell asleep with his head upon a pillow.

Hugh Heller awoke sprawled at the foot of the staircase. He tried to lift his aching head but found it stuck fast.

He attempted to move his arms and found them twisted and pinned beneath his body in some horrific manner. With a great amount of effort and crying, he managed to position his limbs in such a way as to push himself away from the floor. Gradually, he peeled the side of his face from where blood had glued him to the carpet.

With a desperate heave, he ripped free and rolled over onto his back. Fresh blood gushed bright from an opening in his cheek and nylon fibres clung to the wound.

Weeping, he dozed off where he lay on his back and his blood ran into and filled his eye socket.

Days as long as years passed, where Hugh Heller stalked the hallways of his house in one world, alone and cold, and he never quite got the blood out from the foot of the staircase. He stayed indoors on those days and wasted away, waiting to sleep or waiting to wake, waiting to go back to wherever Swan was.

Sometimes he would doze, and when he woke, he would find her there, and she would have warm butternut soup and she smelled like the pale flowers of the magnificent wild almond tree.

Sometimes he wouldn't, and was damned to mourn her pitiful, awful swan song as it echoed through the dark passageways of his memory.

He built fires and burned pinecones in the hearth, rocking gently in her chair and reading one of her books. The cupboards were barren and he ate nothing save medication and the bitter, poisonous fruit of the Brabejum.

He stank, never bathing—sweating and weeping into the same clothing for days. He fell into feverish sleep upon the couch and his notebook was filled cover to cover with the disjointed ramblings of a mad man.

On a frigid, grey morning, he awoke unpleasantly in his wheelchair as it rolled over a stretch of bumpy cobblestones. Consistently oblivious to all of time and place, he had no idea how long he had been out nor where he was headed on this brain-jarring road.

Hugh had been here before, so often.

The large woman behind him pushed him onwards towards the warm house awaiting them and his teeth rattled in his head.

Onwards, to swallowing too much soap water and vomiting.

Onwards, to singing church bells and singing children.

Onwards, to the great wild almond tree and its leaves which smelled of soil and blood.

Onwards, to butternut soup for the thousandth time until he wanted to die.

Onwards, to scribbling round the bend and not knowing which way was up.

Onwards, as the wheelchair vibrated and bounced raucously across the cobblestones.

Onwards, onwards at breakneck speed into the face of the void, to ride pill bottles and dragons and staircase rails until they crashed him down into the sand and the carpet.

Onwards, to stare longingly into the abyss.

The wheelchair rolled onwards and he sat in it, powerless.

He turned his head and cast his gaze up into the gloomy sky above them. "Swan," he murmured. "Is this now?"

Jason Mykl Snyman wasted most of his youth in Johannesburg, trying to kill his brain with Jack Daniels and loud music. Up until now, his writing career consisted of staring out of the window, making inappropriate comments on Facebook and wrestling with blank pages.

He has attempted to study journalism, photography, criminology, psychology, culinary arts and has completed none of them.

Since moving to the Garden Route, he has rediscovered his voice and is finally taking writing seriously. "Blank page," he says. "I'm coming for you."

ESOMNESIA

Phillip Steyn

[BOOTING...]
[CHECKING SYSTEMS...]
[COMPILING DATA...]
[START ESOMNESIA]

Can you hear me?

"Yes, I think so. Where am I? I can't see a thing."

Do not worry too much about that; you will understand soon enough. I am your psychologist. You are here for your check-up.

"Oh... Of course."

I want to focus on your past today. Firstly, I want to know a bit more about your background. What is your earliest memory?

"Wow, let me think... I'm not sure where my memories start."

It does not have to be the first in chronological terms. Think of a memory from your childhood that you can remember more than the others.

"Um... Let me think. Well, I do remember that there used to be a swing set in the backyard of my parents' house, and... Wh-what is this?"

Describe the sensation.

"It feels so weird. It's almost as if I can see the backyard with the swing set; like looking at a picture... but at the same time it's not. I'm not sure how to describe it. Something is missing. I can see the swing set, but it doesn't seem real."

That is perfectly normal. It is usually a very frightening experience for patients to relive memories inside this space. What you are seeing is merely a projection of your own memory.

"Really? Wow. I never knew this kind of technology existed."

It's fairly new. However, the projections can only contain the information you give it. Carry on with the memory. You were talking about the swing set in your parents' backyard. Was it special to you?

"Yes. What kind of kid doesn't like riding on a swing? Our swing set had two swings. The frame was bright red, and the seats were wooden... Wow, I can see what you mean. The picture is somehow becoming clearer now."

What did you experience on the swing?

"I felt happy. I remember swinging on it often with the wind rushing through my hair and my floral dress. I also vaguely remember the sunlight filtering through the trees. This may sound stupid, but because the sun was in my eyes I could see nothing in front of me, and for some reason I felt as if I was in another world. Or, at least, that's how I'd like to remember it."

People recall memories in the manner that they prefer. Sometimes people colour them in such a way that it does not resemble anything relating to the actual event.

"I like this memory… Wait, what was that?"

Describe the sensation.

"I'm not sure what it was. I think I saw something flicker. Kind of like where a vid is broken… Weird… The air feels different."

That's perfectly normal. Let us recap the memory.

"Well, it was my memory of the swing. The memory is actually kind of silly. It was a single swing and it was painted blue… It's strange really. Now that I think about it, I don't remember swinging on it often. I don't remember why… I think I'm getting dizzy."

Good. Okay, tell me a bit more about yourself.

"Shouldn't you know this already? I thought this was a check-up."

That is correct. It is a technique I call identity affirmation. When more memories are recalled in this space, it is important to cement the memories by affirming your own identity. This space is somewhat volatile when it comes to memories.

"Oh, I think I understand now. Well, my name is Mia, I'm twenty-three years old and I live in Cape Town. I like hanging out with my friends and seeing my family. Even though I'm currently unemployed, I would like to do something big with my life."

Tell me about your parents. Start with your relationship with them.

"I guess I have a good relationship with my parents. They are always there for me and they support all the decisions I make. I am an only child, so they gave me all their love. They're always a phone call away."

Parents have a significant impact on—

"There it is again! What is that? Something doesn't feel right... I don't know how to describe it. It is almost as if things vanish and then make no sense."

Don't be alarmed. All is well. What do you remember most about your parents?

"I don't know. Nothing comes to mind... I didn't have any siblings, so I guess I had to go through it alone. My parents died when I was very young. I can't even remember what they looked like..."

How do you think your parents' deaths have affected you?

"There's a part of me that doesn't want to believe it, that it's just one big joke, but that's how life is. Sometimes life is just plain sucks and then you have to struggle through all that. Now I feel really pissed."

Fascinating.

"Actually, my whole childhood seems to be a big blur now, except for Gladys."

Who is this Gladys?

"She was our house-help. Before we got a modmaid, we had Gladys. She was very friendly and very hard working. I liked her a lot. She always made the best sandwiches and took the blame when I did something wrong. She never judged me, even when I was in a lot of shit."

Oh, I see...

"Yes, and— Ow! There's that feeling again. Are you sure everything's all right?"

Yes. Everything is in working order. Maybe the changed memory is too emotionally resilient.

"Wait, what did you say?"

What do you mean?

"Something you said..."

What did I say?

"Um... I don't remember. I must be losing my mind."

Tell me again about the house-help you had before your modmaid.

"All I remember was that she was black. That's about it. It's not like she that important. I have to admit though, she was better than the modmaid that we got after her."

You mean the Ultratech Citizen Models, also known as CitiMods? What is your opinion of them?

"I'm not sure really. I never liked the mods, not just the modmaid. It's quite a controversial topic, especially in South Africa. The only thing you see on the news is how mods are burnt with fire and petrol bombs. They say that it's due to xenophobia, which is probably true."

It sounds as if you have a different theory.

"I just think that it's not the only explanation. There is something strange about those mods. They're supposed to be like real humans, just mechanical. I don't buy that. The only thing that mods do is mimic humans. They don't have real emotions, so how could they be human? I think that's why it's so creepy. You look at them, wearing clothes, talking, showing expressions, but it's never truly genuine."

Are you familiar with Project CitiMod Memory Creation?

"I've heard about it on the news, but I don't know much about it. I remember drinking coffee with a friend of mine in my flat. We were sitting on the couch when the story of Project CMMC came on... My friend was really upset by it. She doesn't like the mods much either. Her family's business got broken into by mods which were supposedly hacked by the technorebels."

Do you think it is possible that the mods acted on their own?

"I'm not sure. It does create a very sensational story for those paranoids out there. Ultimately I would have to say no. I don't think mods are capable of free will—doesn't matter what anyone says."

What do you know of the project?

"All I know is that some scientists are trying to create memories for mods to make them more real... Can they even do that? And even if they do get it right, it doesn't change the fact that they are mods. No matter how close mods resemble and act like humans, a mod is a mod."

Describe any experience you have had with a mod. One that stands out clearly when you think of mods.

"Well, I mostly encounter mods when I'm shopping at PnP Ultramart. Almost all shops nowadays have cashiers manned by Ultratech mods. My experiences with them haven't been unpleasant, just very strange. One day I was doing my normal weekly grocery shopping. I was just browsing the cheese aisle, when an assistant mod came up to me and asked if I—"

"Do you need any help, ma'am?"

"Wha— Did the projection just speak?"

Yes. When the memories recalled are more and more recent, the memories become clearer. This makes speech possible. With the earlier memories we focus more on the visual aspects.

"Okay... Well, he asked,"

"Do you need any help, ma'am?"

"And for a moment I just stared at it. He seemed friendly, but he was a mod, after all... I just replied,"

"No thanks, I'm good. Just browsing."

"Would you like to hear about our specials?"

"That mod was very persistent. Its eyes were what really got to me. They were like two black marbles with red LEDs for pupils. The mod tried to look friendly, but its eyes looked cold and dead."

"No...thank you."

"Okay... Well if you need anything, just let me know."

"He smiled and then walked away. I found it really strange, because for a moment he seemed disappointed—as if he really wanted to tell me about the specials. Can mods really feel disappointment?"

Mods are programmed to exhibit certain emotions for certain situations, to make them seem as human as possible. However programming can only go so far. Giving mods memories will enable them to process responses to situations organically. The only problem is that synthetic memory creation is rather a lengthy and unstable process, which hasn't been perfected yet, but exciting breakthroughs in neuroscience are helping to sidestep that issue.

"What do you mean?"

They have managed to manifest organic memories in a pseudo-physical form. With this it is possible to give mods complex memory structures that would have taken centuries to perfect. *The memories will act as the mod's AI; it will make all its decisions based on a complex value system, rather than having responses pre-programmed.*

"By organic you mean memories belonging to humans?"

Yes, which raises a lot more ethical and philosophical complexities to deal with. The only way that the organic memory matter can be harvested is when it is fresh. This means that one cannot harvest memories from long-deceased persons. Scientists have to wait for fresh specimens. However, it is still illegal to kill, even for memories.

"So you're saying that those scientists just wait for someone to die? That's pretty messed up."

True, it is quite unorthodox. The problem is that memories cannot be duplicated, as of yet, so a person has to be dead for harvesting to be possible. Even though memories cannot be duplicated, they can be manipulated.

"Manipulated?"

Yes. Memories are never constant; they can be easily changed. Manipulating them is necessary, because mods must have memories that are unique to them. Having emotional connections to living people is problematic.

"But then the mods would be living fake lives!"

The memories might not be exactly authentic, but they believe it to be true.

"Is that even ethical?"

Its ethics might be questionable, but it is perfectly legal. You are undergoing memory manipulation right now.

"What? You mean my memories are going to be manipulated? Why?"

You will know soon enough.

"You're not a psychologist, are you?"

Correct. I'm a scientist for Project CMMC. Can we continue?

"Why are you telling me this? Wouldn't it be easier to just change my memories without telling me?"

An experiment. We need to verify if conscious knowledge of memory manipulation has any effect on the process. Let's move on. There is one particular area that I need to cover. Have you ever fallen in love?

"No! You are not touching those memories! How do I leave?"

You cannot leave. When you think of love what do you think of?

"No, stop it!"

Ah! I think I see a face forming. Do you see it? You can see the vague outline of a head. Look at it.

"Why are you doing this to me?"

You can see the short hair and the head shape.

"No, don't make me see his face... please..."

The face is slowly being coloured in. By my estimation, I would say he is in his mid-twenties and has light brown hair. He has a very kind-looking face.

"Please..."

What is his name?

"Please d—"

"Hi! My name is Alex."

"Alex..."

He does have a nice smile. Care to reveal how you two met?

"Please don't, why do you want this memory?"

The fewer connections you have with living people, the better.

"Fuck you! Fuck you and your shit about manipulating memories! Leave him alone! That memory is mine!"

He must have meant a lot to you if you are going to defend it.

"Shut up!"

Alex, Alex, Alex... What do you think every time you hear his name?

"Don't think don't think don't..."

Ah! I think something is emerging. Is that Stellenbosch?

"No please... Ouch, shit! I feel dizzy. What happened?"

We're busy with a memory. This is Victoria Street. It must be winter; the trees have lost their leaves and the sky looks awfully cloudy.

"I think I remember this memory... This is when I met Alex."

Would you like to continue with this memory?

"I was walking to my res with my friend, Jenny. We were in the library doing some research. When we reached the Conserve, Jenny greeted someone in the distance. It was clear that they were good friends. They hugged, and then he turned to me."

"*Hi! I'm Alex.*"

"His smile gave me butterflies."

"*I'm Mia.*"

"Jenny remembered something."

"*Crap! I forgot my external in the library! Wait here, I'll be right back!*"

"And just like that, I was standing alone with Alex. We awkwardly talked about work and classes. Actually, I don't know what we talked about. I couldn't stop staring. He said:

"*I know this is random, but do you want to get some coffee sometime? You seem pretty cool.*"

"My face felt like a tomato. I just nodded quickly."

"*Yes, that would be nice.*"

Did you have coffee with him?

"Eventually, yes. I got his number from Jenny and then we had coffee. And then more than coffee…"

Interesting. Are you sure that you really met him?

"What? What do you mean? You saw the projection."

Yes, I know that is what was projected, but sometimes our memories like to fill in the gaps for us, and then we remember things that did not happen. Human memory is a funny thing.

"I'm not making this up. I'm sure of that."

Can one ever be certain of that?

"What is going on? What is this feeling?"

Describe the feeling.

"No… I can't… think… what… Stop it! Whatever you're doing just stop it!"

Think about it. You obviously saw Alex, but did those events and that conversation actually take place?

"His face… I can see it! And then I spoke to him."

No you didn't. You think you did.

"His mouth is moving. I'm sure there were sounds. Why aren't there sounds? Why?"

You saw him with Jenny, but he didn't say anything. He didn't even seem all that friendly.

"That… Please smile… You seem so distant…"

Alex just greeted Jenny, but he was on his way to somewhere and he couldn't be late.

"Late… Alex… That's his name… Please… Why won't you smile?"

And then they—

"No! It can't be all! Please… Don't do this to me. Don't take him away from me. My memory of him is fading. Please. Just fucking stop!"

Do you want to continue with the memory?

"I spoke with Alex."

"Do you want to—"

No, what really happened?

"I spoke with Alex."

No.

"I spoke with Alex… Please."

No.

"I… wanted to speak to Alex. But why didn't I? I wish I had."

You didn't, because you were shy. You felt that you were inadequate.

"I feel sad. Why am I feeling sad? It feels as if something is missing. What's missing? Tell me. What am I missing?"

You are sad, because you are inadequate.

"I am sad, because he isn't smiling."

Did you speak with Alex?

"No, I didn't, now that I think about it."

How does that make you feel?

"Not much, but I'm used to disappointments. Not like it matters anyway."

Who are you?

"I am Mia and I am twenty-three years old. I don't want to be here. I don't want to be anywhere. Not like anyone needs me."

Good. Interesting… You are making excellent progress, Mia.

"Well, it doesn't feel like it."

The next step in the process is a bit tricky and can get difficult, so I'm going to need all your cooperation.

"What do you mean?"

You are dead.

"Wha— Wait, did I hear you correctly? It sounded like you said that I'm dead."

Yes. It is only your body that is dead, but you are, for all intents and purposes, deceased.

"Wait. I don't get it. If I'm dead, then why am I talking to you?"

Your body may be dead, but your memory matter is still pretty much alive. We are in Esomnesia.

"Eso— What?"

Esomnesia. The state of being within one's memories. A metaphysical state outside of reality.

"Why am I dead?"

You died last night. We were able to harvest your memory matter and stimulate it for Esomnesia. We need your memories for our research with mod memory creation. We are going to process the memory of your death to remove it. This is for the preparation of your memory matter for transfer. We are going to transfer them to a mod brain.

"So, first I'm going to experience my own death, and then I'm going to turn into a mod?"

Basically, yes.

"I can't. I can't do this. This is sick and twisted and just plain wrong."

There is nothing to worry about. You might feel a slight discomfort, but it will be over quickly.

" … "

Can we proceed?

"Yeah, I guess. What exactly do I have to lose, right?"

Good. Let's start with the events of last night. What were you doing last night?

"I was out with my friends. It was my one friend's birthday, so we all went out for drinks at Tiger Tiger. It was fun, but I didn't feel well, so I left early."

When you left, where did you go?

"I parked far away, so I walked up the street. All the lights and loud music, slowly faded away behind me. The further I went, the darker it got. There were a few people around, who were partied out of their minds, so I was pretty much alone."

Why didn't you walk with someone?

"I don't know. Everyone was still having a great time, so I didn't want to spoil it. I was fine, though. I knew the way back."

What happened next?

"I turned into a small street close to the place I parked. I can't remember the name of the street, but it was one of those tiny ones. And then... what..."

What is happening?

"I thought I saw a shadow in the corner of my eye. Is ther—"

"Is there anyone there?"

"There's no reply. Let me just get out of here. Something feels extremely off. There are no lights here. My heart is beating hard. What is happening? I don't like this."

Where are you?

"Still in the tiny street. I need to get out of here. It's extremely dark... What is this feeling? What is going to happen? Shit! I can't move. I don't want to do this!"

Push through. You can do this.

"Oh no... Oh... The shadow. It's there again. Someone is definitely there. What should I do?"

Can you see what he looks like?

"No... Oh crap! Oh crap! He's wearing a hoodie, but his face is completely black. His eyes. His eyes are purple. What... I've never seen purple eyes before."

Purple?

"Maybe I should turn around and run. Okay. Shit, why is this street so long?"

Where is the person with the purple eyes?

"I don't know! Why can't I run?"

"krxxxxzz!"

"Shit! He's got me! Ouch! His fingers are digging into my arm! It hur— *Fuck!*"

"Heeelp! Help m—"

"I can't breathe! I can't breathe! No, no, no… I don't want to die! Help! I can't get his hands off my neck! Aaaahh! It hurts, help!"

Can you get a clearer view of his face?

"Help me! I can't feel my arms… Ouch! I am against the wall. Why do I see blood? Where is it co— Oh no… Shit! My arms… My arms are gone!"

Focus, Mia, focus.

"My arms… Help! My arms… Where are my arms?"

Where is the mod with the purple eyes?

"I can feel myself going… I don't know… Nghh… I don— I don't want to die. Wait, I see his eyes. Big purple orbs… He's coming closer."

What is he doing?

"His face is right in front of mine. I can see his face now. He… He doesn't have a skin. All I can see vaguely are wires and bolts. What is this?"

"Please… Why?"

"Cogito ergo sum…"

Cogito ergo sum… It's definitely him.

"I don't…"

"I don't understand."

"…"

"He's gone. Everything is gone. There is nothing. Even the pain is gone. Am I dead?"

Yes, you are.

"…"

Very good. You've made tremendous progress.

"My head hurts a lot. What happened?"

What do you remember?

"We were talking about a memory. I'm not sure which one it was. For some reason I see Jenny's face, with someone I don't recognise."

Good. Very good indeed. It seems to have been a productive session. I am going to prescribe you some medication for the headache. Please come back to me as soon as possible if the headaches get worse.

"Thanks, doctor, I will."

I just have one more question.

"Yes?"

Do the words 'cogito ergo sum' mean anything to you?

"No, I've never heard them. What does it even mean?"

I think, therefore I am.

"Ah... Cool..."

I am going to count to ten. With every step, you will gradually drift back into reality... one...

[CONNECTION ESTABLISHED]

[COMPILING DATA...]

... two... three... four... five...

[INITIATING TRANSFER...]

... six... seven... eight...

[STABALISING SENSORS...]

... nine... ten.

[TRANSFER COMPLETE]

[DISCONNECTED FROM CMMC TERMINAL]

[END ESOMNESIA]

Phillip Steyn is fascinated by the people around him. At present he is majoring in English literature and linguistics, and tries to find enjoyment in the little things of life. In his spare time he likes to doodle, browse bookstores and stroke his awesome beard.

THE LACUNA

Brendan Ward

It takes a few seconds to spot the plume of smoke rising over the hill, making the air acrid and thick enough to chew. Perhaps the dump—archetype of hell—has had equipment failure again. June is the bitterest month. Winter snaps like a twig beneath my bootsoles on the way off campus. My head aches with dehydration, longing for water, which just now pours from a burst pipe down African Street. My head aches from thinking, drilling first-years on *Hamlet*, on "Words. Words. Words". More than that, my head aches from wrestling with the Soweto poets, with imagining matchbox houses and Bantu Education.

"They sought a new place from which to write. Like other poets about Black Consciousness, LKJ, Langston Hughes, they looked for a new centre, away from the domain of the English canon. Why is this important, do you think?" The seminar is silent a moment, the professor waiting for a response.

"It is a dry white season, brother."

"It is rooted in the same gall as the Bantu Education Act. 'How is one to speak?'—that is the question. How is one to speak? What words can frame these new, vital thoughts? Especially when English and Afrikaans both bear the weight of the prejudices that press on these poets and thinkers.

"It was also the time of banning, and this too must be seen alongside the Bantu Education Act as another travesty in the war of language against language, of words against words. Don Mattera, himself banned, says that the poet must die."

I walk the streets leaning into the wind, struggling to put one foot in front of the other. It is cold, my cheeks sting, and for a moment I consider wrapping my scarf around my face and head like a Halloween mummy, but a foolish smile stretches as the only barrier against the cold. I hunker down and keep walking. The wind tosses leaves, dry and brittle and fading, and plastic bags and empty crisp packets that scratch like alien creatures among a shattered bottle in the gutter.

Someone has sprayed a symbol onto the walls of the substation—an unintelligible alphabet, a hieroglyph. Already in my head I hear my parents' tuts of disapproval, as if this spray-paint, this other kind of art, were the very sign of some deeper decay. This is the thing I struggle to shake—the weight of unknown concepts that sit in my head, scuttling like roaches as I try to look at them. Is this why these lines cannot coalesce into words?

I walk on.

This is a strange town, but only strange in its frankness. Sitting on one hill is the sprawling Settler Monument, like some deranged, rectangular ark moored up there after the flood, while across others clings the location, the township, the apartheid scarf of the town. Not hidden, not knocked down and renamed for triumph, but there, a brazen landmark as notable as the old cathedral that stretches for the darkening sky. Do I even know what to call it? Joza? Have I not lived here for years? I cannot name it, quite, with the correct word, even after all this time.

"My parents kept me from children who were rough." My school tried to, small, elite. The city did so too, placing my small house hiding safe in the suburbs. Not fully safe, no, but where it *looked* safe, with green things growing and dustbin men to make trash vanish once a week and comforting security firm signs watching from walls and gates. Johannesburg nearby is not so simple, the invisible barriers more permeable, in flux. This block will be familiarly generic, that block, a wild unknown, graffiti-branded as *not safe* by the silently conditioned code. Here in this town there are even envoys from across the barrier, divisions clear in streets and zones made moot by the flow of people. Yet there are still places I wish I could want to enter, eyes I want to meet without the surge of confusion, of a kind of shame that won't make itself clear. I still have not taken that Xhosa course, and I still twist with nerves at the thought of going into the places from which the world has kept me away. That I have kept from me. I am a tortoise struggling against its shell.

Maybe we haven't got past our fear of sailing into the unknown and into the clutches of the Cyclops or, worse, off the edge of the world. Is this the thought of a colonist, still so after generations?

It is now dark. I try to imagine Soweto in 1976, even in 2014; how do I speak to you? The image comes out in black and white. I consider walking directly home. Instead I pace down a deserted High Street, silent apart from the donkey eating *something* at the top of the street. I know this street well, now, after days heading to the butcher, the clothing stores, the pharmacy, and nights to the pubs half-hidden down side streets, blaring their location in the air. Tonight is not one of those nights and the air is still apart from the breeze. It is like a close-up of a map, frozen on paper. Why am I out walking? A car passes by, cutting the silence. I see no one, not even the car guards who wait outside the steakhouse franchise in the hopes of a tip. I turn a corner. The streetlights are out and the dark air lies heavy in the street as it climbs a hill. I feel a little disoriented for a moment.

Then I smell it: a reeking, wild and sickly sweet, like the den of some creature. As if this is not a street, but the entrance into the burrow, the den, of something. It overpowers even the smoggy air that billows from the burning trash at the dump, from fires to heat and cook in the township, from the exhausts of cars ferrying children from sport at school. I tense, muscles ready, while my mind runs over a mantra of logical explanations. Maybe it is a chemical spill, or part of the preparations for the National Arts Festival—a rehearsal of a street piece of some kind. Maybe I am imagining the whole thing, a trick of the mind and sinuses in the sensory deprivation of darkness. My nostrils flare despite my decision that this is simply nothing to fear—maybe a lost mongoose in a drain, or feral cats. Or something.

I hear a voice that does not flow over the air. It is as if I am repeating the words myself, an echo of something heard only in my mind. It is crisp and cold, a winter voice, a dark voice, like ice on a deep lake.

At last.

I don't know if I say this aloud: "Who's there?"

The street feels trapped, silent, undisturbed. Although perhaps I did not speak; no one has ever spoken here. Weight, a presence of something large, pressing the space, cuts me off in the gloom.

A shiver runs down my spine. The air stirs, a slow, calculating movement, a muffled footfall. The voice begins again.

Of course you do not know me. I wait in the belly of a beast, in the pit to death, in the singing caves that tempt young maidens to follow the swallows. I have waited for you in the shebeen, the shack, the centre of the city. I have waited for you in the rub-

bish tip, on the streets of Johannesburg, and on dark roads you drive too fast, here in Grahamstown, past the cathedral at night where you've been told to never go alone.

The dark street is a gullet. I turn, wildly, searching for the voice in the shadows. A million images crawl across my mind of monsters from movies, from countless videogames, from hours reading condensed, children's book of Greek myths. Where is my magic sword, my supernatural guide, my gift from the gods?

I can live only where you are in the dark. Of course you do not know me, yet somewhere in your youth I stood in the dark of the passage outside your bedroom, daring you even to go to the toilet. I lurked at the window, and in your closet, invisible and tangible and compounded of all your wildest imaginings and recurring nightmares of being eaten alive by the man with the hairy arms and fiery hair.

Words that aren't mine funnel into my brain, and my lips crack in the dry cold as I mimic them, compelled to try cut the silence. My breath is ragged. Cold air burns my lungs. I whip around again. My feet shift, sore, as if they were turning to stone, melding with the pavement.

And now the chase begins, I suppose. You always run. You have always run to hide. Your species tells itself it is an apex predator, that you ran down your prey until it collapsed from exhaustion. That this guaranteed your rise to dominance over all life. You mythologised your predatory prowess. But what if you did not master fleetness of foot for feeding? You mastered it for your own survival—to flee that which would eat you. Come now, find your feet and move. You dare not disgrace yourself by freezing, like some herd beast now.

I shiver, twisting my neck, and craning to follow where the voice in my head sounds like it is coming from. All directions look the same in the shadows. I am lost in the place that should be my home.

Run! Flee!

I am running, but without knowing where I run. The dark street is a labyrinth of houses, alleyways, twisting shadows, looming shapes in the darkness that mock the mind as it grapples to separate bushes and bears, trees and demons. My footsteps are mirrored in the sounds of something in pursuit.

You know, rats can be conditioned to understand direction, and to understand colour. But, disoriented, they cannot connect location and colour to navigate by landmarks. But you humans, ah-h-h, you humans have your massive minds to help you sort through the noise of the world, while still archiving information to use in times like this. Dodge left!

Instinct kicks in. I step left without thinking, following instruction, avoiding a lamppost that looms out of the darkness like the tail of some burrowing monster. My reactions are slow, however, slower than ever before, never an athlete. I am still lost.

But without language, can this be done? Oh no. Deprived of language you revert to the rat brain, the child brain, the lost mind grappling with the unknown for a foothold in quicksand, for a system to guide you in the absolute chaos. Without language, landmarks become mere shapes, directions disconnect and your mental map breaks down. Your home becomes an alien land, a dark place, an unknown. Do you know why this is?

The Observatory? I'm confused. Buildings loom in darkness. A statue, a figure half seen. I should know it. Terror, I've never felt, grips me now. It is closing on me.

You are barely creatures, despite all your claims to the contrary. All your questions, your questing for that which is elsewhere, for the equation that captures the details of the microscopic universe, cannot raise you from the mire, the foetid swamps in which your species began as little more than bacteria billions of years ago.

Why are buildings so big?

You have stretched your limbs to toddle forward into the dark world, and put names to things to tame them, to separate good from bad, friendly from dangerous. Dog—wolf, cat—lion. Friend—foe. And then you build entire maps of these things to crush each other and struggle blindly for excuses. I know the words that tumble so readily from your mind's tongue, which you push so kindly into my domain. Or else you write poetry to dress the world in mystic hues. For what? Why simply, because without words you lose yourselves in the dark. In the dark I wait for you.

Where are my words?

Your words are drowning in mine. Your words aren't even your own. Where did you find them all, child?

My words—

Their words! They are all so old, so much older than you I have gnawed them for centuries and tasted the changes, and spat them out for you to use. And oh so, so many of my words can lock you out. There are so many languages you cannot speak, languages that deny your access. Of eleven in your supposed home, how many do you speak?

Get out, get out, get

A paltry two!

out!

With so few words you wish to resist me? I speak all words in all tongues. Ek praat alle woorde in alle tale. nDithetha wonke amagama ngazo zonke iilwimi. Je parle tous les mots dans toutes les langues. Jag kan alla ord i alla mål. Pom put di thuk phasa krapb. Sé decir cualquier palabra en todos los idiomas.

All at once. All voices.

Where are you now, lost human? Where? Drowning in language. Adrift in the ocean of forgotten words, foreign sounds. An alien in the very system you love so, need so. Slave to yourself. And there are words I taste that you have mouthed, dark words, mistakes.

Overwhelmed.

I see. Wings. Darkness. Fast. Close.

Ah, now you begin to see me in your wordless terror. It is pitiful to see you clawing for words, burrowing into the corners of your mind to look for a way to see me properly. Can you capture me in words as you drown in the flood of my countless voices? I speak with myriad mouths inside your mind. Look at you, running in circles. You have passed this house before. You twist back in on yourself in terror. Look where you are.

Bridge.

Yes. How far you have run aimlessly in the shadows, trying to steal a glimpse of me and frame me into some system of thought. Let me teach you, if you can keep pace. Repeat after me.

Black wings. Corvid. Crow. Raven. Rook. Igwababa. Nevermore. Huginn and Munnin, Thought and Memory. Nevermore. Valravn, devourer of kings. Nevermore. Nachtkrapp. Babd-Catha, battle crow. Carrion bird. Vulture. Raptor. Impundulu. Nevermore. Birds of ill omen. Thekwane, hammer-head, death's head. Look again. I am no crow, no vulture, no hamerkop. See my vast eyes, my ears? Owl. Isikhova. Strix. Lillith. Blodeuwedd. Messenger to Xibalba. Silent hunter. Crushing talons. Calling your name, announcing your death. Run rat! But no, not an owl either. Serpent. Snake. Viper. Constrictor. Adder. Niddhogg. Grootslang. Basilisk. Zahhak. Nakhásh. The Beast. Ophis. Jörmungandr. Apep, sun devourer. Scales scratch as I slither swift so as to strike. Ouroboros, infinite, skin shed to be reborn. What am I, rat? Do you feel my paw behind you? The black cat to cross your path. Witch's familiar. Sekhmet. Manticore. Leo Nemaeus. Matagot. Lion. Panther. Pard. Tiger, Tyger, burning bright, in the forests of the night. What immortal had or eye could frame my fearful symmetry? I pounce, rat.

Lost.

Lost between the walls of buildings, and lost among the walls of words; a little rat in a maze and so far from the cheese. To think the stories limit my kind to the darkness of caves, of dungeons, of empty wildernesses, deserts, desolate badlands, the dry and empty lands, the depth of the seas, the bottom of black lakes, the dark edge of space. Where better to lurk than alongside you, in the cracks between buildings, between districts, along the lines where cities and lives were butchered to suit a social order. Ah-h-h how I may flourish in these spaces, the dark gaps you dare not look down for fear of finding yourself on the other side. The map is where we grow, in the places without borders, without lines, scratched off as terra incognita, full of monsters, dragons, headless humans, cannibals, storm-breeding beasts. Your ancestors even did the honour of sketching things, approximating the least part of me in the corners of their maps as a warning. Then they spread into the corners, and became as monsters themselves. And now as your satellites spy upon all the corners of the earth your maps look complete, but not these ones in your head. I thrive in the holes where other

*tongues should be, the gaps of experience you shut yourself away from in a cage
of privilege and guilt and shame. I grow as you hide shyly, fail to greet, avert your
eyes, lie about having no change in your pocket, agonise over slips in your words,
over unbidden thoughts you cannot contain. I live in the unfilled spaces of your
world. The map is still my domain, little rat, and all it takes is my words to tear
it from your paws and make you squirm. Make you obey. Run, little rat! Flee!
Escape! Bolt, dash, fly! Run!*

Running,

And now cease, halt, give up. Stop!

Stopped,

Genuflect, bow, scrape, make obeisance, cower. Kneel!

Kneeling.

Cold.

Quiet.

Dark.

Lost.

Empty space.

Dark, light, dark.

Shapes. Light. Dark. Shadow.

Shapes in shadows. Where is voice?

Gaps in the light, shadows. Still silent.

Look around. Cold lines curve, run together.

Train tracks under bridge. Posters peel from wall.

How am I here?

Standing, limbs ache. Blisters burst. Sharp breath.

Cold air on face. Where is the voice? Look for light, walk toward it, walk
along tracks. Trip. Pain. Hand wet, dark. Blood?

Stand again. Stumble forward to light. Head aches, throbs, eyes closing. Silence everywhere, just feet on stones. Drag. Crunch. Drag. Crunch. Breathing.
Drag. Crunch. Shadow. Light. Shadow. Light. Bars, street light, streaks shine on
tracks.

A voice. Terror. Turn. Stumble. Stones, sharp.

No! Voices. Talking to each other. Breathe. Walk. Two humans in shadows, talking on the street. What are they saying? Hand stretches out. Head shakes. Parting. One looks at me. I raise an empty hand, not quite a wave.

Brendan Ward grew up in the little town of Benoni, and fights the temptation to tell people he is from Joburg instead. He is currently studying his Masters in English at Rhodes University, researching some of his great interests: speculative fiction and the environment. He graduated with a joint Honours in English and journalism from Rhodes. So far, he has managed to convince one other publication, the Eighty-Eight Journal, *to print a short story of his. He currently lives in Grahamstown, being unable to escape small town life.*

THE CARTHAGION

Sarah Jane Woodward

The sharp scent of the cordite filled the boy's nostrils. He was hunkered down, two brown scabby knees on either side of his face, and tense with concentration. The tip of his tongue poked through his cracked lips as he struck the flint again and again, willing the dry grass to ignite.

"Come *on*," he pleaded, and though his voice was not yet broken, it had a hard edge. The small pile of dry twigs had caught light twice that evening, but had gone out each time, leaving only blackened, curled shapes between the boy's dirty feet. He rearranged the sticks for the umpteenth time and shoved the bits of grass and leaves between the small strips of bark.

"Ag man, *come* on!" the boy said, getting more frustrated, "you blêrrie schtupit thing!" His voice was beginning to wobble. This was his first night doing guard duty on his uncle's farm—Jakkelsplig they called it. He wasn't alone. Kobus would be there too, but Kobus had asked him to make the fire while he caught something for dinner. Now the fire wasn't ready and he had been crouched here for ages and he felt so useless. He was twelve years old and couldn't even make a dumb fire.

"Howzit going there, boytjie?" Kobus's voice startled Jan, and he turned to see Kobus.

His half-cousin was more than twice his age, with a thick ginger beard, and a veld hat on his head. He towered over Jan, and had a small blue duiker slung over his shoulder.

"It's fine, I'm doing it." Jan struck the two pieces of flint together, but rather half-heartedly this time.

"Never mind, boy, I'll do it for you." Kobus gently removed the two stones from the boy's hands. He struck once, twice. Soon there was a pile of glowing coals in the small circle of stones, with a haunch of venison roasting on the grill above it.

Kobus ruffled Jan's hair as he sat on a tree stump near the fire. "Moenie worry nie, boy. One day you'll get the hang of it." Kobus chuckled while he drew on his long-stemmed pipe, leaned back, and stretched out his long legs. He looked up, and indicating with his pipe at the sky, said, "Isn't it beautiful? Look, there's Orion with his belt, and there quite close are the Seven Sisters, also you can see Taurus's horns. And if—" He grunted then turned to look behind him. "If you look that side, you can see the Southern Cross. Look, over there."

As he lay on his back staring up at the inky night sky, Jan had the peculiar sensation that the world had tipped forward, and it was he who lay suspended above the Milky Way. Whole constellations stood out in relief; tiny stars seeming to grow bigger and smaller as Jan glimpsed them from the corner of his eye—stars that were actually twinkling. The night breeze ruffled his hair. He breathed in the smell of the roasting meat, and listened for the *kriek kriek* of the crickets nearby.

Jan closed his eyes, and for an instant completely forgot his script, and sighed "God, it's like the one thing I really I miss, you know. The sky." The night seemed to go very still. A small buzzing came from the implant in Jan's right ear, but before it could get any louder, he stammered: "I-I mean, when I have to go to school, you know in the term time, they don't let us out of the koshuis much. I hardly ever see the sky."

There was a small pause then the breeze shifted and the crickets sang. Jan turned slightly to catch Kobus's eye. His complexion darkened, and his eyes were black with anger. He stared at Jan, who stared back, his mind racing.

"U-um, Kobus, please tell me that story again? You know, that story where you killed a lion that one time? Please?"

Kobus was still for a moment then his face relaxed somewhat. He didn't look happy but he didn't look murderous either.

He turned to look into the darkness, pulled on his pipe and let out a long curl of blue smoke. The fire sparked and sent a glowing red ember zig-zagging up into the darkness. The meat smelled as if it was burning. A moment passed.

"Fine," said Kobus. "You get that steak off the fire and I will tell you the story while we eat."

Jan scuttled towards his canvas backpack, where he removed two yellow enamel plates and two steak knives. Deftly he cut the meat into halves and handed the larger piece to Kobus. He took his plate back to the small stone on which he had been sitting. Kobus took his plate without thanks, and between bites of slightly charred flesh, began his tale.

"The year was nineteen eighty-seven. I was a young lad in the Sixth Battalion, stationed not far from here, at Madimbo, two hundred kilometres north of Massina in the middle of bloody nowhere. Very close to place where the three borders, Mozambique, Zimbabwe and South Africa join. There were two of us standing guard..." Kobus's voice grew softer and more gruff as he spoke.

Jan leaned forward, his hands clasped around his knees, and his gaze fixed on his half-cousin. Gradually, his heart rate began to slow down, and the utter terror that had gripped him moments before began to subside.

It wasn't just that he had nearly ruined the session; it was that there were actual physical dangers of having a client turn against one, especially when they had chosen an alpha male, prototype 2.1 to embody. The AL-M pr2.1 was a particularly aggressive model, with a military background and a penchant for hunting. Jan hardly listened while Kobus told the story of how a lion had crept into the tent of his buddy, and had tried to drag him out by the boots. This would be the sixty-third time he had heard this story, so he didn't really have to concentrate too hard on the appropriate interjections. A couple of "oohs" and "jislaaiks!" at appropriate moments was all it took for Kobus to get completely carried away with his tale.

"...and then Frikkie Marais grabbed the blêrrie thing by its tail, what a doos! It turned on him and with a mighty roar, sprang on to the oke's back. But luckily Fossie and Piet were there as well so all together we..." Kobus was totally absorbed in the telling of his exploits, the script deviation seemingly forgotten.

It was just hard sometimes. Jan *did* miss the sky. The only time he saw it— the only time any of them saw it—was during these sessions, and no matter how rigorous the training, sometimes looking up at the vastness of the universe was just...well, just overwhelming.

It was a mark of his training that he thought of himself as "he" during these sessions, because Jan was only one of the characters Bella inhabited.

"So, anyway, we soon put that mangy cat out of its misery, and do you know, to this day, I still have the skin upstairs in my pa's attic. It used to live on the hall floor but Ma got too freaked out by it. She said it looked at her funny." Kobus chuckled.

He stood, stretched and took his sleeping bag out of his backpack. "Here you go my boy, you sleep first and I'll keep an eye out for the jackals. Goodnight."

Jan quickly brushed his teeth with water from an enamel mug, pissed on the fire and crawled into the sleeping bag. As his eyes closed, he slipped momentarily into unconsciousness until—

"Oh shit Bella, you are in like, deep, deep trouble!" Debulon's voice was the first thing that shrieked into her ear. The feeling of disassociating was always disorienting and Deb's voice was not helping. Bella sat up on the white table. Her muscles ached, and she ran a hand over her legs to ease the cramps. Her techie stood over her, holding up a square of white cloth to cover her body. The company preferred their characters to associate in the nude; there was less restriction of movement, apparently.

"Idiot." Bella snarled at Deb as she snatched the cloth from his robotic hand and took a deep breath. Debulon was AI, and a rather exasperating trait for scandal and gossip mongering had been built into his personality. He was annoying, but completely harmless. The clear, smooth voice that now spoke directly into her ear however, wasn't.

"BelPascione, please come to my cubicle. As soon as possible. Thank you."

Bella zipped up her regulation shell suit and placed her identity clip reading BelPascione345 on the upper left pocket. She ran her fingers through her hair to compose herself and checked her face in the small mirror inset into her locker's door panel. The panel slid back into place as she turned away, melting back into a wall of hundreds of similar storage units.

As she turned into the corridor that led away from the tech rooms, the light pulsed slightly ahead of her, drawing her forward through the labyrinth. She had no choice but to follow, or be left in complete darkness. The director didn't like to be kept waiting.

As Bella travelled the corridors, she caught glimpses of the embedded holographs displaying the latest citizen directives. A wall flickered with the message: "The Carthagion! It's the only way!" It seemed somebody had come up with a new slogan for the latest placatory campaign. The illumination mechanism didn't allow for pauses, so Bella was forced to continue on her way. She felt slightly nauseous as she travelled the twisting passages. There was such a disconnection between the world she inhabited as Jan, and the reality of the underground city. Sometimes she wished she could stay above ground, but knew that it wasn't a possibility. Not for a few thousand years at least.

As she approached the director's cubicle, Bella went over the three main tenets of her training in preparation for the meeting: *Number one, always remain on script. No matter what happens, it is vital. Number two, always remain within the designated playing area, and number three, never, ever contradict the client.*

I only broke one of those rules. And it was such a small slip that I am sure Kobus probably didn't even notice. Even as she told herself that, she knew it was a lie. She had seen his expression; he had known exactly what had happened.

Bella arrived at the cubicle threshold slightly out of breath. She paused. The transition from the cramped corridor of the Carthagion into the vast expanse of the cubicle was always a little disconcerting. The room was enormous, long white walls, stretching away from the door, and at the end of the room, was a desk, where a small, neat man was seated. The smooth voice again spoke through Bella's implant, "Come closer, BelPascione" His mouth did not move. She moved closer.

The man seated at the desk didn't look up.

"Ignore him," said the voice. "He is busy at the moment and doesn't wish to be disturbed. You will talk with me."

Bella nodded hastily, recognising the voice of the supreme director.

She stammered: "As you wish, madam director."

"Do you know why you are here?"

Bella considered denying what she had done, but knew it was ultimately futile. "Uh… yes."

"Explain it to me."

"I… Uh, I went off script. I said something I shouldn't have?"

"Exactly. Tell me, BelPascione, why is it that the first rule of your training is to never deviate off script?"

Bella opened her mouth to answer, but nothing came. Why? She had never thought about why before. It had been an order, direct and simple, and always unquestioned.

"Uh… I don't know why, madam director." Bella was beginning to feel nauseous. The circulated air of the Carthagion was tinged faintly with the smell of roses. It was cloying.

"Repeat that please."

"I don't know, madam director."

"Perhaps if I explained it to you, you may understand the gravity of the situation?" The voice spoke softly, intimately into Bella's ear, and a shudder, of either pleasure or disgust, she couldn't quite tell, ran down Bella's spine.

"Yes please." Bella's voice came as a whisper.

There was a soft whooshing, and as Bella turned, one of the white walls of the cubicle lit up as the room dimmed behind her. On the wall was displayed a series of blue and yellow interconnecting dots, arranged in a hexagonal formation, small beams of light connecting each one to another.

The speaker said, "What do you see?"

"The Pantetra, madam director."

"Explain."

Bella, squirmed. She hated this. She felt like a child, being asked to explain her first lessons back to a grim, unsmiling teacher.

"The Pantetra is at the heart of the Carthagion. It is what makes our company work, and it is the living mechanism by which we fulfil our function," Bella intoned in a sing-song lilt.

"Yes, but what is it?"

Bella paused. She had just said hadn't she? "Um… the Pantetra is the heart of…" She faltered. The silence grew. Bella had never been asked these questions before. What was going on? She was starting to feel rebellious; if she was going to be punished for her mistake why didn't they just get it over and done with?

The madam director started again, as smooth and as calm as before, but Bella thought she detected a hint of impatience beneath the rounded vowels.

"Each blue dot that you see represents the mind of a client. Each yellow dot is the mind of an associate, such as yourself, BelPascione. The particular blue dot that you were connected to in your last session belongs to this man."

A smooth, handsome face appeared on the wall. He was a well-known politician, a man renowned for his strong views on quelling the violent outbreaks in the underground city. Bella knew his face well. His name was Endwald Grobler.

Her breath caught. She had always hidden her background from the Carthagion. She had been recruited at a young age, and had lied on countless forms and in the evaluation tests, because one of the excluding factors was a childhood trauma of any kind. She had never told anyone who had murdered her parents, let alone that they had been killed. This is who had been inside the mind of Kobus.

"Tell me, BelPascione, why do you think the session terminates exactly at the point when the boy known as Jan closes his eyes?"

Bella swallowed hard, trying to control her panic. "Um. Because he falls asleep?"

"Well, that is what you have always believed, but the truth is that the real Jan was brutally murdered by the real Kobus, stabbed over one hundred times with a hunting dagger, and decapitated. We always pull *you* out moments before, but we leave the client there. Can you imagine why?"

Bella started to shake even harder. She knew why. So that whoever was inside Kobus could do whatever he liked in the safe space of the session. As this man grew in political power, so did his predilections for violence.

"We found that in our research, the memories of a certain type of man living at a particular age were so violent, so devoid of feelings, that they suited our purpose absolutely. Here, below what used to be known as South Africa, we resourced a particularly brutal section of history. Many of these men who returned from the border wars were so traumatised by what they had seen and done that they were quite psychotic. It serves our purpose well."

Wait. Memories? Bella had always believed that these sessions were VR, created by computers, fiction.

"Memories?" she said.

"Well, technically, yes. More like time travel. Dr Minnaar is rather good at inserting the minds of the clients into the subjects, leaving two consciousnesses, but only one awareness. It's astonishing, really. The client pays handsomely for this outlet, this moment of release, and we cannot afford to lose him nor you. So do you understand the danger now?"

The madam director fell silent. The man at the white desk still hadn't looked up at Bella; she was completely unimportant to him. It was unnerving being interrogated by a woman who wasn't there, yet ignored by a man who was. Bella knew it was deliberate. She wasn't a part of the company in order to be comfortable; she was here to do a job.

The information she had been given was a lot to comprehend all at once. Every time Bella associated, she was putting her life, her mind in danger, and that if she wasn't pulled out in time, she would be erased from this world. She also understood something else. That little, snotty barefoot Jan was real, forced to play out his horrific end over and over to entertain this disgusting brute of a man, and the Carthagion was a willing participant in this unspeakable act of violence.

"You may go," the madam director dismissed her.

Bella turned and ran from the cubicle, down the corridor, the pulsing light following her as she tried to escape from what she had just learned. She put her wrist to her mouth. "Deb?" She spoke into her transmitter. "Deb! Are you receiving?"

There was slight sigh. "Oh it's you. What do you want?"

"Deb, I'm sorry I called you an idiot. You're not an idiot."

Bella heard a slight sniff.

"Deb? You're not an idiot. You are the best AI techie a gal could wish for and I love you with all my heart and you're amazing."

"Ha. Now you're just being silly." Bella could hear that he was mollified. "All right, what do you need?"

It had been two months since Bella had been called in front of the director. In that time, Bella had behaved impeccably in all her associations, sticking perfectly to her scripts. But she had been waiting, and now it was time. Debulon had intercepted the Pantetra transcript and had seen that Endwald Grobler had booked a session.

Bella once again lay on the white table in her session room.

She said: "Ready."

Debulon pressed a button on the left side of the table at the same time as he placed one robotic finger on her temple. He whispered, "Good luck."

She wasn't sure if this was the best plan in the world, but it was all she could think of. She no longer could bear the thought of association, but neither could she leave this man, this treacherous deceiver, to play out his desires in this never-ending cycle of violence. She had to do something. There was nobody left for her here anyway.

She closed her eyes.

And Jan opened them. It was a beautiful afternoon. The late summer sun was low in the sky, and Jan was walking down a dusty road kicking up gravel with his bare feet. He looked up to see his tall half-cousin Kobus walking with him, backpack slung casually over one shoulder, hunting knife in the sheath hanging from his belt.

Kobus looked down at him, and ruffled his hair. "Hey boytjie, are you looking forward to this as much as I am? It's gonna be a great night!"

Jan smiled and nodded.

Everything went as usual. Jan struggled to make a fire, until Kobus said, "Never mind, boy, I'll do it for you." They ate meat under the wide Bushveld sky, and Jan listened to a heroic tale of lion slaughter near the border.

As the fire sputtered and sent glowing embers into the sky, Jan looked up at the stars. He felt so small, so insignificant against this majestic backdrop. His heart swelled and he glanced over at Kobus, who squatted by the fire.

"Kobus?" Jan said. "Can I ask you something?"

"Ja, sure, boytjie," said Kobus.

"Why did you do it?" asked Jan.

"What? Kill the lion?" Kobus grinned.

"No, Endwald," said Jan. "Why did you kill my parents?"

When he reached for it, Kobus found that his hunting knife was not in the sheath at his waist. Jan stood, blade at the ready and struck.

There was a small pause. The breeze shifted and the crickets sang. As Jan walked away from the bushfire into the night, he left behind him the tiny buzzing from the small voice-transmitting implant. It lay there in the dust, next to the rapidly cooling body of Kobus Malan.

Sarah Jane Woodward holds an MA in Theatre and Performance from UCT, and has been a lecturer with the Drama Division at Wits University since 2008. She has dabbled in poetry and performed some of her own work at various poetry events. Much of her writing up to this point has been for academic or teaching purposes, and this is her first foray into speculative fiction. She lives in Johannesburg with her husband, two children, two cats and her dog.

THE CORPSE

Sese Yane

I

The coroner, a pitiful recluse, once found himself burdened with a so-called occurrence at the morgue that he could not retell his wife, but could not keep from her either, it seemed to him. He lay next to his wife that night, listening to his silence and how it was being shattered in a manner that amused him. His silence, it occurred to him, was persisting throughout his speech, and therefore, in a way, he was never robbed of it; that overwhelming will to silence, that is—that fundamental part of his being. Naturally, as long as he avoided talking about this so-called occurrence, he was not saying anything at all, and that's how we can only assume it seemed to him.

One warm Tuesday afternoon, a middle-aged man snaked his way onto the bus, where he sat by the window and waited. His window was slightly open and he thought he might close it later when the bus got into motion and the wind became too much for his face.

The middle-aged man, it's important to say, had sideburns that sloped sharply along his cheekbones to join his moustache. Naturally, this gave him a wolfish appearance.

A young man occupied the seat next to him, but the middle-aged man, a very private man, despite being the proud owner of very public sideburns, did not notice this young man. He only concerned himself with the general happenings inside and outside the bus, without focusing on anything in particular. Therefore it's true to say that he indeed noticed the general fact that a young man had taken up the seat next to him but beyond that general activity of this sitting down by a young man, he noticed nothing about the particulars of the person doing the sitting. This was because, naturally, he was not interested, for sitting down has always been a mundane activity to some people. This folding up of one's body, halving of oneself, so to say, has, for some curious reason, never interested many people in the world.

When the bus left the station, the middle-aged man kept himself occupied with the illusory movement of buildings and trees along the way. This illusory movement had always fascinated him since childhood. He'd kept his eyes so focused on things rushing by that by the time he got to the country, his head was pounding with a headache. But now, as a grownup, he knew how to regulate his observation. He did not, so he thought of his art, have to pour himself out of his eyes, because, so he said to himself, his eyes were narrow, far too small for the act of seeing, and to see, he thought, one had to be artful.

He would focus on something definite that was far away and watch how it slowly changed position almost anonymously, until it slid out of the window of perception again, almost anonymously. And so in this art of his, he followed a house perched like an old bird at the top of a distant hill, its red tiles fascinating him, its hedge of evenly spaced trees that had arrow-tipped crowns... He followed a purple-crowned tree by the ravine, and for the next few kilometres found himself counting every purple-crowned tree that appeared, without keeping up with the number—counting by beginning over and over, but counting every purple-crowned tree nonetheless.

On this day, he was greatly pleased, because he didn't have to close his window. Its angle of opening and his angle of sitting allowed just enough wind without irritating his ears or his face, and just enough wind to allow him to keep his coat on, for, out of lethargy, he didn't want to remove his heavy coat. Besides, it would have meant extra luggage for his hands, which were already busy drumming the briefcase on his lap.

The road that cut through the township was damaged from a poor drainage system that floods the asphalt surface, and here the bus had to slow down. At this point, there were more passengers alighting than those who were boarding. The middle-aged man had about three kilometres to go, he thought. As the bus slowed down once again to negotiate a puddle that might or might not have been concealing a pothole, the middle-aged man saw the rotting remains of a dog on the shoulder of the road. The smell of death hit his nose from the open window before he immediately decided to hold his breath. It was quicker than closing the window.

But as the bus tore its way farther and farther away from the black dead dog, the middle-aged man could still see behind his eyelids the sardonic smile of the black dead dog, that disturbing smile we see on naked skulls and rotting carcasses. The middle-aged man continued holding his breath out of disgust. Minutes rushed past his open window and they dragged with them trees and houses and people, and still the middle-aged man held his breath, amazed that he could do this. His eyes actually lit up as eyes do when they're threatening to smile...way past a minute, past two minutes, past three minutes, passengers alighting, someone excusing themselves for stepping on another's shoes, a hearty laugh somewhere at the front, perhaps the driver's, or the conductor's, still holding his breath out of fascination of his ability to do so.

But past ten minutes, and fifteen, he was no longer amazed but afraid that he could do such a thing. He decided, against this childish merriment, to get his lungs back to their use. Something was terribly amiss. No matter how hard he tried, he couldn't suck in air from the outside world. His lungs impenetrable, his nose a pair of blocked tunnels, he seemed not to remember how to breathe in.

He dropped his briefcase to the floor.

Why won't they fix this road anyway, he thought.

The young man who had sat next to the middle-aged man had already alighted from the bus, the man now noticed.

God! I have overshot my destination...

When the bus conductor found the middle-aged man, sprawled out, half on the seat and half on the floor, it was the hideous sideburns that struck him first. He prodded the body with the tip of his boot, and once he was sure, took the seat directly on the other side of the aisle and stared at the corpse for a while before calling out to the driver.

II

*D*eath by asphyxia, the coroner wrote in his report then quickly moved the body to a small moveable freezer, covered it with rags and a broken squeegee, and pushed the small freezer into the store. For a moment, he could not decide what corridor to follow, and made his way for the toilet, but changed his mind halfway. He returned to the store and reset the squeegee, nervously patted the rag then hurriedly walked all the way past the lockers until he came to the fire exit. He ran down the stairs all the way to a dead end in what looked like it used to be a vestibule but was littered with all manner of equipment.

The effect it had on him was sudden. Entrapment. He forgot he had come down on a stairwell. Lost in this sea of broken chairs, broken lamps, broken trolleys, and bed-stretchers, old buckets, old stained books, and strewn papers, as three fluorescent tubes widely spaced above him illuminated this dusty sea of broken things. Under a sustained hum, he remembered, almost with what can be said to be an exaggerated childlike triumph, where he had run up the stairwell again, until he came to the correct corridor and made for the glass doors, heaving past the human-traffic, trolleys, stretchers, breathing hard but breathless nonetheless.

"No one saw me," he said to himself, almost too loudly. *What a moustache! But of course no one will suspect me,* the coroner thought at the gardens. He didn't notice the bench until he had sat on it. *It is not unusual for the morgue to lose a body. They lose bodies all the time, all the time, certainly, and people pick up wrong bodies all the time. In any case, I won't be here. I should call in sick tomorrow just in case. A headache, yes a headache, I have a headache, after all. It won't be lying...*

He fumbled a cigarette from his breast pocket and stared at it thoughtfully. What he felt was fear, not that he was afraid of being found out. After all, he wouldn't be caned if he were to be found out. He was too old for the cane, it now occurred to him; he was afraid entirely for something else—the unnameable fear of being a source, or perhaps being at the source, of some vague disorder in the world.

The coroner lay next to his wife that night and thought of the moustachioed corpse, now lying in an old, unused water tank in his garden shed.

After several attempts at words, just as someone might wait impatiently for the mocking swash of a wave to lick their foot, he spoke, "This corpse, Honey, beautiful moustache, you see. That's the first thing that tells you that he's different, but that's a disguise too… I'm standing there, I'm thinking… I have done this over a hundred times, right, but for some reason, and I don't know how. I must say, one usually gets the feeling that something is about to happen before it happens… I may say I don't believe what I finally see, but at the same time it's as if I'm opening him up with the specific intention of seeing what I'm now seeing," said the coroner and went quiet for a while, for it now occurred to him that he could not retell his story with the accuracy of how it had unfolded itself to him; the suspense and alarm of it all was now, to his frustration, being lost in his narration.

"Anyway, I write *asphyxia* in my report," said the coroner, "because it's asphyxia too… But I believe, strongly believe, the reverse is what happened. Not the reverse as we might know it but the reverse as we might speculate a new kind of reverse no one has ever experienced before. Well until this man.

"The man had no lungs," said the coroner.

"Born without lungs, can you believe it? Ah, but that's a ridiculous story. It's unscientific." The coroner laughed a silent laughter of embarrassment.

The coroner had not intended to disclose the incident of the strange corpse to anyone, or at least not yet. As he lay next to his wife, he thought how curious it was that his intern, this day of all days, had not shown up to work. She had offered the most ridiculous of excuses for her absence. "It's as if the universe knew," said the coroner to himself. *I should not have known what to do in such event…*

III

"Well, I guess, in a way, someone can," said the coroner to his wife, absentmindedly, pulling the bed sheet to his side. There's always an excuse, wouldn't you say, one way or the other. I think people are naturally lazy. A word here to replace an activity there; you don't have to show up if you can explain your absence. The grand miracle of words, so to speak, but don't get me wrong. There's a good reason for laziness, certainly. There's always a good reason for everything, otherwise there would be nothing."

The coroner was trying to avoid thinking about the corpse; trying to conceal his enthusiasm from himself. He was half tempted to jump out of bed and run to the garden shed to be with his corpse, but was held back by the even greater beauty of procrastinating and having something interesting to look forward to in the morning.

But he also wanted to talk about the corpse.

He sighed against his wife's neck, ecstatic with this beautiful dilemma, and searched for her hand under the sheets until he found the small hand and clasped it tightly over her warm thigh. He closed his eyes and smiled to himself, snuggled closer to her so that he felt his skin being warmed up by her nightshirt as his body pressed hard against her behind. The coroner again sighed that sigh of defeat, and watched the back of his wife's head. She had been quiet all the while and was looking away from him.

The coroner had never talked so much to his wife, he now thought. If he had to keep talking, he would have to explain his years of silence too—a silence that had always seemed to him to be executed by malicious will. Unless he was giving his report, and in a mathematical language, the coroner found it unbearable to talk to people. At home, he usually stayed in the library, dissolving himself in the dark timber shelving, and in the panelling, or turning the pages of one of his numerous books… or looking outside the window, at the twittering long-tailed birds jumping from tree to tree in the garden, now at the changing blue of the sky, now at the different shades of green on the foliage—basically hiding from his wife but trying not to think of it as such…

When his daughter stood at the door, watching him, (if he called her she would hide behind the door but if he decided not to notice her she would keep coming piecemeal until she reached his leg) he would sit her down by his side and passionately instruct her from one of his books, or from a train ticket for a journey he once took to Tbilisi from Batumi, or from a receipt for a latte in Turin, from anything, really. All this was to avoid or to atone for this avoidance, or even to punish himself for this avoidance, of talking to his wife, who might be in the kitchen or somewhere in the house.

You see, even after eight years of marriage, he still dreaded running into her in the corridors of their house. He got into bed with the airs of one too tired for a conversation; his consciousness of the exaggeration of conversation crippled his relationship with everyone. But this particular night, certainly because of the strange corpse, he had already said too much, and now he kept talking because he thought stopping abruptly would interfere with the equilibrium of a room he had already filled with his sound. In his estimation, he should perhaps keep talking until his words died naturally and proportionately to the falling volume of his sound.

"This intern," said the coroner, "Apparently I'm too old-school. I know and yet… makes you think, though, so much has happened around you. Where were you, all this time… Christ! There's nothing left for me to do. I've done everything. I've got everything. I don't want anything. What am I going to do now? That's exactly what I was thinking, standing there… before her frog-like eyes, big, beautiful," said the coroner to annoy his wife.

"I've never been so scared in my life, I'll tell you that. Have you ever lost something that never existed? That's the greatest loss… and yet how careless of us? I mean the garret. I was thinking about the garret. It's been years… all these years, so many years…

"Why was I still holding onto all these inaccurate tales? I'm thinking, it all comes back to me, flood-like, but I can't discern a thing. Mr Monkey, that's all I have on my mind, this vague memory, a silly sock monkey. I didn't lose Mr Monkey. I threw him in the garret, and I lied because I love Father. Father thought I was afraid of him. I could see through him clear like glass. I am the one who made him," said the coroner…

"*Bring a cane!* he would pretend to shout to me after being given the report of one thing or the other I had done during the day, *a good cane!* But I was never afraid of him. I pitied him instead. Brought him the best cane. I was very confident that he wouldn't, but I wanted him to cane me too, badly... but, by my foolishness, I had already manipulated him by bringing him the best cane. Naturally he couldn't cane me. The cane was too perfect," said the coroner, "simply too perfect... Had I brought him a bad cane, a poor cane, so to say, there's no doubt he should have gotten angry and used it. But the perfect cane incapacitated him, always...

"I used to wait for him at the gate every day as he came home from work. I don't know, perhaps a little afraid that he wouldn't come. And when I saw his figure in front of the sunset, like an apparition, as if he were walking from inside the sunset itself, I ran to my room and hid. In my childish soul I thought he was overburdened by his own presence. In a way, that's why I believed I had lost Mr Monkey, for Father's sake. I could never lie to him. I had to believe that I had lost the toy and not thrown it away, naturally for Father's sake. I never attempted to fool Mother, though, never pitied her that way. We were equals in pitying Father, I thought," said the coroner, "but I've always pitied her in her own way, and I've always pitied everyone else in their own way too...

"But it was those frog-like eyes of hers that reminded me of the long-forgotten, inaccurate tale I had made up for myself to protect Father from a lie. She's *young*," said the coroner, hoping this would enrage his wife, excited by the thought of the corpse in his garden shed. "Timid, like a sweet little kitten, domineering when talking to those corpses. In fact, she's more eloquent when talking to them than when she's talking to the living. She's got a natural stammer, but very comprehensible when talking to a corpse, can you believe that? When I ask her a question, for instance, because she's somehow comfortable in my presence, because apparently I'm too 'old-school', as she puts it, she answers me by way of telling the corpse and so I have to listen to what she's telling the corpse because that's meant for me.

"But she can't do this when talking to the other staffers. For some reason, she chooses the option of stammering. I guess you can say I'm special in that regard," said the coroner hoping to irritate his wife... "And so, for a laugh, because, naturally, that's what she wants, you see, I will sometimes talk to her through all these things in the morgue. For instance I'll ask the fluorescent tube to tell her to hand me a scalpel, the window to tell her that I need some cotton wool, etc, etc, and how she laughs when I do that."

The coroner was overwhelmed with excitement just thinking of the strange corpse in his garden shed.

IV

*O*h, how right I was to be brave enough to move the corpse from the hospital's storeroom this evening instead of waiting to come up with a better plan, thought the coroner.

There was no better plan, and it now indeed surprised him that he had gone along with what now looked like the worst plan. He could obviously not have gone through with such a poor plan the following day, he thought as he started talking about the lung-less man to his wife, again—talking of the lung-less man as if he were not real but a story he was inventing for the sole purposes of annoying her. Indeed, he talked about the corpse with the intention of annoying his wife; he described the corpse in flowery language, because poetry can never be believed, and is proof of madness. Similarly, according to him, verbosity was proof of deceit, for he had already talked too much. To justify this unnatural occurrence, the coroner was trying to convince his wife, but also more himself, that he had lost his mind.

He squeezed his wife's small hand again, put his lips to her neck and, with that little touch, his mind dissolved into vertigo. He thought he heard the distant howling of dogs, the whistling of trees. Oh how beautiful life is, especially whenever his wife wore a pinafore dress, how beads of rain trickled down the windowpane, how nothing seemed to exist when you pulled away from the eyepiece of the microscope... How small and ridiculous and yet amazing everything seemed to be, especially because it was small and ridiculous. His eyes misted. To disclose by concealing, or to conceal by disclosing. This sharing with his wife was a truth he could not tell anyone else, not even her, and it gave him a thrill this making of himself unbelievable... and he, for his own amusement, and also to his utter disbelief, which was also part of his own amusement, was at this time convinced that he was making up the story about the corpse.

At that very moment, after his unprecedented monologue, loneliness finally crept in to claim what had always belonged to it, just what the coroner, unbeknown to him, had been desperately waiting for. He turned onto his side and slept.

There was once a time that nothing in the world mattered more to Sese Yane than art. That was before he was introduced to his first novel in high school. When he is not reading Kafka – in his opinion, the only true, if blasphemous, genius – he practises law in Nairobi.

ACKNOWLEDGEMENTS

A good writer possesses not only his own spirit but also the spirit of his friends.
– Friedrich Nietzsche

Every publication is the result of a team effort, and none more so than this. It's therefore our great pleasure to welcome Nick Mulgrew onto the Short Story Day Africa team. Nick proved to be an invaluable help in 2013, designing the adult anthology and, when he offered to do the same in 2014, we jumped at the chance to invite him to join the team permanently. Nick will take on the role of Deputy Chair on the SSDA board, as well as many of the practical aspects of running the project.

Beyond the core team of Tiah, Nick and myself, there are many that contributed to this year's anthology. Special thanks to Nerine Dorman, lead editor on *Terra Incognita*. It is our great fortune that Nerine is blessed with keen eyes and extreme patience. Her dedication added shine and polish to these stories.

Thanks also to Nick Mulgrew for the cover and page design, as well as his encouragement, enthusiasm and support; Colleen Higgs and Emily Buchanan of Hands On Books/Modjaji Books, our publishing partner, for their support and publishing advice, and for taking SSDA under their experienced wings; the team at Worldreader for their support, encouragement, cash and endless offers of extra help should we need it.

We are eternally grateful to the Terra Incognita competition judges Richard de Nooy, Jared Shurin and Samuel Kolawole, and the team of readers who helped us compile the longlist: Aoife Lennon-Ritchie, Ayesha Kajee, Beatrice Lamwaka, Bontle Senne, Bronwyn Stewart, Carine Englebrecht, Cat Hellisen, Dave de Burgh, Dominique Phoeleli, Gail Schimmel, Henrietta Rose-Innes, Iain Thomas, Judy Smee Dixon, Karen Jennings, Lisa Lazarus, Maya Fowler, Margot Bertelsmann, Rahala Xenopolous, Sharon Tshipa, Sheryl Kavin, Summaya Lee and Susan Newham Blake.

Thank you also to the judges of the Brave New World competition: Beatrice Lamwaka, Bwesigye Mwesigire, Dorothy Dyer, Elizabeth Wood, Kathryn Torres, Lauren Beukes, Lauri Kubuitsile, Sean Fraser and Yewande Omotoso; and to Máire Fisher for editing the resulting children's anthology, *Follow the Road*.

And thank you especially to every writer who entered either competition, whether they made it into an anthology or not.

The prizes for the competitions were donated by All About Writing, Books Live, The Book Lounge, Cover2Cover, Fredrick J. Carleton Attorney at Law, Helen Moffett, Louis Greenberg, Modjaji Books, NB Publishers, Paige Nick, Rory's Story Cubes, VTS Communications and The Caine Prize for African Writing.

Without the sponsorship, financially and in kind, of the following organisations and individuals, our scope would have been much smaller:

ALL ABOUT WRITING • ALEX LATIMER • AOIFE LENNON-RITCHIE • BEATRICE LAMWAKA • BEN WILLIAMS • BOOKS LIVE • THE BOOK LOUNGE • BONTLE SENNE • BRONWYN STEWART • THE CAINE PRIZE FOR AFRICAN WRITING • CAT HELLISEN • CANDACE DI TALAMO • CINDY DE BRUYN • CHRIS DI TALAMO • CRISTY ZINN • CRYSTAL WARREN • DIANE AWERBUCK • DEVILLIERS USA • DREAM CIRCLE • DR SUESS • E DE VILLIERS • FIONA DAVERN • FIONA SNYCKERS • FREDERICK J. CARLETON • FOX AND RAVEN PUBLISHING • HANDS ON BOOKS • HELEN BRAIN • HEART & SOUL PHOTOGRAPHY • HENRIETTA ROSE-INNES • HELEN MOFFETT • IAIN THOMAS • ISLA HADDOW-FLOOD • I WROTE THIS FOR YOU • JILL SHURIN • JO LINDSAY WALTON • JOANNE MACGREGOR • JOHN SCHAIDLER • KARINA MAGDALENA SZCZUREK-BRINK • KERRY HAMMERTON • THE KITCHIES • LAURI KUBUITSILE • LOUIS GREENBERG • MARIUS DU PLESSIS • MICHAEL SWEENY • MODJAJI BOOKS • NB PUBLISHERS • NELLA FREUND • NICK MULGREW • PAIGE NICK • PAPERIGHT • PHILLIP STEYN • PRUFROCK • RAHLA XENOPOULOS • RICHARD DE NOOY • RORY'S STORY CUBES • SARAH LOTZ • SEAN FRASER • SHERYL KAVIN • S.L. GREY • SUSIE DINNEEN • TIAH BEAUTEMENT • VERUSHKA LOUW • VTS COMMUNICATIONS • WORLDREADER

And to all the writers and readers of African fiction, we thank you.
RACHEL ZADOK

OCEANVS

ATHLAN

TICVS

Libya

deſertum

Cano r.

regio Aethiop

Tombu
Tombutto

Agiſymba

Mellir

Gago

Benin

C. de las palmas

C. de las bayas   C. de la Mota   I. del Principe

S. Paulo   S. Thomæ

300   10   Circulus   20   ſequinoctialis

Santa Croce

S. Matthæo   Iſla de Nobon

C. de S. Catrina

Occaſione   C. primero

N. de Fernando   Fremo flu
de lorenns

Americe pars   O   C   E   A   N   V   S   C. Almadi
de S. Auguſtino

la Aſcenſion   AETHI   C. Le

C. de

OPI   C. de Ar

C Neg

A   C. de
PHRI
CA   Tropicus

Plaia

CVS

Printed in the United States
By Bookmasters

Inſula de Priſcam
de leuna

Ihan Bußemecher ex